Computer Accounting
Essentials
With
Microsoft®
Office Accounting

Carol Yacht, MA
Software Consultant

Susan V. Crosson, MS, CPA
Santa Fe Community College

**McGraw-Hill
Irwin**

Boston   Burr Ridge, IL   Dubuque, IA   Madison, WI   New York   San Francisco   St. Louis
Bangkok   Bogotá   Caracas   Kuala Lumpur   Lisbon   London   Madrid   Mexico City
Milan   Montreal   New Delhi   Santiago   Seoul   Singapore   Sydney   Taipei   Toronto

McGraw-Hill
Irwin

About the Authors

Carol Yacht is a textbook author and accounting educator. Carol contributes regularly to professional journals and is the Accounting Section Editor for *Business Education Forum*, a publication of the National Business Education Association. She is the author of Microsoft Office Accounting, Dynamics-GP (Great Plains), Peachtree, QuickBooks, and Excel textbooks and Carol Yacht's General Ledger and Peachtree CD-ROMs (www.mhhe.com/yacht). In 1978, Carol started using accounting software in her classes at institutions including California State University, Los Angeles; West Los Angeles College; Yavapai College; and Beverly Hills High School.

Carol Yacht is an officer of the American Accounting Association's Two-Year College section and recipient of its Lifetime Achievement Award. She has worked for IBM Corporation as an education instruction specialist, and served on NBEA's Computer Education Task Force. Carol is a frequent speaker at state, regional, and national conventions. Carol earned her MA degree from California State University, Los Angeles; BS degree from the University of New Mexico, and AS degree from Temple University.

Susan V. Crosson is Professor and Coordinator of Accounting at Santa Fe Community College in Gainesville, FL. She previously taught on the faculties of University of Florida, Washington University in St. Louis, University of Oklahoma, Johnson County Community College, and Kansas City Kansas Community College. Susan is known for her innovative application of pedagogical strategies online and in the classroom. She likes to speak and write on the effective use of technology throughout the accounting curriculum. Susan is co-author of several accounting textbooks including the Computer Accounting Essentials series.

Susan serves on the AICPA's Pre-certification Education Executive Committee and on the Accounting Careers and Members in Education committee for the Florida Institute of CPAs. She is active in the American Accounting Association and has served it as a Vice President of Sections and Regions, Chair of the Membership Committee, Council Member-at-large, and Chair of the Two-Year Accounting Section. Susan has received the Outstanding Educator Award from the American Accounting Association's Two Year College Section, the Florida Association of Community Colleges Professor of the Year Award for Instructional Excellence, and University of Oklahoma's Halliburton Education Award for Excellence. Susan earned her Master of Science in Accounting from Texas Tech University and her undergraduate degree in accounting and economics from Southern Methodist University. She is a CPA.

COMPUTER ACCOUNTING ESSENTIALS WITH MICROSOFT® OFFICE ACCOUNTING
Carol Yacht and Susan V. Crosson

Published by McGraw-Hill/Irwin, a business unit of The McGraw-Hill Companies, Inc., 1221 Avenue of the Americas, New York, NY 10020. Copyright © 2008 by The McGraw-Hill Companies, Inc. All rights reserved.

1 2 3 4 5 6 7 8 9 0 QPD/1PCC 0 9 8 7

ISBN: 978-0-07-352703-1
MHID: 0-07-352703-3

Editorial director: *Stewart Mattson*
Senior sponsoring editor: *Steve Schuetz*
Editorial assistant: *Colleen Honan*
Project manager: *Dana M. Pauley*
Senior production supervisor: *Carol A. Bielski*
Designer: *Matthew Baldwin*
Marketing manager: *Dean Karampelas*
Media project manager: *Matthew Perry*

www.mhhe.com

Preface

Computer Accounting Essentials with Microsoft Office Accounting teaches you how to use Microsoft Office Accounting Professional 2007 software (MOA). Microsoft Office Accounting is a financial management program created for businesses with fewer than 25 employees.

Read Me: Microsoft Office Accounting or Small Business Accounting?

The former name of Microsoft Office Accounting 2007 was Microsoft Office Small Business Accounting 2006. Small Business Accounting 2006 became two products: Microsoft Office Express 2007 and Microsoft Office Accounting Professional 2007. Microsoft Office Accounting Professional 2007 and Windows XP Pro (SP2) were used to write the textbook.

MOA has the look and feel of Microsoft's popular Office Suite software and works well with either the 2003 or 2007 editions. You will notice immediately that MOA looks like Microsoft Outlook and Dynamics-GP software. Once MOA is installed, it is listed as one of the Microsoft Office applications.

Microsoft Office Tools ▶
Microsoft Office OneNote 2003
Microsoft Office Access 2003
Microsoft Office Excel 2003
Microsoft Office Outlook 2003
Microsoft Office PowerPoint 2003
Microsoft Office Publisher 2003
Microsoft Office Word 2003
Microsoft Office Accounting 2007 Tools ▶
Microsoft Office Accounting 2007

MOA is a comprehensive accounting program that includes sales order and purchase order processing, banking, inventory management, fixed assets, job tracking, and payroll. You can also share information with other Office programs, such as Word, Excel, Access, and Outlook.

```
    Read Me
```

School computer labs can Install the software packaged with the textbook, Microsoft Office Accounting 2007. This ensures software compatibility between the school and students' off-site installation on their personal computers.

Additional resources are on the textbook website at www.mhhe.com/moaessentials. The website includes resources for each chapter, including troubleshooting tips, online quizzes, flashcard templates, Internet activities, etc.

MICROSOFT OFFICE ACCOUNTING 2007

Each textbook includes a copy of the software, Microsoft Office Accounting Professional 2007. Install the software included with the textbook in the school's computer lab to ensure compatibility with the software that students install on their individual computers.

Computer Accounting Essentials with Microsoft Office Accounting shows you how to set up and operate a merchandising business. When you complete the textbook you will have a working familiarity with Microsoft Office Accounting Professional 2007 software.

MICROSOFT OFFICE ACCOUNTING PROFESSIONAL FEATURES

- ❖ Familiar Microsoft Office interface.
- ❖ Customizable chart of accounts and reports.
- ❖ General ledger, customer, vendor, inventory, fixed asset, payroll and job tracking.
- ❖ Create quotes, invoices, and purchase orders.
- ❖ Backup and restore.
- ❖ Audit trail for tracking transactions.
- ❖ Financial statements—income statement, balance sheet, cash flow.
- ❖ Microsoft Office integration.
- ❖ Built-in security roles and internal controls.
- ❖ Export to Excel, Word, or Access
- ❖ Create charts, graphs, and pivot tables.
- ❖ Transfer company files to the Accountant.

TEXTBOOK ORGANIZATION BY CHAPTER

1: INSTALLATION AND OVERVIEW
There are two sample companies included with the software: Northwind Traders, a product company; and Fabrikam, Inc., a service company. You install MOA and open, backup, and restore the product-based sample company, Northwind Traders. You then explore Northwind Traders to learn about MOA's user interface and help resources.

2: SECURITY AND INTERNAL CONTROLS
In this chapter you turn on the change log, review the built-in security roles, add and customize a role for yourself, disable multi-user access, create an accountant transfer file, and then e-mail it to your professor.

3: NEW COMPANY SETUP FOR A MERCHANDISING BUSINESS
In this chapter, you set up a retail business called Your Name Retailer. You enter beginning balances for October 1, edit the chart of accounts, record and post bank transactions, complete bank reconciliation, and print reports. Detailed steps and numerous screen illustrations help you learn how to use MOA. The business that you set up in this chapter is continued in the rest of the text.

4: WORKING WITH INVENTORY, VENDORS, AND CUSTOMERS
In this chapter you complete two months of transactions for a retail business to learn basic business processes. You set up vendor preferences, defaults and inventory items, record vendor transactions, make vendor payments, record sales transactions, and collect customer payments. You also complete a bank account reconciliation, display various reports, and prepare financial statements.

5: ACCOUNTING CYCLE AND YEAR END
In this chapter you review the accounting cycle and complete end-of-year adjusting entries, print financial statements, and make closing entries. You send files to your Accountant (your professor) using the Accountant Transfer feature and print the Change Log.

6: FIRST MONTH OF THE NEW YEAR
In this chapter you open the new fiscal year, record one month of transactions for your business, make adjusting entries, print reports, and send files to your Accountant (your professor) using Accountant Transfer.

Project 1, Your Name Hardware Store, is a comprehensive project that incorporates what you have learned.

Project 2, Student-Designed Merchandising Business, asks you to create a merchandising business from scratch.

7: MICROSOFT OFFICE ACCOUNTING TOOLS AND FIXED ASSETS

In this chapter you learn about fixed assets, Accountant View, and MOA analysis tools which use built-in Access reports and Excel pivot tables.

8: INTEGRATION WITH MICROSOFT OFFICE-- EXCEL AND WORD

This chapter shows you how to export data to Excel and Word and how to protect documents.

Project 3, Student-Designed Forms, gives you an opportunity to design an invoice and purchase order.

MICROSOFT OFFICE ACCOUNTING DATA FILES

Microsoft Office Accounting stores data in six separate files which are identified with the following extensions:

1. **.sbd**—data file, stored by default in the SQL server folder (Program Files\Microsoft SQLServer\ MSSQL$MICROSOFTSMLBIZ\Data).
2. **.sbc**—company file, a shortcut pointing to the location of the data file, stored by default in the My Documents\Small Business Accounting\Companies folder of the administrator who set up the MOA company.
3. **.sbl**—SQL log file, generated when you create a new company, import data from an XML file, or restore a backup file to a new company. SBL files are stored by default in the SQL server folder (Program Files\Microsoft SQLServer\ MSSQL$MICROSOFTSMLBIZ\Data).
4. **.xml**—XML file, containing data exported from Microsoft Office Accounting, stored by default in the My Documents\Small Business Accounting\Exported Data folder of the administrator who set up your company in Microsoft Office Accounting. You can create a new company from an existing company file by exporting your company data from one data file and then importing it into a new data file.

5. **.log**—log file, generated by migrating QuickBooks data, by repairing a data file, by upgrading your software, and by accessing online banking or payroll processing by ADP (if you selected Log online activities in Company Preferences). Log files are stored by default in the My Documents\Small Business Accounting\Logs folder of the administrator who set up the MOA company.

6. **.sbb**—created when company data is backed up. SBB files are stored by default in the My Documents\Small Business Accounting\Backups folder of the administrator who set up the MOA company. Create a backup file to protect your company data, to send to your accountant, to import into a new company file, or to move Microsoft Office Accounting to a different computer.

CONVENTIONS USED IN TEXTBOOK

As you work through the chapters in this text, read and follow the step-by-step instructions. Numerous screen illustrations help you check work.

1. Information that you type appears in **boldface**; for example, Type **Melody Harmony** in the Customer name field.

2. Keys on the keyboard that are pressed appear like this: <Tab>; <Enter>.

3. Words that are shown in boldface and italics are defined in Appendix B, Glossary; for example, *vendors*.

4. Unnamed buttons and icons are shown as they appear on the window; for example, [start] , [refresh] (refresh), [export to Excel], [Save and New] (post and start new transaction), etc.

5. Read Me boxes go into more detail about the task you are completing. Whenever you see a Read Me box, review this information.

6. Footnotes provide information about the task you are completing.

Chapter	Backup Names (.sbb extensions) and Files Saved (.xls and .doc extensions)	File Size	Page No.
1	Northwind Traders XXX	37,783KB	14
	Chapter 1 End XXX	37,785KB	31
	Exercise 1-2 XXX	39,797KB	38
2	Chapter 2 End XXX_200X-XX-XX	39,124KB	51
3	Chapter 3 Begin XXX	31,946KB	77
	Chapter 3 Check Register October XXX	31,300KB	89
	Chapter 3 October End XXX	32,139KB	101
4	Chapter 4 Vendors XXX	32,221KB	129
	Chapter 4 End XXX	32,295KB	154
	Exercise 4-2 December XXX	32,345KB	160
5	Chapter 5 December UTB XXX	32,383KB	170
	Chapter 5 ATB XXX	32,399KB	179
	Chapter 5 EOY XXX	32,410KB	181
	Yournameretailers_Date	32,415KB	182
6	Chapter 6 January UTB XXX	32,506KB	199
	Chapter 6 ATB XXX	32,545KB	203
Project 1	Your Name Hardware Store Begin	31,988KB	216
	Your Name Hardware Store January	32,223KB	218
	Your Name Hardware Store Financial Statements	32,275KB	220
7	Services Sales Report [first and last name].xls	120KB	229
	Payments List [first and last name].doc	62KB	231
	Suggested Fixed Asset Schedule	24KB	236
	End Chapter 7 XXX.sbc	38,166KB	236
8	Northwind Traders XXX	38,055KB	250
	Balance Sheet [first and last name].xls	33KB	253
	Last Fiscal Income Statement [first and last name].xls	33KB	256
	Comparative Income Statement [your first and last name].xls	36KB	258
	Brenda Diaz letter [first and last name].doc	21KB	261
	Password protected [first and last name].doc	21KB	263
	Exercise 8-2 Cash Balance Sheet [first and last name].xls	35KB	268
	Exercise 8-2 Letter [first and last name].doc	26KB	270

Table of Contents

> **Comment:**
> The Timetable for Completion below is meant as a guideline for hands-on work. Work can be completed in class or as a stand-alone outside of class project.

TIMETABLE FOR COMPLETION		Hours
Chapter 1	Software Installation and Overview	2.0
Chapter 2	Security and Internal Controls	1.0
Chapter 3	New Company Setup for a Merchandising Business	2.0
Chapter 4	Working With Inventory, Vendors, and Customers	2.0
Chapter 5	Accounting Cycle and Year End	2.0
Chapter 6	First Month of the New Year	1.0
Project 1	Your Name Hardware Store	3.0
Project 2	Student-Designed Merchandising Business	3.0
Chapter 7	Microsoft Office Accounting Tools and Fixed Assets	2.0
Chapter 8	Integration with Microsoft Office—Excel and Word	1.0
Project 3	Student-Designed Business Forms	1.0
TOTAL HOURS:		**20.0**

<table>
<tr><td>**Chapter
1**</td><td># Software Installation
and Overview</td></tr>
</table>

OBJECTIVES: In Chapter 1, you will learn about:

1.   System Requirements.
2.   Software Installation.
3.   Starting Microsoft Office Accounting.
4.   Opening starting data for a sample company.
5.   Backing up[1] and restoring sample company starting data.
6.   Overview of Office Accounting, pages.
7.   Microsoft Office Accounting Help, Preferences, and Product Information.
8.   Backing up your work.
9.   Flashcard Review.

 Read Me: Microsoft Office Accounting or Small Business Accounting?
The former name of Microsoft Office Accounting 2007 was Microsoft Office Small Business Accounting 2006. Small Business Accounting 2006 became two products: Microsoft Office Express 2007 and Microsoft Office Accounting Professional 2007.   Microsoft Office Accounting Professional 2007 and Windows XP Pro (SP2) were used to write the textbook.

SYSTEM REQUIREMENTS

These are the system requirements for Microsoft Office Accounting Professional 2007. Microsoft Office Accounting Professional 2007 is the software packaged with the textbook.

*   1 GHz or faster processor.
*   512 MB of RAM or more.
*   2 GB of available hard-disk space; a portion of this disk space will be freed after installation if the original download package is removed from the hard drive.
*   CD-ROM or DVD drive.

---

[1]The chart in the Preface shows you the size of each backup file. Refer to this chart for backing up data. Remember, you can back up to a hard drive location or external media.

The McGraw-Hill Companies, Inc., *Computer Accounting Essentials with Microsoft Office Accounting*

- 1024 x 768 or higher-resolution monitor.
- Vista-all editions, Microsoft Windows® XP with Service Pack (SP) 2 or later, or Microsoft Windows Server® 2003 with SP1 or later operating system.
- Microsoft Office Small Business Edition 2003 or later is required to create customized invoices, sales orders, quotes, customer credit memos, customer statements, and purchase orders.
- Microsoft Office XP or later is required to export data to Microsoft Office Word or Excel®.
- To share data among multiple computers, the host computer must be running Vista-all editions, Windows Server 2003 SP1 or later, or Windows XP Professional SP2 or later.
- Microsoft Internet Explorer® 6 or later, 32-bit browser only.
- Internet functionality requires Internet access (fees may apply).
- **External media for backups:** One 1GB or higher USB drive; Zip™ drive disk; CD-R; or, DVD-R. (CD-RW or DVD-RW required for backing up to CD-R or DVD-R.) See the Part openers for backup files sizes. The default location for backing up is C:\.....\My Documents\ Small Business Accounting\Backups. You may also specify a hard-drive or network location for backups.

Actual requirements and product functionality may vary based on the system configuration and operating system. For complete requirements, visit http://www.microsoft.com/office/products/. Third-party services are available for additional fees.

SOFTWARE INSTALLATION

This section gives you instructions for installing Microsoft Office Accounting 2007 (MOA) software. (Instructions for deleting MOA are included in Appendix A.) *Check with your professor to see if MOA has already been installed in the classroom or computer lab.*

Microsoft Office Accounting 2007 works with the following operating systems:

❖ Microsoft Windows XP Service Pack (SP) 2 or later; Vista; Microsoft Windows Server SP 1 or higher.

Follow these steps to install MOA 2007.

Step 1:   Turn on your computer. Close all programs. Microsoft Outlook should *not* be open. If Microsoft Outlook is open, close it, along with other programs that may be open.

Step 2:   Place the Microsoft Office Accounting 2007 CD into the CD-ROM drive.

Step 3:   If Autorun is enabled, Setup will start automatically. If Setup does *not* start, open Windows Explorer and double-click the Setup.exe file on the CD.

Step 4:   Office accounting 2007 uses Microsoft .NET framework 2.0. If .NET is *not* installed on your computer, the following dialog box will appear:

Step 5:   If necessary, click OK to install Microsoft .NET framework 2.0. This may take a few minutes.

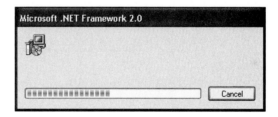

Step 6:   During the installation of .NET, you may be asked to install additional hotfixes. Click OK to install the hotfixes.

Step 7:   The Microsoft Office Accounting 2007 Setup Wizard window appears.

Step 8: Click [Next >]. The Destination Folder window appears.

Step 9: The setup wizard allows you to pick an installation folder. The authors suggest you accept the C drive default. (*Or*, click [Browse...] to select a folder.) Click [Next >]. The Begin installation window appears.

Step 10: Click [Install]. An Installation in progress window appears. This process may take several minutes. The setup wizard will continue with the installation of SQL Server 2005 Express and Microsoft Office Accounting 2007. Microsoft SQL Server 2005 Express is installed with the folder name MSSMLBIZ. Refer to the two illustrations below to see the progress of SQL installation and MOA.

Note: If any Firewall or Security pop-up windows occur during setup, select Always Allow.

Step 11: An Installation Complete window appears.

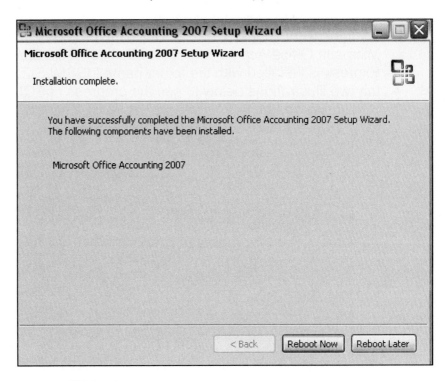

Step 12: Click Reboot Now or Finish depending on your screen. Remove the Microsoft Office Accounting 2007 CD.

Step 13: The software included with the textbook is a 120-day trial version. Write down the date of software installation here.

Note: Instructions on how to delete MOA are located in Appendix A.

Read Me: What happens after 120 days?

See the READ ME FIRST! Important Information for Your 120-Day Trial of Microsoft Office Accounting Professional 2007 included with your software.

STARTING MICROSOFT OFFICE ACCOUNTING

Follow these steps to start MOA.

Step 1: Click ; All Programs, Microsoft Office, Microsoft Office Accounting 2007. (*Hint:* You may want to set up an icon on your desktop. To do that, right-click on Microsoft Office Accounting 2007, left-click Copy. Right-click on the Windows desktop; left-click Paste. To start MS Office Accounting, double-click on the Microsoft Office Accounting 2007 icon.)

Step 2: The Enter Product Key window appears. Enter the Product Key located on the READ THIS FIRST! Information included with your software. Enter the Referral Code which is the Referral Key located on the back of your software envelope.

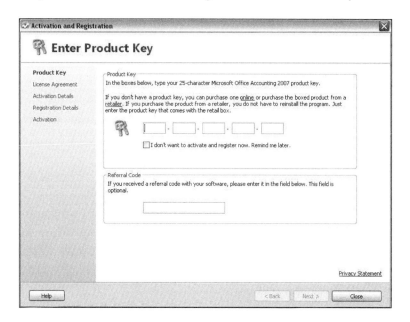

Click Next >.

Step 3: Accept the license agreement by selecting I accept the terms of this license agreement. Click Next >.

Step 4: The Activation window appears. Select radio button for I want to activate the software over the Internet (Recommended).

Click .

Step 5: The Activation Registration window appears. Complete the colored required fields using the following information:

Company Name:
       Your
       Name
       Retailers
       (use your
       first and
       last
       name)
Street: Your
       address
City: Reno
State: Nevada
Zip: 89557
Phone: Your phone
       number
E-Mail: Your e-mail
Role: Owner
Industry Type:
       Retail
No. of Employees:
       1-5

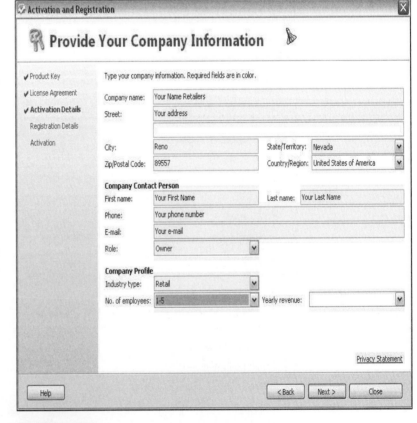

When satisfied, click .

Step 6:   The Select Contact Preferences screen appears. Uncheck all
          boxes and click send to complete activation and registration.

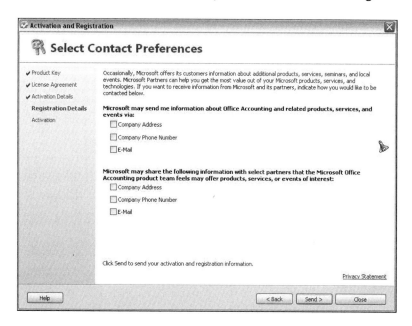

Step 7:   The Start - Microsoft Office Accounting window appears.

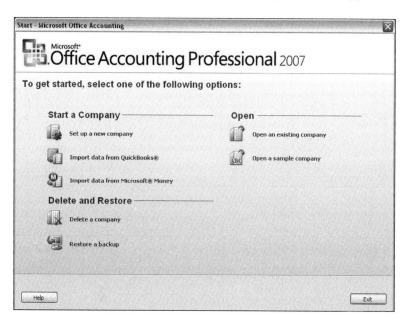

Step 8:   Review what is shown on the Start window. Exit or continue
          working on the next section.

OPENING STARTING DATA FOR A SAMPLE COMPANY

Sample company data files for Northwind Traders and Fabrikam, Inc. are included with the software. Follow the steps below to open starting data for Northwind Traders, the product based sample company. Similar steps can be followed to open data from the service based sample company, Fabrikam, Inc.

1. Begin in the Start – Microsoft Office Accounting window. (If necessary, select, Start; All Programs, Microsoft Office, Microsoft Office Accounting 2007. The Start -Microsoft Office Accounting window appears. If a company opens, click File; Close Company.) The Start – Microsoft Office Accounting window appears. Click on the link to <u>Open a sample company</u>.

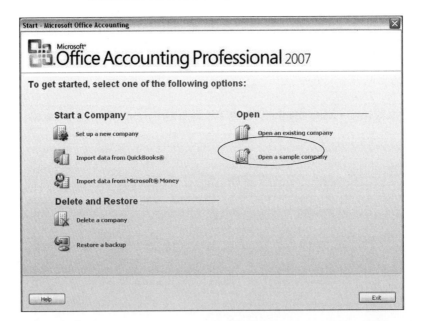

2. The Select Sample Company window appears. Select Product based sample company.

3. Click OK .

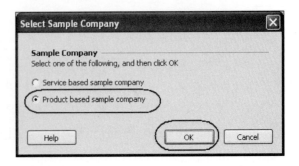

A product based company purchases merchandise from vendors, then sells that merchandise to customers. Products fall into two categories: inventory and non-inventory items. Another way to describe a product based company is to call it a merchandising or retail business. The sample company that you are going to use, Northwind Traders, is a product based business.

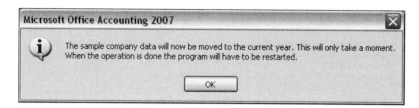

4. When the window prompts The sample company data will now be moved to the current year, click [OK].

5. When the window prompts, The program will be closed for the changes to take effect, click [OK].

6. Restart MOA. (*HINT*: See Step 1 on page 10.) The Product Activation (Trial) window appears. Write down the date the 120 day trial period ends.

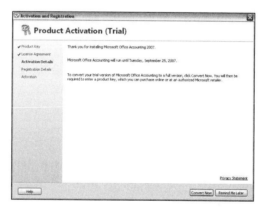

Click [Remind Me Later].
Note: Each time you open MOA you will see this window.

7. The Northwind Traders – Microsoft Office Accounting 2007 window appears. When the sample company is started for the first time, the current year (system date year) is established.

8. The company home page appears. Compare your window with the one shown on the next page. The various parts of the MOA home page willl be explained later in the MOA's Graphical User Interface section.

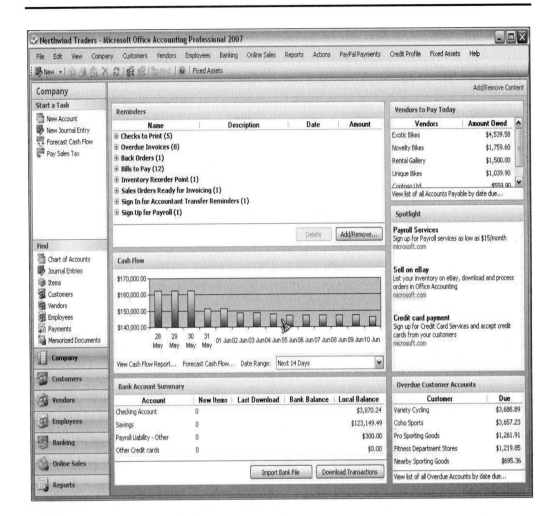

BACKING UP NORTHWIND TRADERS

When using MOA, information is automatically saved to the hard drive of the computer. In a classroom setting, a number of students may be using the same computer. This means that when you return to the computer lab or classroom, your data is gone. *Backing up* your data means saving it to a hard drive, network drive, or external media. Backing up insures that you can start where you left off the last time you used Microsoft Office Accounting.

In this section you will create a backup of the original starting data and then restore this backup file. This backup is made *before* any data is added to the sample company so if you want to start with fresh, starting data again, you can restore from this backup file of the original data.

Comment

The authors suggest backing up the sample company. In this textbook, you are shown how to backup to a hard drive location. Backing up to a drive other than the hard drive or network drive is called backing up to *external media*. The instructions that follow assume you are backing up to the hard drive of your computer. If you are working in the computer lab, this may not be possible. **Instead, backup to a 1GB USB flash drive or to your desktop.**

When you back up, you are saving to the current point in MOA. Each time you make a backup, you should type a different backup name (file name) to distinguish between them. In this way, if you need to *restore* an earlier backup, you have the data for that purpose. See Preface for a list of backups you will make in this text and their file size.

In the business world, backups are unique for each business day. Daily backups are necessary. If you are working in a computer lab, *never leave the computer lab without first backing up your data to external media, i.e., your USB flash drive.*

The text directions assume that you are backing up to the *default* hard drive location. Defaults are defined as an option that is already selected for you and will be used unless you change it. Follow these steps to back up Microsoft Office Accounting.

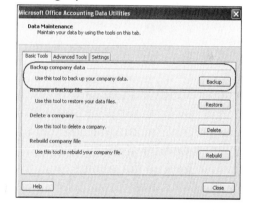

1.   From the menu bar, select File; Utilities, Data Utilities. The Microsoft Office Accounting Data Utilities window appears.

2.   Click [Backup]. The Backup window appears. (The software defaults to the current date.)

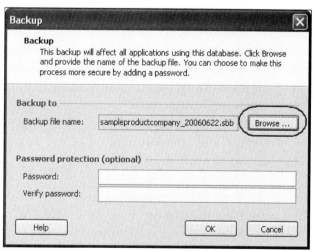

3.   Click [Browse ...]. The Select Backup File window appears. Observe that the Save in field defaults to the Backups folder.

Delete the file name shown in the File name field. Type **Northwind Traders and your initials,** i.e., Northwind Traders XXX, in the File name field. (Use your initials in place of the XXX.) Observe that you are creating a Backup File with an .sbb extension.

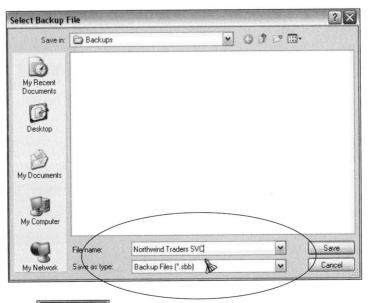

4.   Click [Save].

5.   The Backup window appears showing the Backup file name: C:\....\My Documents\Small Business Accounting\Backups\ Northwind TradersXXX.sbb. (Remember your backup file name will also include your initials.) *If you are working in the computer lab, the Backup location must be on your Desktop!*

DO NOT PASSWORD PROTECT!

6. Click . The Backup please wait; Backup in progress window appears. The backup file is being created/compressed (made smaller.)

7. When the window appears saying the Backup was completed successfully, click [OK].

8. Close the Data Maintenance window.

9. Click File; Exit to exit Northwind Traders and return to the windows desktop. (*Or,* continue with the next section without exiting.)

If you want to back up the starting data for Fabrikam, Inc. (the service based sample company) follow similar steps to create its backup file.

Read me: Data Files

Refer to the Preface, to review information about the seven types of MOA files and where these files are stored. The Preface also lists the names of all the backups you will make in this text.

Locate the Backup File

You can use either My Computer or Windows Explorer to identify where your backup file has been saved. In the example that follows, My Computer is used.

The steps that follow assume that the backup file was saved to the default location—C:\.....\My Documents\Small Business Accounting \Backups. Follow these steps to locate the backup file using My Computer.

1. Click Start; My Computer. The My Computer window appears. In the Files Stored on This Computer area, select your computer's Documents. The My 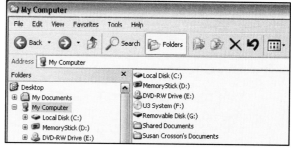 Computer window shows the author's Documents folder.

2. Double-click on the XXXX Documents folder to open it. (Substitute your name, or Administrator, for the XXXX's.)

3. The My Documents window opens: C:\Documents and Settings\Your Name or computer's name\My Documents.

4. Double-click on the Small Business Accounting folder. Observe the folders, Backups, Companies, and possibly Logs.

5. Double-click Backups. The Northwind Traders XXX.sbb file is shown. (Substitute your initials for XXX) Observe the address of your backup file. This is the location of the file. File size may differ.

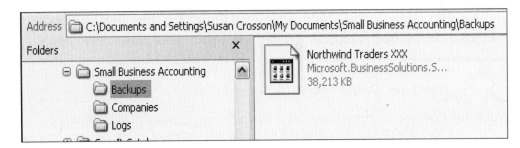

Copy Northwind Traders XXX.sbb to External Media

1. Click on Northwind.sbb to select it. In the File and Folder Tasks list, link to <u>Copy this file</u>.

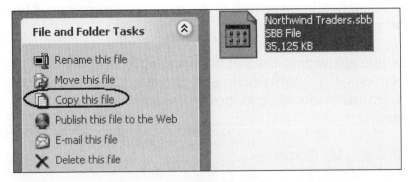

2. The Copy Items window appears. Select your USB drive (*or* other external media drive). Click Copy . The file copies to external media.

3. Close the Backups window. To make sure you copied the backup

file, go to My Computer (or Windows Explorer); then browse to the location of Northwind Traders XXX.sbb (Substitute your initials for XXX) to make sure it is there.

RESTORING STARTING DATA FOR A SAMPLE COMPANY

1. Begin in the Start – Microsoft Office Accounting window. (If necessary, select, Start; All Programs, Microsoft Office, Microsoft Office Accounting 2007. The Start -Microsoft Office Accounting window appears. If a company is open, click File; Close Company.) The Start – Microsoft Office Accounting window appears.

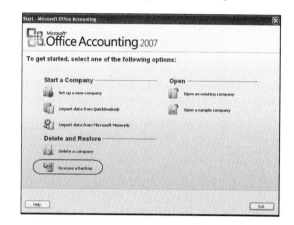

2. Link to <u>Restore a backup</u>.

3. The Database Restore window appears. In the Backup filename field, click Browse ... . Browse to the location of your backup file. The steps that follow assume you backed up to the hard drive location My Documents \Small Business Accounting \Backups\Northwind Traders XXX.sbb. If necessary, in the Look in field, go to the appropriate location of your backup file.

4. Click Northwind Traders XXX.sbb. (Substitute your initials for XXX) Compare your Select Backup File to the one shown here. Click Open .

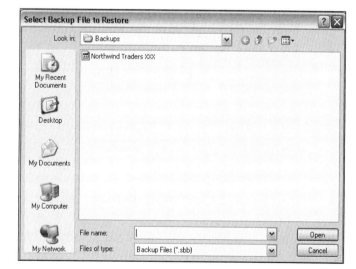

5. The Database Restore, Restore a Backup window appears. In the Restore backup file to field, click [Browse ...]. The Select Company File window appears. Select sampleproductcompany.sbc. Click [Save]. When the window appears that says this file already exists, click [Yes]. Compare your Database Restore, Restore a Backup window to the one shown below.

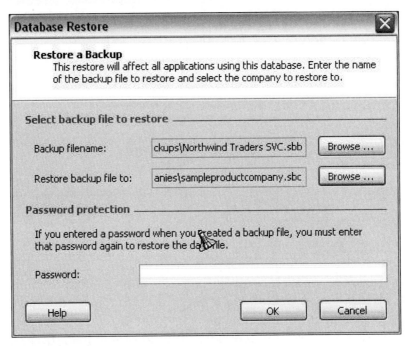

6. Click [OK]. The file starts to restore.

7. When the window prompts, the restore process was completed successfully, click [OK].

8. From the Start – Microsoft Office Accounting window, link to <u>Open a sample company</u>, click [OK].

9. From the Select Sample Company window, select Product based sample company. Click [OK].

10. Close the Microsoft Office Accounting Utilities window.

GRAPHICAL USER INTERFACE (GUI)

The general look of a program is called its graphical user interface. As you know, most Windows programs include the mouse pointer, icons, toolbars, menus, and a navigation pane. One of the benefits of Windows is that it standardizes terms and operations used in software programs.

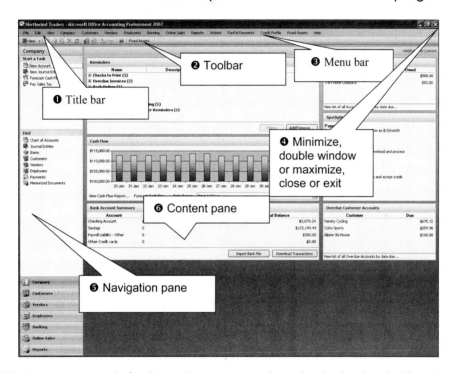

MOA's home page defaults to the current date (today's date). Your home page may differ; for example, the Cash Flow bar chart may show different dates and amounts.

The Northwind Traders – Microsoft Office Accounting 2007 window here shows how MOA's windows are organized. In this textbook, you will use both menu bar selections and Navigation Pane selections to complete work.

For now, let's study the parts of the window. Some features are common to all software programs that are written for Windows. For example, in the upper right corner is the Minimize ▬ button, Double Window ▣ button, and the Close ✕ button. The title bar, window border, and mouse pointer are also common to Windows programs. Other features are specific to MOA: menu bar, toolbar, and navigation pane.

Windows programs use menus in the form of horizontal menu bar selections. The contents of these menus differ depending on the application.

❶ *Title Bar*: Contains the company name and the program name, Microsoft Office Accounting 2007.

❷ The *Toolbar* displays a set of buttons –

New, E-mail, Print, Export to Excel, Delete, Refresh, Send Books, Receive Books, Find, and Help. It also shows Fixed Assets which is an add-on feature you will learn about later in the text.   If a button appears dimmed, it is unavailable.

❸ *Menu Bar*: Contains the menus for File, Edit, View, Company, Customers, Vendors, Employees, Banking, Online Sales, Reports, Actions, PayPal Payments, Credit Profile, Fixed Assets, and Help. You can click on the menu bar item to see its selections, or you can press **<Alt>** plus **<F>** to see the File menu. Once you click **<Alt>** plus **<F>**, notice that your menu bar selections have an underlined letter. If your menu bar selections have an underlined letter that means you can make a selection by typing **<Alt>** and the underlined letter. For example, in Windows XP if you press the **<Alt>** key then press the **<F>** key, the menu bar shows underlined letters as well as the submenu. You can also click with your left-mouse button on the menu bar headings to see the submenu selections.

❹ Minimize ▬, Double Window ▢, or Maximize ▣, and Close or Exit ✖ buttons: Clicking once on Minimize ▬ reduces the window to a button on the *taskbar*. In Windows, the 🏁 start button and taskbar are located at the bottom of your window. Clicking once on Double Window ▢ returns the window to its previous size. This button appears when you maximize the window. After clicking on the Double Window ▢ button, the symbol changes to the Maximize ▣ button. Click once on the Maximize ▣ button to enlarge the window. Click once on the Exit or Close ✖ button to close the window, or exit the program.

❺ ***Navigation Pane*[2]**: Microsoft Office Accounting offers a graphical alternative to the menu bar. The Navigation Pane on the left side contains the following areas: Start a Task list, Find list, and Navigation buttons. The Navigation buttons for the home pages are: Company, Customers, Vendors, Employees, Banking, and Reports.

❻ ***Content Pane:*** Displays information on your company. The following content appears when you first open the Company home page: Today's Reminders, Cash Flow, Bank Account Summary, Vendors to Pay Today, Spotlight, and Overdue Customer Accounts list. You can also Add/Remove Content from the Company home page.

NAVIGATION PANE

The Navigation Pane contains the following areas: Start a Task list, Find list, and Navigation buttons for the home pages. In the information that follows, the Navigation Pane [Company] button was selected.

Start a task: The Start a Task list contains links to help manage the company.

Find: The Find list contains links to records and the ***chart of accounts***. The chart of accounts is a list of all the accounts used by a company. A partial chart of accounts is shown below. Observe that it shows up-to-date balances. In a future chapter, you will explore the chart of accounts in more detail (after you have added transactions). Scroll down the list to familiarize yourself with Northwind Traders accounts.

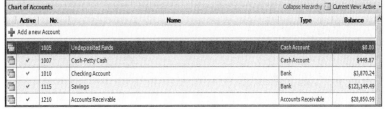

Chart of Accounts			Collapse Hierarchy ☐ Current View: Active ▾	
Active	No.	Name	Type	Balance
➕ Add a new Account				
	1005	Undeposited Funds	Cash Account	$0.00
✓	1007	Cash-Petty Cash	Cash Account	$449.87
✓	1010	Checking Account	Bank	$3,870.24
✓	1115	Savings	Bank	$123,149.49
✓	1210	Accounts Receivable	Accounts Receivable	$28,850.99

[2]The Navigation Pane can be widened or narrowed. Move the cursor over the Navigation Pane's right border. The cursor changes to a cross-bar, left-click to move the pane wider or narrower.

Navigation Buttons: Select a navigation button to go to home pages: Company, Customers, Vendors, Employees, Banking, and Reports.

TYPICAL MICROSOFT OFFICE ACCOUNTING WINDOWS

When one of the Navigation Pane's buttons (Company, Customers, Vendors, Employees, Banking, Reports) is selected, a home page appears. For example, click [Banking], and the Banking home page is shown. Compare your Banking; Start a Task window to the one shown here.

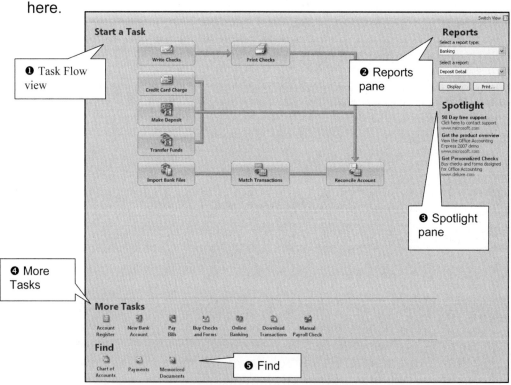

Clicking on an icon takes you to that task. Observe that the Banking home page includes: ❶ Task Flow view, ❷ Reports pane (right side, ❸ Spotlight pane (right side), ❹ More Tasks (bottom), and ❺ Find.

Observe there is also a Switch View 🔳 icon on the Banking title bar. If you click 🔳; a Start a Task and Find list appears instead of the Task Flow view. Observe that the Reports choices and Spotlight list are included when you selected Switch View. Click 🔳 again to go back to the task flow view.

MENU BAR

Northwind Traders menu bar has 15 selections: File, Edit, View, Company, Customers, Vendors, Employees, Banking, Online Sales, Reports, Actions, PayPal Payments, Credit Profile, Fixed Assets, and Help. The sample companies show MOA's complete menu bar. Some of the selections require third-party software (for example, PayPal Payments, Credit Profile.)

1. If necessary, enlarge Northwind Traders.

   (*Hint:* Click 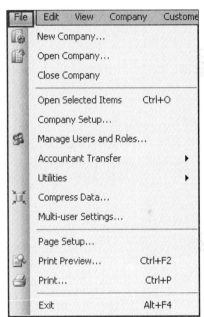 on the taskbar.) From the menu bar, click File to see the file menu options. The file menu includes selections for New Company, Open Company, Close Company, Open Selected Items, Company Setup, Manage Users and Roles, Accountant Transfer, Utilities, Compress Data, Multi-user Settings, Page Setup, Print Preview, Print, Exit. If any of the items are grayed out, they are inactive. In order to show all File menu selections, from the Navigation Pane's Company Find list, select Chart of Accounts.

   Menu choices that are followed by an ***ellipsis*** (...) are associated with ***dialog boxes*** or windows that supply information about the open window. An arrow (▶) next to a menu item (for example, Utilities) indicates that there is a submenu with additional selections. Also, observe that pressing **<Ctrl>+<O>** can be used to open selected items.

2. From the menu bar, click Edit. The edit menu includes selections for Delete, Select All, Make Active (grayed out because it is inactive), Make Inactive. Observe that keyboard shortcuts such as **<Ctrl>+ <D>** can be used to Delete.
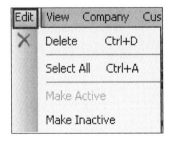

3.   From the menu bar, click View. The View menu allows you Arrange By, Filter By, Refresh, Switch view (grayed out selections are inactive), and Add/Remove Content.

4.   From the menu bar, click Company. The Company menu bar has selections for Company Home, Business Services, Company Information, Preferences, Integrates with Business Contact Manager, Forecast Cash Flow, Create a Budget, New Journal Entry, New Cash Basis Journal Entry, New Account, Merge Accounts, Sales Tax, Manage Support Lists, Manage Fiscal Year, Write Letters, Manage Word Templates, and Company Lists.

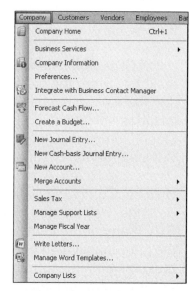

5.   From the menu bar, click Customers. This selection includes Customers Home, New, Receive Payment, Customer Refund, Finance Charge, Create Statement, Credit Card Processing, Price Levels, Write Letters, Manager Word Templates, Customer Services, Customer Lists.

6. Click on Vendors to see its menu. This selection includes Vendors Home, New, Receive Items, Enter Bills, Pay Bills, Issue Payments, New Vendor Payment, Record Expenses, Physical Inventory Worksheet, Change Item Prices, Adjust Inventory, Write Letters, Manage Word Templates, Vendor Services, Vendor Lists, and Display 1099 Report.

7. Click Employees. This selection includes Employees Home, New Employee, New Time Entry, New Timesheet, Online Payroll, Payroll, Download Pay Runs, Manual Payroll, Reimburse Employee, Write Letters, Employee Services, and Employee Lists.

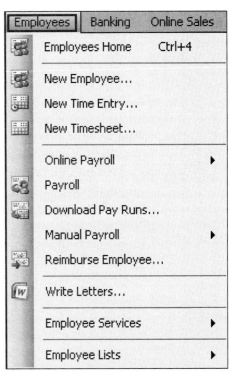

8. Click Banking. This selection includes Banking Home, New Bank Account, Account Register, Write Checks, Make Deposit, Transfer Funds, Pay Bills, Enter Payments, Bank Online, Import Bank File, Credit Card Processing, Match Transactions, Credit Card Charge, Reconcile Account, Print Checks, Banking Services, and Banking Lists.

Banking	Online Sales	Reports	A
Banking Home		Ctrl+5	
New Bank Account...			
Account Register		Ctrl+R	
Write Checks...			
Make Deposit			
Transfer Funds...			
Pay Bills...			
Enter Payments			
Bank Online			▶
Import Bank File			
Credit Card Processing			▶
Match Transactions			
Credit Card Charge			
Reconcile Account...			
Print Checks...			
Banking Services			▶
Banking Lists			▶

9. Click Online Sales. This selection includes Online Sales Homes, Set Up To Sell Online, List Items to Marketplace, Download Orders and Fees, Manage Online Sales, and Online Sales Lists. Online Sales appears on the menu bar, when the company preference has been selected to enable online sales.

10. Click Reports. This selection includes Reports Home, Saved Reports, Company and Financial, Customers and Receivables, Sales, Vendors and Payables, Purchases, Inventory, Banking and Employees and Payroll, and Fixed Asset Manager.

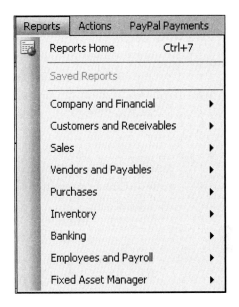

11. Click Actions. This selection includes Find, Export to Excel, New Account, and New Journal Entry. (*Hint:* In order to see the Actions selections, the Chart of Accounts was selected.)

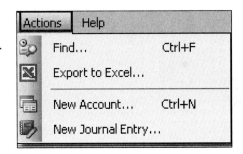

12. Click PayPal Payments. This selection shows PayPay Settings, Import Payments, and PayPal Help.

13. Click Credit Profile. This selection shows Sign Up for Credit Profile, Manage Credit Profit, Get Your Company's Credit Report, and Credit Profit Help.

14. Click Fixed Assets. This selection includes Fixed Asset Manager, Fixed Asset Depreciation Schedule, Fixed Asset Projection, and Fixed Asset Help.

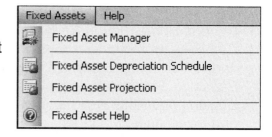

15. Click Help. The Help selection includes Microsoft Office Accounting Help, Help with this Window, Office Online, Check for Updates, Activate and Register Product, Contact Us, Support Services, Find an Accountant, Community, Customer Feedback Options, Submit Feedback, and About Microsoft Office Accounting.

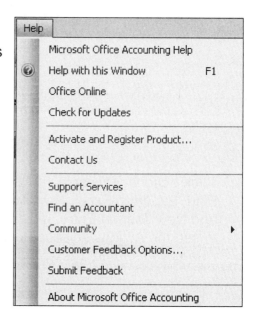

MICROSOFT OFFICE ACCOUNTING HELP

Microsoft Office Accounting includes a couple levels of Help. The instructions that follow demonstrate MOA's Help files.

1. From MOA's menu bar, click Help; Microsoft Office Accounting Help. The Contents tab is selected.

2. Click on the plus sign next to Data Files.

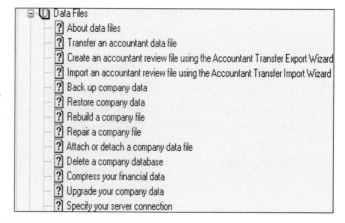

3. Click on the question mark next to Back up company data. Read the information on the Back up company data window.

4. Click on other areas to explore. Read the information on various help windows. For example, click on the question mark next to Restore company data.

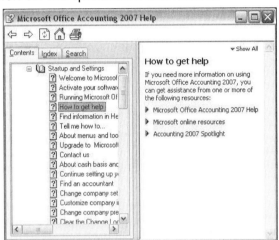

5. Before exiting the Help windows, click How to get help.

6. Read about the different ways to get Help when using MOA.

7. Link to each area. When you are through, close the Help window.

COMPANY PREFERENCES

Follow these steps to look at the User Preferences for Northwind Traders.

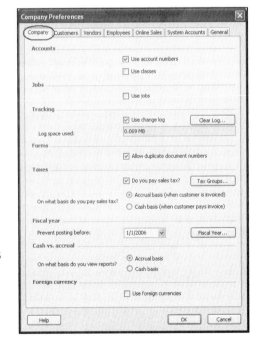

1. From the menu bar, select Company; Preferences. The Company Preferences window appears. If necessary, click on the Company tab.

2. Read the information on the Company Preferences window. Observe where the checkmarks are placed. To see other preferences, click on the tabs for Customers, Vendors, Employees, System Accounts, and General.

3. Close the window, click [X] on the Company Preferences title bar.

DISPLAYING PRODUCT INFORMATION

1. From the menu bar, click on Help;
   About Microsoft Office Accounting. The
   About Microsoft Office Accounting
   window appears. (Your Product ID and
   Registration fields will be completed.)
   Version 2.0.7024.0 was used to write
   the textbook.

2. After reviewing the window, click
   | Close |.

USING WINDOWS EXPLORER

The instructions that follow show you how to identify MOA's program
path, directories, and subdirectories on the hard drive of your computer.
You also see the size of the MOA and sample company data.

Follow these steps to use Windows Explorer to identify MOA's location
on your computer system.

1. If necessary, minimize Microsoft Office Accounting. Your Windows
   desktop should be displayed.

2. If your desktop has a Windows Explorer icon, double-click on it. *Or,*
   click ; All Programs, Accessories, Windows Explorer.
   (These instructions are consistent with Windows XP. If you are
   using another version of Windows, make the appropriate elections.)

3. In the Address field, select drive C, then double-click on the
   Program Files folder to open it. The address field shows
   C:\Program Files. Now double-click on the Microsoft Small
   Business folder to open it. The Address field shows C:\Program
   Files\Microsoft Small Business. This is the location (program path)
   of Microsoft Office Accounting on your computer.

4. Notice on the left side of your
   window, there is a Folders list

and that the Small Business Accounting folder has a plus sign next to it. Click on the plus sign.

5. Right-click on the Small Business Accounting 2007 folder. A drop-down list appears. Left-click on Properties. The Small Business Accounting 2007 Properties window appears. Compare your Small Business Accounting 2007 Properties window to the one shown here.
    Observe the Location (program path) of Microsoft Office Accounting is C:\Program Files\Microsoft Small Business. The size of the file is 320 MB or 335,793,388 bytes and contains 180 files and 18 folders. Your file size, number of files, and folders may differ.

6. Click **OK** to close the Microsoft Office Accounting Properties window.

7. Close Windows Explorer.

BACKING UP YOUR WORK

At the end of each chapter or part, the authors recommend that you backup. Backing up insures that you have data to restore. For example, let's say you would like to start Northwind Traders from the beginning. The backup made on pages 12-17, Northwind Traders XXX.sbb, has fresh, starting data. If you back up your work now and restore this backup file, you can start the sample company from the end of the Software Installation and Overview part.

Follow these steps to backup your work now.

1. Click File; Utilities, Data Utilities.

2. In the Backup company data area, click **Backup**.

3. In the Backup file name field, click **Browse ...**.

4. Type **Chapter 1 End and your initials**, i.e., Chapter 1 End XXX, in the File name field.

5. Click [Save].

6. When the Backup window appears, click [OK]. Wait a few moments while the file is being backed up.

7. When the window prompts that the Backup was completed successfully, click [OK].

8. Close the Microsoft Office Accounting Data Utilities window.

9. Exit MOA or continue.

> Read **me:**
> Periodically copy backups to external media. First, backup data; then copy the files from My Documents\Small Business Accounting\Backups\[filename.sbb] to a USB drive. (*Hint: You may have saved your backups to a different path.*)

You may need to transport data from one location to another. The authors suggest that you copy the backup file to USB media. Then copy the backup file from USB media to the Desktop of Computer 2. This way when you want to restore data, it is easy to find the backup file. The flowchart below illustrates how to transport data from one computer to another computer.

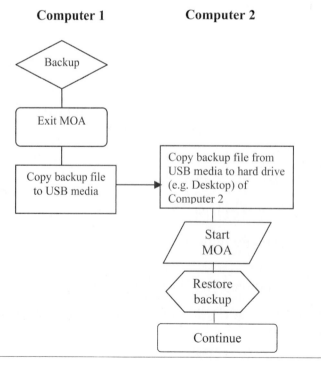

FLASHCARD REVIEW

This section demonstrates how to prepare flashcards. Each chapter requires flashcard preparation to reinforce what you have learned. Keep all of your flashcards handy, just in case you need to know how to do something in MOA in a flash!

To create flashcards, use index cards or use PowerPoint or Word. For example, if you use Word to create a flashcard on how to install MOA, type the heading **Installation of Microsoft Office Accounting Software** on page 1. On page 2, type the installation steps (see example below). Save your file. Print the pages back-to-back. You should have the title of the flashcard on one side of the paper and the steps on the other side of the paper.

Page 1

INSTALLATION OF MICROSOFT OFFICE ACCOUNTING SOFTWARE

Page 2

---

1. Insert the MOA CD into your computer's CD-ROM drive. *Note:* If Setup does not start, open Windows Explorer and double-click the Setup.exe file on the CD.
2. If necessary, install the Microsoft .NET framework 2.0 and the appropriate hotfixes.
3. When the Setup Wizard window appears, follow the prompts to install. Install SQL Server 2005 Express and MOA 2007.
4. When the Wizard is complete, click Finish.
5. Start MOA.

You can also use PowerPoint to create flashcards. Templates for making flashcards are located on textbook's website: www.mhhe.com/moa**essentials**

SUMMARY AND REVIEW

OBJECTIVES: In Chapter 1, you learned about:

1. System Requirements.
2. Software Installation.
3. Starting Microsoft Office Accounting.
4. Opening starting data for a sample company.
5. Backing up and restoring sample company starting data.
6. Overview of Office Accounting's user interface.
7. Microsoft Office Accounting Help, Preferences, and Product Information.
8. Backing up your work.
9. Flashcard Review.

GOING TO THE NET

Comment

For the Going to the Net exercises, go online to **www.mhhe.com/moa**essentials. Link to Student Edition; choose the appropriate chapter, then link to Going to the Net Exercises.

Access the Microsoft Office Accounting Express website at:
http://office.microsoft.com/en-us/accountingexpress/default.aspx
and Microsoft Office Accounting Professional 2007 website at:
http://office.microsoft.com/en-us/accounting/default.aspx

1. What are the standard features of Office Accounting Express?
2. Who should use Office Accounting Express?
3. What additional features does Office Accounting Professional provide? Who should use it?

FLASHCARD REVIEW

To review how to use Microsoft Office Accounting, create flashcards. For example in this chapter you learned to prepare a flashcard for installing MOA by writing Installation on one side of the card; and on the other side, writing the steps for software installation. Create flashcards for the following.

1. Software installation.

2. Starting Sample Company.

3. Backing up data.

4. Restoring data.

5. Copying backup data to external media.

6. Using Windows Explorer to determine file size.

True/Make True: Write the word True in the space provided if the statement is true. If the statement is not true, write the correct answer.

1. After the 120 day trial period ends, all of MOA's features and data cannot to be used.

   _____

   _____

2. Your Name Retailers is located in Reno Nevada.

   _____

   _____

3. Shortcut keys enable you to use Microsoft Office Accounting's mouse.

_____

_____

4. In this book, the greater and lesser signs are used to indicate individual keys on the keyboard; for example <Tab>.

_____

_____

5. You can close the application you are working with if you single click with your mouse on the close button ().

_____

_____

6. It is a good idea to regularly copy backups to external media such as a USB drive.

_____

_____

7. The default location for Company data is My Documents\Office Accounting\Backups.

_____

_____

8. The Navigation Pane is shown at the top of the home page.

   _____

   _____

9. When backing up, files are compressed or made smaller.

   _____

   _____

10. The extension added to files that have been restored is .MOA,
   Microsoft Office Accounting.

   _____

   _____

Exercise 1-1: Follow the instructions below to complete Exercise 1-1:

1. Start MOA. Open the service-based sample company, Fabrikam, Inc.
   (*HINT:* See pages 10-12.)

2. Continue with Exercise 1-2.

Exercise 1-2

1. Follow these steps to backup.

   a. Click File; Utilities, Data Utilities.

   b. In the Backup company data area, click [Backup].

   c. In the Backup file name field, click [Browse ...].

d. Type **Exercise 1-2 and your initials** in the File name field.

e. Click [Save].

f. When the Backup window appears, click [OK].

g. When the Backup was completed successfully window appears, click [OK].

h. Close the Microsoft Office Accounting Data Utilities window.

i. Exit MOA.

2. Copy the backup file to external media. (*HINT:* See pages 31-32.)

Analysis Question: How many menu bar selections does Fabrikam, Inc. have? List the menu bar selections that are available.

Chapter 2
Security and Internal Controls

OBJECTIVES: In Chapter 2, you use software to:

1. Start Microsoft Office Accounting (MOA).
2. Restore and open the product-based sample company, Northwind Traders.
3. View Change Log and confirm that it is in use.
4. Understand User's pre-built security roles and permissions.
5. Modify a user role and try to add a user.
6. Disable Multi-user access.
7. Transfer company data file to your accountant (professor).
8. Use your Internet browser to go to the book's website. (Go online to www.mhhe.com/moaessentials.)

In Chapter 2, you become familiar with some of the MOA features that protect business data and keep it safe. You become familiar with Microsoft Office Accounting's various preset user roles and the internal controls prescribed for each user group. You learn about the change log, multi-user access, and how to share your company's database with your Accountant.

GETTING STARTED

1. Start Microsoft Office Accounting.

   1. Begin in the Start – Microsoft Office Accounting window. (If necessary, select, Start; All Programs, Microsoft Office, Microsoft Office Accounting 2007.

   2. Click Remind Me Later when the Product Activation (Trial) window appears.

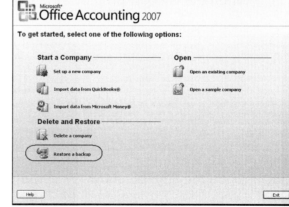

The McGraw-Hill Companies, Inc., *Computer Accounting Essentials with Microsoft Office Accounting*

3. The Start -Microsoft Office Accounting window appears. If a company is open, click File; Close Company.) The Start – Microsoft Office Accounting window appears.

4. Link to Restore a backup.

5. The Database Restore window appears. In the Backup filename field, click [Browse ...]. Browse to the location of your backup file. The steps that follow assume you backed up to the hard drive location My Documents \Small Business Accounting \Backups\. If necessary, in the Look in field, go to the appropriate location of your backup file.

4. Click Chapter 1 End XXX.sbb. Click [Open]. (Substitute your initials for XXX)

5. The Database Restore, Restore a Backup window appears. In the Restore backup file to field, click [Browse ...]. The Select Company File window appears. Select sampleproductcompany.sbc. Click [Save]. When the window appears that says this file already exists, click [Yes].

6. Click [OK]. The file starts to restore.

7. When the window prompts, the restore process was completed successfully, click [OK].

8. From the Start – Microsoft Office Accounting window, link to Open a sample company, click [OK].

9. From the Select Sample Company window, select Product based sample company. Click [OK].

10. When the title bar shows Northwind Traders – Microsoft Office Accounting Professional 2007, the product based sample company is open.

[Northwind Traders - Microsoft Office Accounting Professional 2007]

CHANGE LOG

The Change Log tracks who changes company data and what changes were made. This ability to monitor changes occurring in the accounting system and who is doing them is an essential internal control for any business. Data tracking allows managers who are responsible for safeguarding data and maintaining its confidentiality assurance that the system is secure. Follow these steps to confirm the Change Log is working and to view the Northwind Traders Change Log.

1. To confirm that the Change Log is monitoring Northwind Traders accounting system changes, open Company; click Preferences.

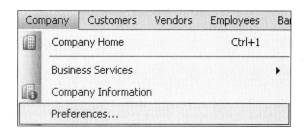

2. When the Company Preference window appears, confirm that the Use Change Log check box is checked.

3. Close the Company Preferences window to return to Northwind Traders desktop.

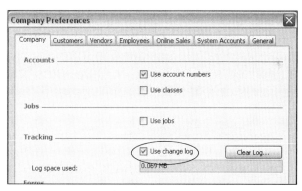

4. Open the Reports menu; select Company and Financial, click Change Log.

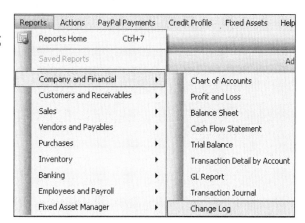

5. The Change Log appears. Yours will differ from what is shown here.

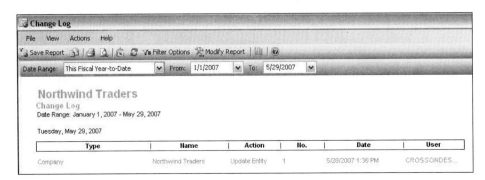

6. Review entry then close the Change Log.

UNDERSTANDING USER ROLES AND PERMISSIONS

Having user roles with preset permissions allows MOA to keep sensitive financial data secure and maintain good company internal controls. Good internal controls reduce a business' risk for wrongdoing and fraud by limiting what users can do or see. What a user can view or do in MOA is limited by the role assigned to them. Each role permits different authorized access to MOA. Only authorized Windows users can be assigned one of the following preset roles:

- Read-only User-can view customer and vendor transaction information but cannot add, delete, or update any information.
- Salesperson-can handle customer transactions and most vendor transaction but cannot do any banking, accounting, or payroll transactions.
- Office Manager-can manage the day-to-day financial records of the company, including customer transactions, vendor transactions, banking transactions, and payroll. The Office Manager role has full access to most product areas but cannot open a closed fiscal year, setup a company, manage user roles, set up access for multiple users, install add-ins, create or import an accountant's backup copy, or use the Data Utilities commands on the File menu.
- Accountant-can manage and update company financial data. The Accountant role has all the permissions of the Office Manager and can open a closed fiscal year.
- Owner-can only be assigned to users with Windows Administrator

privileges since a Windows Administrator has full access to MOA. If an Owner is later removed as a Windows Administrator, they will only have access to the MOA features not requiring Administrator access.

- Windows Administrator-can access all aspects of MOA including installation, company setup, user roles and permissions, archiving, setting up multiple users , setting up add-ins, creating or importing an accountant's backup copy, and using the Data Utilities commands on the File menu.

If one of the pre-built roles does not meet the needs of a business, additional customized roles can be added. To add a role, follow these steps:

1. From Northwind Traders desktop, open the File menu; click on Manage Users and Roles.

2. The Manage Users Dialog box appears. Click on Add...

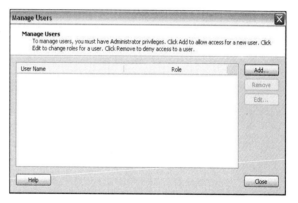

3. In Add User window, before you add yourself as a user, click on Manage Roles... to see the permissions each role has.

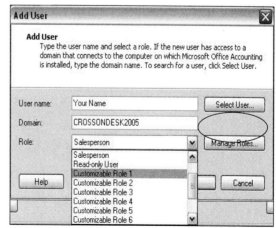

4. The Manage Roles window appears. The permissions associated

with the Salesperson role is shown here. Scroll through all the roles and note each role's ability to interact with the company data then click OK .

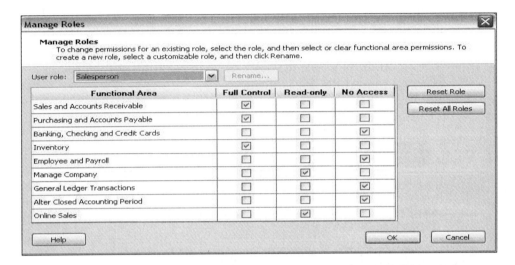

5. To rename a customizable role, use the pull down menu for User role and select Customizable User 10. Click Rename... .

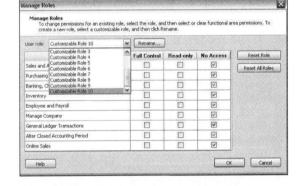

6. Type **Your Name** (type your first and last name) for New role name. Click OK .

7. The Manage Roles window

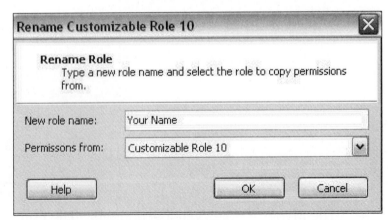

shows that the Your Name role currently has no permissions. To assign the role access company data, check various boxes to assign Full Control, Read-only, or No Access rights. Notice how checking one box activates other check marked boxes. These are good internal controls preset by MOA. For example a user with Full Control access to Purchasing and Accounts Payable should have similar access to Inventory, only Read-only access to Sales and Accounts Receivable, and No Access to Banking or other company tasks.

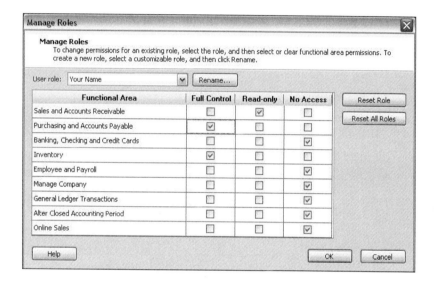

8. Assign Your Name various rights and click [OK]. You can always modify these rights later for the role titled Your Name.

9. To add yourself as a user, in the Add User window, for User Name type **Your Name** (type your first and last name).

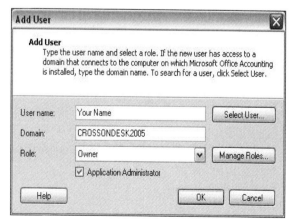

10. Select Owner from the pull down menu for Role. The Application Administrator box should be checked. Compare your screen to the one shown here. Your Domain name will differ.

11.   Click .

12.   One of two screens will appear:

   a.   If you are working on your personal computer which means you are an authorized Windows user, the following warning will appear. Click [Yes].

Then the Manager Users window will appear and show your user name and role. Click [Close].

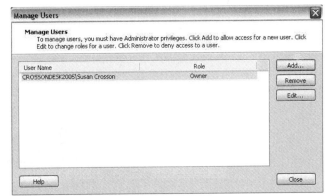

   b.   Or, if you are not an authorized Windows user for the computer (i.e., you are working on a computer lab computer), the following message will appear instead. Read it and click [OK].

13.   Close the Manage Users window to return to Northwind Traders desktop.

MULTI-USER ACCESS

If MOA is installed on computers using Windows XP Pro, Windows 2000 SP3, or Vista, then more than one user and more than one computer can simultaneously work with MOA and access the company database. This is possible since MOA only allows one user to update one record at a time and no other user can be working in that specific area simultaneously. For a business with multiple office staff, this multi-user feature is essential to running an efficient and effective operation. Each member of the staff must be belong to the Windows group that has access to the computer running MOA and have an assigned role within MOA. To confirm that multiple user access is currently disabled, do the following steps:

1.   Open the File menu; and select Multi-user Settings.

2.   When the Multi-user Settings box appears, confirm that multi-user access is disabled. Compare your screen to what is shown here.

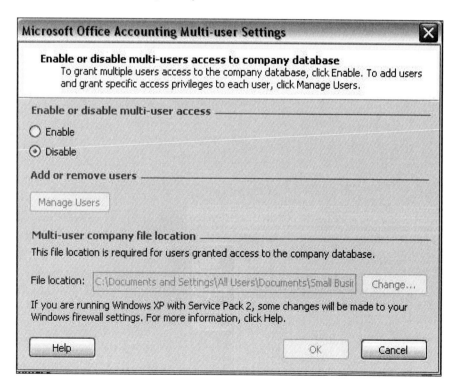

3.   Click [Cancel] to return to Northwind Traders desktop.

ACCOUNTANT TRANSFER FILES

When a company wants their external accountant to review their accounting records, the accountant generally must physically visit the business. With MOA's Accountant Transfer feature, a physical visit is no longer necessary and both the company and the accountant can continue to work simultaneously with the data. Company data can be shared with the accountant various ways. It can be shared using a CD or USB flash drive, or sent via e-mail as an attachment, or uploaded to a shared secure website. In this text, your Accountant is your professor. Periodically through out the text, you will be sending your company files via e-mail to you professor. In other words, you will be submitting your work for grading purposes. To create an accountant transfer file, complete the following steps:

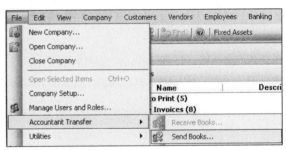

1. Open File menu; select Accountant Transfer, and click on Send Books…

2. The first Send Books window appears. Select Send books manually. Click Next >.

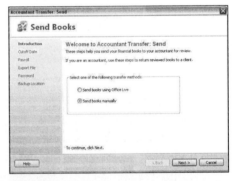

3. For Select Cutoff date, accept default which is the last day of previous month. The Cutoff date stops you from making changes to transactions, changing company preferences, and doing many other tasks prior to the cutoff date. Click Next >. (Your cutoff date will differ from this screenshot.)

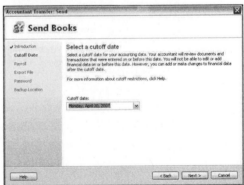

4.   For Payroll, select I will run my payroll. click 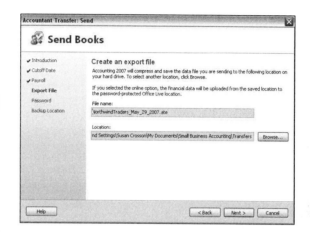 .

5.   In Create an export file window, click Next > . Your date will differ.

6.   In Set export file password window, click Next > . Do not password protect!

7.   In Backup file window, click Browse... to go to the backups folder.

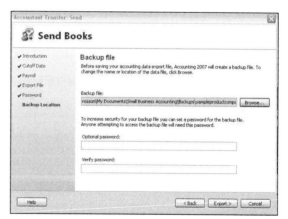

8.   For File Name, delete sampleproductscompany and type **Chapter 2 End and your initials** before the date. Click Save . (Your initials and date will differ from this screenshot.)

9.   The Send Books window now shows Chapter 2 End and your initials and today's date as the Backup file. Click Export > .

10. The send books window appears and shows the progress of your export. When complete, the following window appears:

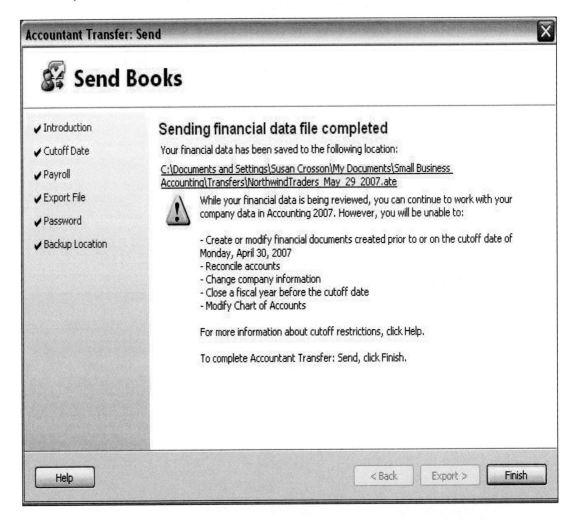

11. Note the location of your Transfer file. In Exercise 2-1, you will send it as an e-mail attachment to your professor. Read all the tasks you are unable to do while the file is being reviewed by your professor.

12. Click Finish.

BACK UP OF CHAPTER 2 DATA

Follow these steps to confirm you have made a back up of Chapter 2 data.

1. From MOA desktop, open File menu; Utilities; Data Utilities.
2. Click [Backup] in the MOA Data Utilities window.
3. In the Backup file name field, click [Browse ...]. Browse your backup folder to confirm Chapter 2 END and your three initials and date file exists. Click [Cancel].
4. When the Backup window appears, click [Cancel].
5. Close the MOA Data Utilities window.
6. Make a backup copy on your USB flash drive of your Backups folder.

   a. Start Windows Explorer (*Hint:* Right click on the Start button; left click Explore).
   b. Display your external media (i.e., USB drive in the left pane of Windows Explorer and the backups folder in the right pane. Highlight the backups folder and drag it on to the external media to copy it.
   c. Double click on your external media to display its contents to confirm that you successfully copied the Backups folder and its contents. Close Windows Explorer. (Substitute the X's for your initials.)

7. Exit MOA or continue with the next section.

SUMMARY AND REVIEW

OBJECTIVES: In Chapter 2, you used the software to:

1. Start Microsoft Office Accounting (MOA).
2. Restore and open the product-based sample company, Northwind Traders.
3. View Change Log and confirm that it is in use.
4. Understand User's pre-built security roles and permissions.
5. Modify a user role and try to add a user.
6. Disable Multi-user access.
7. Transfer company data file to your accountant (professor).
8. Use your Internet browser to go to the book's website. (Go online to www.mhhe.com/moaessentials.)

GOING TO THE NET

From MOA's menu bar, select Help; Microsoft Office Accounting Help, and search for About roles and permissions to answer these questions.

1. Why is MOA's system of permissions for accessing data a security feature?

2. To use MOA, is a Microsoft Windows user name and password required?

3. List the preset user roles in MOA.

4. Which preset role has the most privileges? Which preset role has the least privileges?

FLASHCARD REVIEW

Create the following flashcards.

1. What are the steps to add a user role?

2. What are the steps to transfer a company file using e-mail?

Short-answer questions: In the space provided write the answer to the question.

1. Why is good internal control important?

_____

_____

_____

2. What is the purpose of the Change Log?

_____

_____

3. What are the pre-built user roles in Microsoft Office Accounting 2007?

_____

_____

_____

4. Rank the built-in security roles from the one with the most access to company data to the one with the least access to company data.

_____

_____

5. What is the value of the feature, Multi-user Settings?

_____

_____

6. What is the value of the feature, Accountant Transfer?

_____

_____

7. List three ways you can transfer company data files to the accountant.

_____

_____

_____

8. Why is the cutoff date important when transferring data files to the accountant?

_____

_____

9. Describe what you cannot do while the accountant works with your company data.

_____

_____

_____

10. Explain why businesses password protect company data files while for the purposes of this text the files should not be protected when transferred to the accountant (professor).

_____

_____

_____

Exercise 2-1: Follow the instructions below to complete Exercise 2-1.

1.   Start your e-mail program.

2.   Create an e-mail message to your professor. Type **Your Name Chapter 2 End** for the Subject. (Use your first and last name)

3.   Attach the accountant transfer file you created this chapter. Recall its location is: C: ....\Small Business Accounting\Transfers (or on your desktop if you are working in the computer lab).

4.   CC yourself on the message to be sure the message sends.

5.   Send the message to your professor. You should receive a copy of it as well.

Exercise 2-2: Follow the instructions below to complete Exercise 2-2.

1. Start MOA. Open service-based sample company, Fabrikam, Inc.

2. View Fabrikam's Change Log.

3. Print the Change log. Write your name and Exercise 2-2 on it.

ANALYSIS QUESTION: Why are there up to 10 customizable roles?

Chapter 3 — New Company Setup for a Merchandising Business

OBJECTIVES: In Chapter 3, you learn to:

1. Set up a new company called Your Name Retailers.
2. Edit the chart of accounts.
3. Enter beginning balances.
4. Record check register entries.
5. Void and correct an error.
6. Complete account reconciliation.
7. Print the trial balance.
8. Print the financial statements.
9. Make backup of your work.[1]
10. Use your Internet browser to go to the book's website. (Go online to www.mhhe.com/yachtmoaessentials.)

In this text you are the sole stockholder and manager of an online merchandising corporation that sells inventory from its website. Merchandising businesses are retail stores that resell goods and services.

In this chapter, you set up your merchandising business called Your Name Retailers. First, you set up a business using MOA's new company setup. Then, you complete the accounting tasks for the month of October using your checkbook register and bank statement as source documents.

In accounting, you learn that source documents are used to show written evidence of a business transaction. For Your Name Retailers, the source documents used in this chapter are your checkbook register and bank statement.

---

[1] The chart in the Preface shows you the size of each backup file. Refer to this chart for backing up data. Remember, you can back up to a hard drive location or external media.

The McGraw-Hill Companies, Inc., *Computer Accounting Essentials with Microsoft Office Accounting*

GETTING STARTED

1.   Start MOA. Click [Remind Me Later] when the Product Activation (Trial) window appears.

2.   If a company opens, from the menu bar select File; Close. The Start – Microsoft Office Accounting 2007 window appears.

3.   Link to Set up a new company.

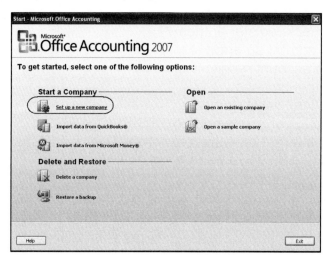

3.   The Company Setup; Company and Preferences window appears. Read the information. Observe that company setup includes the following lists on the left side of the window: Company (Introduction, Company Details, Accounts, Start Date); and Preferences (Introduction, Jobs, Sales Tax, Forms Layout, Numbering, Currency, Payroll Online Sales, Cash vs. Accrual, and Add-in packs). When you go through company setup, required fields are a different color. This means the field *must* be completed. Compare your Company Setup window to the one shown here.

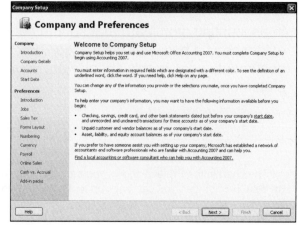

---

4. Before you click Next, read the information in Welcome to Company Setup. Click [Next].

5. Read the information on the Company Introduction window. This information includes adding company details, how to set up accounts, defining the fiscal year, and selecting preferences. After reviewing the information, click [Next]

6. The Add company details window appears. Notice that in the Company list, Introduction is checked. This means you have completed the Company Setup's Introduction. Complete the following fields in the Add company details screen:

Company & Legal Name: [Your Name] **Your Name Retailers** *(use your first and last name then Retailers)*

Street: **Your Street address**
City: **Reno**
State/Province: **NV**
ZIP/Postal Code: **89557**
Country/Region: United States
Phone: **Your phone number**
Fax: **775-555-2802**
E-Mail   **Your e-mail address**
Web site: **www.retailer.biz**
Federal Tax ID: **27-5662211**

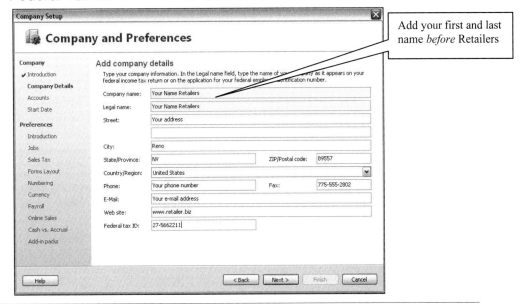

Comment
Since you use your name in the Company Name field, the name of your company will appear on all printouts.

7. Check the information you just typed, then click .

8. The Set up accounts window appears. The default selection is Select your business type and have Accounting 2007 suggest accounts.

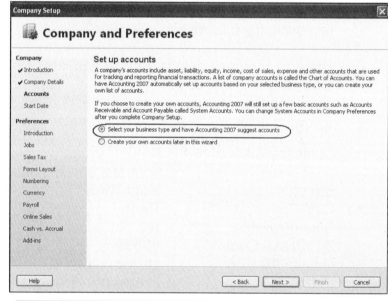

9. Click .

10. The Set up accounts (Cont.) window appears. In the Business Type field, select Retail.

11. Click .

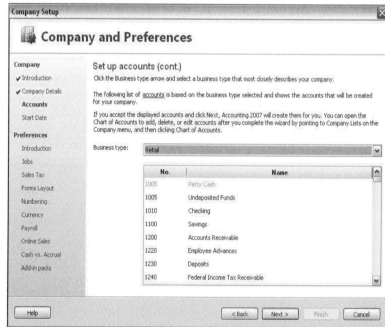

---

12. The Select a fiscal year and start date window appears. Read the information. Make these selections:

     Beginning of the first fiscal year: **1/1/200X** (Use your current year)
     End of the first fiscal year: 12/31/200X **(Use your current year)**
     Start date: 10/1/200X **(Use your current year)**

     Compare your Select a fiscal year and start date window with the one shown below. **This is important! Make sure the dates selected are correct for your current year. For example, if you are currently living in 2009, use 2009 as your fiscal year and start date. If it is currently 2008, use 2008.**

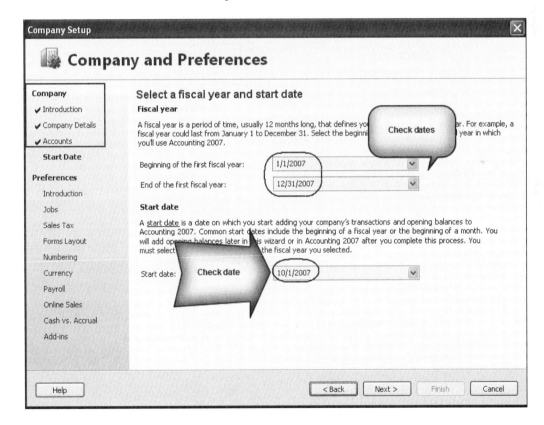

     Check the dates carefully for your current year. Observe that the Company list shows that you have completed three tasks: Introduction, Company Details, and Accounts.

13. Click [Next].

14. The Preferences introduction window appears. Read the information. Click Next .

15. The Select jobs preferences window appears. Since you are *not* going to track jobs, accept the default selection for No. Click Next .

16. The Select sales tax preferences window appears. Accept the default for No by clicking Next . (The company is located in Nevada where there are no sales taxes.)

17. The Select form layout preferences window appears. Select Sells products, or both products and services. Click Next .

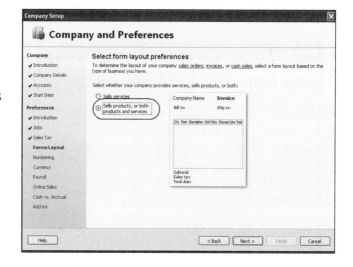

18. The Select numbering preferences window appears. Click on the boxes next to Customers, Vendors, Employees, Products and Services to place a checkmark. This allows for numbering. Click Next .

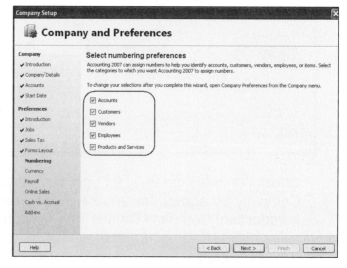

19. The Currency preferences window appears. Since you are not going to use foreign currency, accept the default for No by clicking Next.

20. The Set up payroll window appears. Since Your Name Retailers is not going to use the ADP payroll service, accept the default for No by clicking Next.

21. The Online Sales window appears.. For now, make the selection, No, do not enable online sales at this point. Remember, you can change preferences. For now, select No.

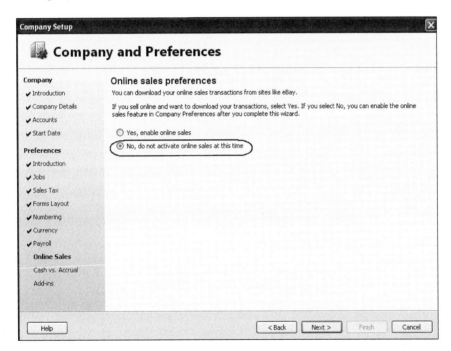

22. After selection No, click Next.

23. The Select cash basis or accrual basis reporting window appears. Accept the default for Accrual basis reports (Recommended) by clicking Next.

24. The Select Add-in packs window appears. Uncheck Fixed Asset Manager, PayPay Payments, Equifax Credit Profile, and ADP

Payroll Addin. (*Hint:* Since you are not going to use these services, you should uncheck them. Remember, you can change preferences. For now, uncheck.) Compare your selections to the one shown here. If these selections are enabled, the menu bar includes more selections.

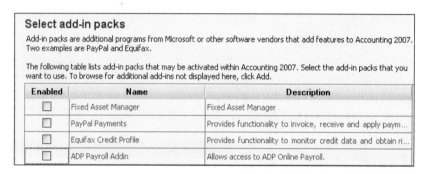

25. After making sure you unchecked the boxes on the Select add-in packs window, click Next

26. The Company details and preferences completed window appears. Observe that checkmarks are placed next to the Company list and Preferences list. You have completed all the company details and preferences.

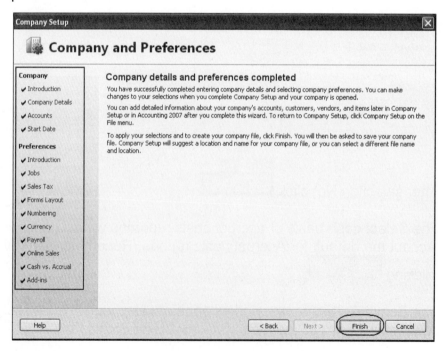

27. Click [Finish].

28. The Select company file window appears. Observe that the Save in field shows the Companies folder. The File name field shows yournameretailers.sbc. MOA has automatically assigned a company name to Your Name Retailers. Since you used your first and last name, your company name differs. MOA companies end in the extension .sbc. (*Hint:* Observe that the Save as type field shows Company files (*.sbc). This field indicates the extension used.)

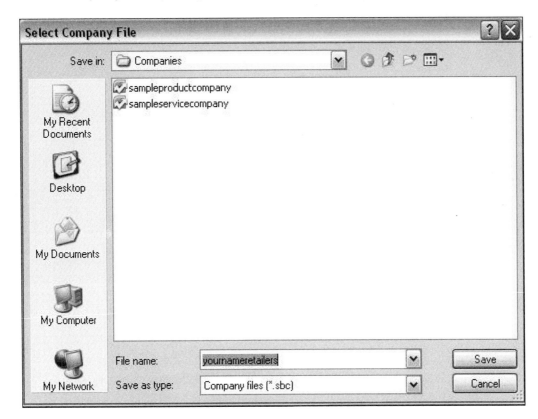

29. Click [Save]. A window prompts that a new company is being saved and that a company database is being created.

The Microsoft Office Accounting Startup Wizard progress checklist appears. Observe that Company and Preferences is checked. In the next section of the book you will edit the chart of accounts. Compare your Microsoft Office Accounting Startup Wizard progress checklist window with the one shown below.

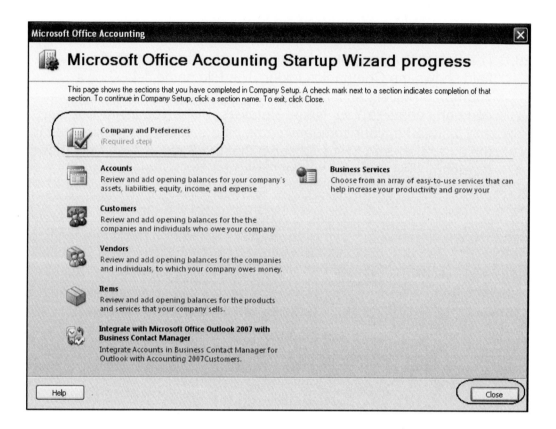

Read the information on this window. In this chapter you will set up accounts. In the next chapter, you will set up Customers, Vendors, and Items.

25. Click [Close] . The Company home page for Your Name Retailers – Microsoft Office Accounting 2007 window appears. (Since you used your first and last name, your name, Retailers is shown.)

COMPANY PREFERENCES

Follow these steps to check the company preferences.

1. From the menu bar, select Company; Preferences. The Company tab shows Use account numbers checked.

2. For Company tab; Tracking, place a check mark next to Use Change Log.

3. The Customers tab shows Use customer ID checked.

4. The Vendors tab shows Use vendor ID, Use item numbers, and Check for item quantity on hand is checked.

5. The Employees tab shows Use employee ID checked and I would like to be able to run Payroll.

6. The Online Sales tab shows Enable online sales unchecked.

7. Click on System Accounts. In the Opening balances field, scroll up to select Account No. 3010, Common Stock.

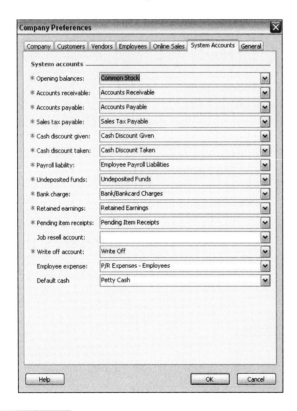

8. Click OK.

CHART OF ACCOUNTS

Examine the Company home page. (If necessary, click

[Company] on the Navigation Pane.) Observe that there is no information recorded in the Reminders, Cash Flow, and Bank Account Summary sections. Since you have not entered any transactions, the company home page's sections are mostly blank.
In accounting you learn that the chart of accounts is a list of all accounts in the general ledger. Follow these steps to add, edit, and change accounts.

Delete Accounts

Follow these steps to delete accounts.

1. If necessary, on the Navigation pane click [Company]; in the Find list, select Chart of Accounts. The Chart of Accounts appears.

2. Right-click on Account No. 1220, Employee Advances. Left-click Delete.

3. When the window prompts Are you sure that you want to permanently delete the selected items(s)? appears, click [Yes]. Account No. 1220, Employee Advances, is removed.

4. MOA's chart of accounts is extensive. For now, delete the accounts shown on the table below.

No.	Name
1230	Deposits
1240	Federal Income Tax Receivable
1420	Interior
1475	A/D Interior
1730	Start-up Costs
1740	Accum Amortization
2050	Trust Payable
2225	Payroll Liability: 401k
2230	Payroll Liability: Profit Sharing
2235	Payroll Liability: Medical & Dental
2240	Payroll Liability: Section 125
2245	Payroll Liability: Union Dues

2250	Payroll Liability: Other
2310	Salaries Accrued -FYE
2320	Customer Deposits
2400	Shareholder/Stockholder Loan
3115	Distrib-Life Insurance
3120	Draws
4022	Consignment Sales
4024	Merchandise
4026	Service
4030	Cash Over/Short
4190	Refunds $ Adjustments
5010	Inventory Adjustment
6015	Marketing/Printed Materials
6020	Website
6025	Amortization
6055	Bad Debts
6070	Contract Labor
6080	Contributions/Donations
6100	Dues, Publications, Books
6165	Ins-Disability
6175	Ins-Liability
6180	Licenses & Permits
6190	Meals & Entertainment
6195	Music & Entertainment
7015	Salary
7020	Life Insurance
7025	Medical
7030	Personal Use of Auto
7125	P/R Expenses-Bonuses
7135	Employee-Meals 100%
7140	Medical
7145	Morale
7150	Retirement
7185	P/R Tax Expense-L&I-Company
7200	Printing & Reproduction
7210	Postage & Delivery
7234	Employment Services Fees
7236	Retirement Plan Administration
7238	Payroll Processing Fees
7260	Consulting
7265	Legal
7292	Building/Janitorial
7294	Computer
7296	Equipment
7320	Storage Off-site
7342	Computer
7346	Office

7352	Business Taxes
7354	Personal Property
7515	Cell
7520	Internet
7525	Telephone
7715	Lodging
7720	Parking
7725	Transportation
7730	Vehicle/Rental/Fuel
7915	Vehicle Insurance
7920	Vehicle Repair & Maintenance

Make an Account Inactive

Follow these steps to make Account No. 1000, Petty Cash, inactive.

1. Right click on Account No. 1000, Petty Cash. Left-click Open selected items.

2. Click on the box next to Active to uncheck it.

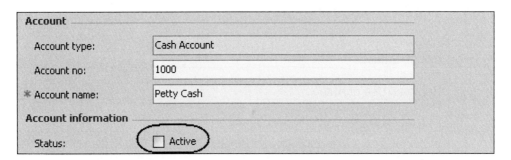

3. Click ![Save and Close]. The Chart of Accounts list starts with Account No. 1005, Undeposited Funds. Notice Petty Cash is *not* shown because it is inactive.

4. Make the following account inactive.

No.	Name
8170	Penalties & Fines

Change Accounts
Follow these steps to change an account name.

1. Right-click on Account No. 1010, Checking.

2. Left-click Open Selected Items.

3. Change the Account name field to **Reno Bank**.

4. Click [Save and Close] . Observe that Account No. 1010 name is Reno Bank.

5. Change the following accounts.

No.	Name
1100	Prime Savings and Loan
1810	Prepaid Insurance
3110	Dividends
5015	Cost of Goods Sold
6090	Depreciation Expense
6150	Insurance Expense

Add Accounts

1. Link to [+ Add a new Account] . (*Hint:* Under Chart of Accounts title bar.)

2. To add Account No. 1420, Computer Equipment, select Fixed Asset. Click [OK].

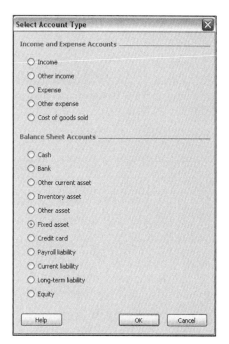

3. Complete the following field. Press <Tab> between fields.

   Account no.:   1420
   Account Name: Computer Equipment

4. Click . Observe that Account No. 1420 has been added to the chart of accounts.

5. Add the following accounts.

No.	Name	Account Type
1240	Supplies	Other current asset
1470	A/D-Computer Equipment	Fixed assets Account No. 1470 is a Subaccount of No. 1460 Accumulated Depreciation

6. When done adding accounts, click ⊟ Save and Close.

7. Scroll through your chart of accounts to make sure you made the

changes shown on in this section. If necessary, click 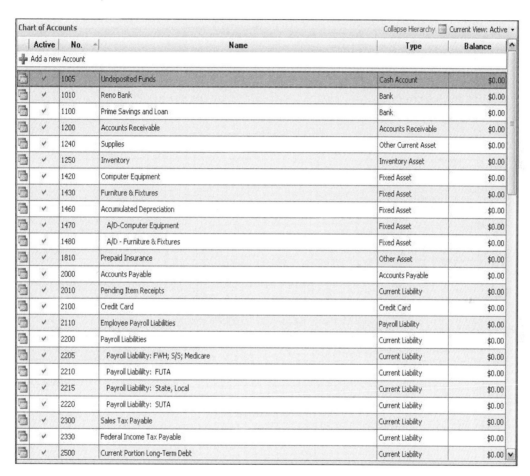 [Refresh] to see the accounts deleted, added, and changed. If necessary, click on the header, No., to see the accounts in numeric order. Here is a partial chart of accounts for Your Name Retailers:

Chart of Accounts				Collapse Hierarchy	Current View: Active ▾
Active	No. ▲	Name		Type	Balance
➕ Add a new Account					
✓	1005	Undeposited Funds		Cash Account	$0.00
✓	1010	Reno Bank		Bank	$0.00
✓	1100	Prime Savings and Loan		Bank	$0.00
✓	1200	Accounts Receivable		Accounts Receivable	$0.00
✓	1240	Supplies		Other Current Asset	$0.00
✓	1250	Inventory		Inventory Asset	$0.00
✓	1420	Computer Equipment		Fixed Asset	$0.00
✓	1430	Furniture & Fixtures		Fixed Asset	$0.00
✓	1460	Accumulated Depreciation		Fixed Asset	$0.00
✓	1470	A/D-Computer Equipment		Fixed Asset	$0.00
✓	1480	A/D - Furniture & Fixtures		Fixed Asset	$0.00
✓	1810	Prepaid Insurance		Other Asset	$0.00
✓	2000	Accounts Payable		Accounts Payable	$0.00
✓	2010	Pending Item Receipts		Current Liability	$0.00
✓	2100	Credit Card		Credit Card	$0.00
✓	2110	Employee Payroll Liabilities		Payroll Liability	$0.00
✓	2200	Payroll Liabilities		Current Liability	$0.00
✓	2205	Payroll Liability: FWH; S/S; Medicare		Current Liability	$0.00
✓	2210	Payroll Liability: FUTA		Current Liability	$0.00
✓	2215	Payroll Liability: State, Local		Current Liability	$0.00
✓	2220	Payroll Liability: SUTA		Current Liability	$0.00
✓	2300	Sales Tax Payable		Current Liability	$0.00
✓	2330	Federal Income Tax Payable		Current Liability	$0.00
✓	2500	Current Portion Long-Term Debt		Current Liability	$0.00

BEGINNING BALANCES

The *Balance Sheet* will establish your beginning balances. In accounting you learn that a Balance Sheet lists the types and amounts of assets, liabilities, and equity as of a specific date. A balance sheet is also called a *statement of financial position*. The October 1 balance sheet for the current year is shown on the next page.

Your Name Retailers Balance Sheet, October 1, 200X (current year)		
ASSETS		
Current Assets:		
1010 - Reno Bank	$60,000.00	
1100 - Prime Savings and Loan	20,500.00	
1240 - Supplies	2,000.00	
Total Current Assets		$82,500.00
Fixed Assets:		
1420 - Computer Equipment	7,500.00	
1430 - Furniture & Fixtures	5,000.00	
Total Fixed Assets		12,500.00
Other Assets		
1810 – Prepaid Insurance	5,000.00	
Total Other Assets		5,000.00
Total Assets		$100,000.00
LIABILITIES AND STOCKHOLDERS EQUITIES		
Long-Term Liabilities:		
2600 - Long-Term Notes Payable	20,500.00	
Total Long-Term Liabilities		$20,500.00
Equity:		
3010 - Common Stock		79,500.00
Total Liabilities & Equity		$100,000.00

The information on the October 1 balance sheet will be the basis for recording your business' beginning balances.

Follow the steps shown on the next page to enter opening balances for Your Name Retailers.

1. The Chart of Accounts list should be displayed. (If *not*, click

; in the Find list, select Chart of Accounts.)

2.   Right-click Account No. 1010, Reno Bank; left-click Open Selected Items.

3.   Type **60000.00** in the Opening Balance field. This is the Reno Bank balance from the October 1, 200X balance sheet shown here. Press <Tab>. For As of: enter the date **1001200X** (use your current year).

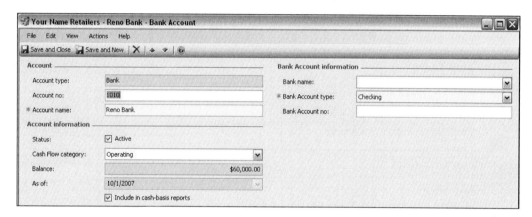

4.   Click [Save and Close]. Continue to record the account balances shown on the balance sheet on the previous page. Be sure correctly enter amounts and 10/01/200X date before you save and close each account. Observe that the balance, $79,500.00, for Account No. 3010, Common Stock is automatically completed.

October 1 Balance Sheet

To make sure that you have entered the October 1 balances correctly, display a balance sheet and compare it to the previous page. Follow these steps to do that.

1.   From the menu bar, select Reports; Company and Financial, Balance Sheet.

2.   Type **10/1/200X (use current year)** in the Date field. Press <Tab>. The 10/1/200X balance sheet appears. Compare the account balances to the one shown here.

Your Name Retailers
Balance Sheet
As of: 10/1/2007
Report Basis: Accrual
Wednesday, May 30, 2007

	As of 10/1/07
Assets	
Current Assets	
Cash	
1010 - Reno Bank	60,000.00
1100 - Prime Savings & Loan	20,500.00
Total Cash	**80,500.00**
Other Current Assets	
1240 - Supplies	2,000.00
Total Other Current Assets	**2,000.00**
Total Current Assets	**82,500.00**
Fixed Assets	
1420 - Computer Equipment	7,500.00
1430 - Furniture & Fixtures	5,000.00
Total Fixed Assets	**12,500.00**
Other Assets	
1810 - Prepaid Insurance	5,000.00
Total Other Assets	**5,000.00**
Total Assets	**100,000.00**
Liabilities & Equity	
Liabilities	
Long Term Liabilities	
2600 - Long-Term Notes Payable	20,500.00
Total Long Term Liabilities	**20,500.00**
Total Liabilities	**20,500.00**
Equity	
3010 - Common Stock	79,500.00
Total Equity	**79,500.00**
Total Liabilities & Equity	**100,000.00**

3. Click ⊠ on the Balance Sheet's title bar to close.

4. Click [No] when the screen prompts do you want to save.

BACKING UP COMPANY DATA

Follow these steps to backup Chapter 3 data.

1. Click File; Utilities, Data Utilities.
2. In the Backup company data area, click [Backup].
3. In the Backup file name field, click [Browse ...]. Browse to the appropriate location for your backup file.

4. Type **Chapter 3 Begin and your initials** in the File name field.

5. Click [Save].

6. When the Backup window appears, click [OK].

7. When the window prompts, Backup was completed successfully, click [OK].

8. Close the Microsoft Office Accounting Data Utilities window.

9. Exit MOA.

RESTORING COMPANY DATA

After setting up a new company, editing the chart of accounts, and entering beginning balances, you backed up (saved) Your Name Retailers company information. In order to start where you left off the last time you backed up, you use MOA's Restore a backup feature.

Remember, backing up data saves to the current point in MOA. Restoring a backup file allows you to start where you left off the last time you used MOA. If you exited MOA, and want to restore your file, follow these steps.

1. From the Start – Microsoft Office Accounting window, select Restore

a backup. (If a company is open, click File; Close Company to go to the Start window.)

2.   In the Backup filename field, click [Browse ...]. Go to the location of the Chapter 3 Begin and your initials.sbb file. Select the Chapter 3 Beginand your initials.sbb file. Click [Open].

3.   In the Restore backup file to field, click [Browse ...]. Select yournameretailers.sbc. (*Hint:* Since you used your first and last name, your company name differs.)

4.   A window appears saying that C:\......\yournameretailers.sbc already exists. Do you want to replace it? Click [Yes].

5.   You are returned to the Database Restore window. Review the information in the Backup filename field and Restore backup file to field. Check the filename at the end of both fields: ....\Chapter 3 Begin.sbb *and* .....\yournameretailers.sbc. Click [OK].

6.   The Restore Complete window appears. Click [OK].

7.   You are returned to the Start – Microsoft Office Accounting window. Select Open an existing company; then double-click yournameretailers.sbc to open it. The Your Name Retailers – Microsoft Office Accounting home page appears. (*Hint:* Since you used your first and last name for the company name, your name appears on the title bar.)

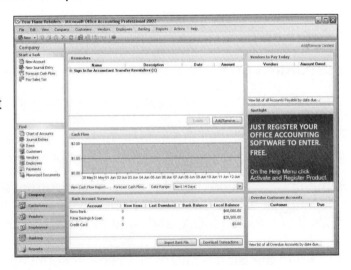

ACCOUNT REGISTER

MOA's account register is a listing of all deposits and checks. It is similar to your checkbook register. Your Name Retailers' check register is shown here.

Check Number	Date	Description of Transaction	Payment	Deposit	Balance
					60,000.00
	10/1	Deposit (Acct. No. 3010, Common Stock)		1,500.00	61,500.00
	10/2	Transfer funds (Acct. No. 1100, Prime Savings and Loan)	5,000.00		56,500.00
4002	10/4	The Business Store (Acct.1420, Computer Equipment) for computer storage	1,000.00		55,500.00
4003	10/25	Office Supply Store (Acct. No. 1240, Supplies)	300.00		55,200.00

In accounting, you learn that source documents are used to show written evidence of a business transaction. Examples of source documents are sales invoices, purchase invoices, and in this case, your check register for your Reno Bank account.

Make Deposits

Follow these steps to use MOA's Account Register to record your check register entries.

1. On the Navigation Pane, click **Banking**. The Banking home page appears. Observe that the Banking Start a Task flowchart shows icons for Write Checks, Credit Card Charge, Make Deposit, Transfer Funds, and Import Bank Files.

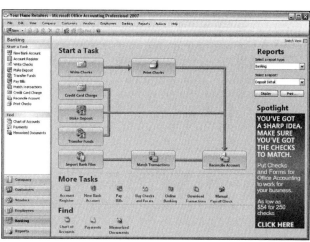

2. Since the first transaction on your check register on the previous

page is a deposit, click .

3. Type **10/1/200X** (use your current year) in the date field.

4. Observe that there is an asterisk (*) next to the Deposit in field. This means it is a required field. In the Deposit in field, select Account No. 1010, Reno Bank.

5. Place your cursor is on the first row in Date field. 10/1/200X appears.

6. Now place cursor in the Account field, select Account No. 3010, Common Stock from the pull down menu.

7. Type **1500** in the Amount field. Press <Enter>. Compare your Untitled – Deposit window to the one shown here.

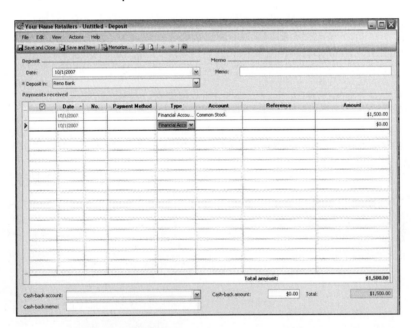

8. Click Save and Close . Close the Deposit window. You are returned to the Banking home page.

Transfer Funds

The October 2 transaction on your check register is a transfer of $5,000 to Account No. 1100, Prime Savings and Loan Account. Follow these steps to transfer $5,000 from Account No. 1010 Reno Bank to Account No. 1100 Prime Savings and Loan.

1. From the Banking Start a Task flowchart, click .

2. Type **10/2/200X** (use your current year) in the Date field. (Observe that it is a required field, which is indicated by an asterisk next to it.)

3. In the Transfer from area, select Account No. 1010, Reno Bank. Observe that the Balance field shows $61,500. This is consistent with the check register balance on page 79.

4. In the Transfer to area, select Account No. 1100, Prime Savings and Loan. Observe that the Balance field shows $20,500. This is consistent with the October 1 balance sheet shown previously.

5. Type **5000** in the Amount field. Press <Tab>.

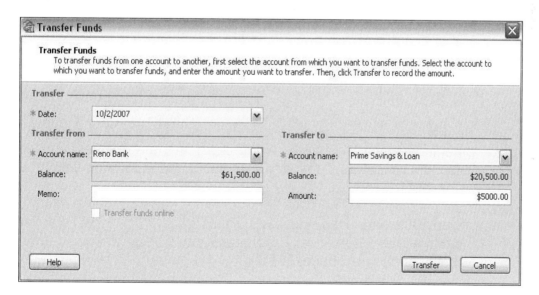

6. Click   Transfer .

Write Checks for Assets

Follow these steps to record a purchase of computer storage.

1. From the Banking Start a Task flowchart, click .

2. The Untitled – Check window appears. In the Bank Account field, select Account No. 1010, Reno Bank. Observe that the Balance field shows $56,500. This is the same balance as on the check register on page 79.

3. Click on the To be printed box to uncheck it.

4. Type **4002** in the No. field. (*Hint*: Click on the box next to To be printed to uncheck it.)

5. Type **10/4/200X (use your current year)** in the Date field.

6. Type **1000** in the Amount field.

7. In the Pay to field, type The Business Store. Press <Tab>. When the window appears asking to add the payee to the list, click [Yes]. Add The Business Store as a vendor. Click [OK]. When the Untitled Vendor window appears, click [Save and Close]. You are returned to the Untitled – Check window.

8. In the Items and expenses table, expense [icon] should be selected in the first column (next to the Name field). In the Name field, select Account No. 1420, Computer Equipment. In Description field type **Computer Storage.**

9. Type **1000** in the Unit Price field. Press <Tab>. The Line Total field is completed automatically. Compare your Check window to the one shown on the next page.

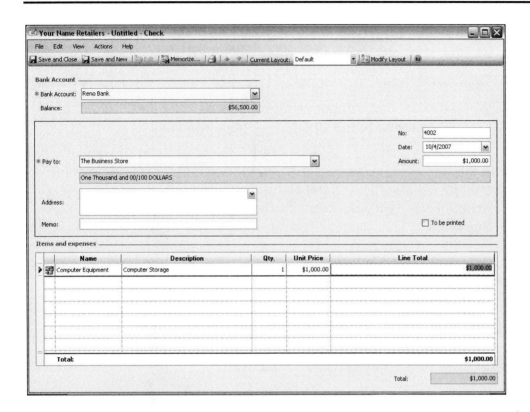

10. Click to begin to record the next check. *Hint:* When you record successive checks, the Untitled – Check window will show a balance. Compare the Balance field on the Check window to the check register shown previously. After completing a transaction, click the Save and New icon to record successive checks; for example, Check Nos. 4002 - 4003.

11. The Untitled – Check window appears. In the Bank Account field Account No. 1010, Reno Bank should appear. If not, select it. Observe that the Balance field shows $55,500. This is the same balance as on the check register on the previous page.

12. The To be printed box should be unchecked. (If not, click on the box next to To be printed to uncheck it.)

13. The No. field displays 4003. If not, type **4003** in the No. field.

14. Type **10/25/200X (use your current year)** in the Date field.

15. Type **200** in the Amount field.

16. In the Pay to field, type Office Supply Store. Press <Tab>. When the window appears asking to add the payee to the list, click Yes. Add Office Supply Store as a vendor. Click OK. When the Untitled Vendor window appears, click Save and Close. You are returned to the Untitled – Check window.

17. In the Items and expenses table, expense should be selected in the first column (next to the Name field). In the Name field, select Account No. 1240, Supplies. In Description field type **Store Supplies.**

18. Type **200** in the Unit Price field. Press <Tab>. The Line Total field is completed automatically. Compare your Check window to the one shown here.

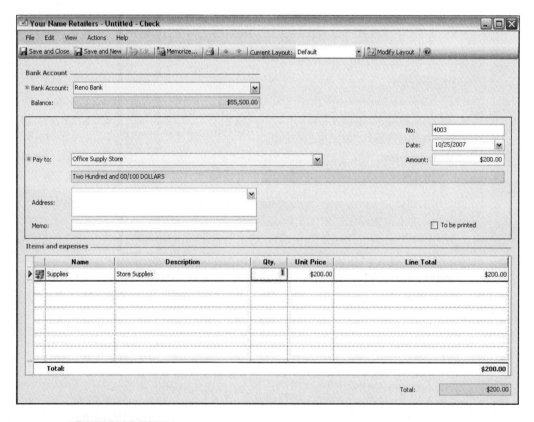

19. Click Save and Close.

20. When the window prompts that you have changed the Home Address field, click [Yes].

21. Close the Check window.

Reno Bank Account Register

Periodically check the account register to confirm the account balance equals what is shown on the check register and that there are no errors. To view the Account Register, follow these steps.

1. From the Banking Home page, More Tasks area, link to

2. The Reno Bank – Account Register window appears. Select Account No. 1010, Reno Bank, in the Bank Account field. Notice the last row shows the current date or *system date*. Your date will differ from what is show here.

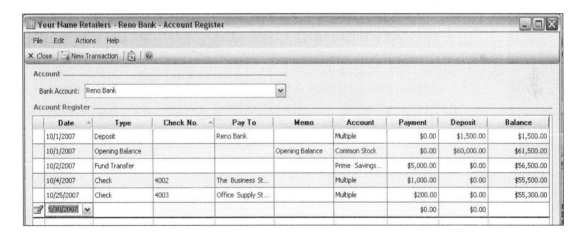

Date	Type	Check No.	Pay To	Memo	Account	Payment	Deposit	Balance
10/1/2007	Deposit		Reno Bank		Multiple	$0.00	$1,500.00	$1,500.00
10/1/2007	Opening Balance			Opening Balance	Common Stock	$0.00	$60,000.00	$61,500.00
10/2/2007	Fund Transfer				Prime Savings...	$5,000.00	$0.00	$56,500.00
10/4/2007	Check	4002	The Business St...		Multiple	$1,000.00	$0.00	$55,500.00
10/25/2007	Check	4003	Office Supply St...		Multiple	$200.00	$0.00	$55,300.00
5/30/2007						$0.00	$0.00	

3. Compare the account register to your check register on page 79 as of 10/25. Notice the balances are not the same. An error was made in writing check # 4003. The check was written incorrectly for $200 instead of $300.

4. To correct, you must void the check and entry.

5. Close the Reno Bank – Account Register window. You are returned to the Banking Home page.

VOID AN ENTRY

When you notice a mistake, you can void the entry and change it. Since MOA includes an audit trail, MOA tracks every transaction and shows when and how an entry was changed. You can view this audit trail using MOA's Transaction Journal. When you void a transaction, MOA's transaction journal shows the original entry (with a checkmark next to it); the reversing entry (with checkmark); and the new entry.

Follow these steps to void and correct the error.

1. Click **Reports**; Company and Financial, Transaction Journal.

2. Type **10/01/200X** in the From field, in the To field make sure it shows **10/31/200X (use current year).**

3. The Transaction Journal should be displayed. Move your mouse over 10/25 transaction you want to change. Observe that the mouse changes to a hand icon.

4. Double-click on the transaction. This takes you to the original entry. To void an entry, select Actions; Void. A large VOID appears on Check No. 4003. Click **Save and New** to write the correct check (Check No. 4004) from the account register information:

4003 4004	10/25	Office Supply Store (Acct. No. 1240, Supplies)	300.00		55,200.00

5. When satisfied, click **Save and Close**.

6. You are returned to the Transaction Journal. Click the Refresh icon ( ). Select **Yes** when the window prompts The data in this report may have changed, do

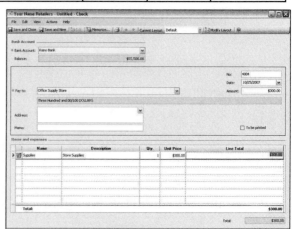

you wish to refresh?. Observe that the Transaction Journal shows a checkmark next to the edited transactions. These checkmarks verify that the transaction was changed. Accountants and managers know that the records show a changed transaction.

7.   Close the Transaction Journal. If prompted, do not save changes.

Write Check for Dividends

Follow these steps to record the payment of a cash dividend to the sole stockholder, Your Name. The check register states:

4005	10/30	Your Name (Acct. No. 3110 Dividends)	200.00		55,000.00

1.   From the Banking Start a Task flowchart, click 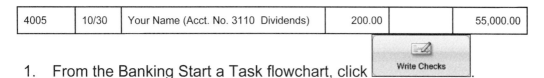.

2.   The Untitled – Check window appears. In the Bank Account field, Account No. 1010, Reno Bank appears. Observe that the Balance field shows $55,200. This is the same balance as on the check register.

3.   To be printed box should be unchecked.

4.   Type **4005** in the No. field.

5.   Type **10/30/200X (use your current year)** in the Date field.

6.   Type **200** in the Amount field.

7.   In the Pay to field, type Your Name. Press <Tab>. When the window appears asking to add the payee to the list, click [Yes]. Add yourself as a vendor. Click [OK]. When the Untitled Vendor window appears, click [Save and Close].

8.   In the Items and expenses table, expense [icon] should be selected in the first column (next to the Name field). In the Name field, select Account No. 3110, Dividends. Leave Description field blank.

9. Type **200** in the Unit Price filed. The Line Total automatically completes.

10. On the next line select comment and add the following: **Paid Cash Dividend to Stockholder.** Compare your screen to the following one, when satisfied click 💾 Save and Close .

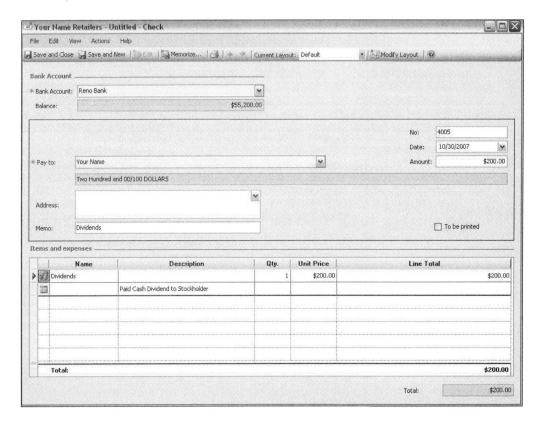

11. You are returned to the Banking Home page.

BACKING UP THE OCTOBER CHECK REGISTER

Before you complete account reconciliation, back up your data.

1. Click File; Utilities, Data Utilities.

2. In the Backup company data area, click Backup .

3. In the Backup file name field, click [Browse ...]. Browse to the appropriate location.

4. Type **Chapter 3 Check Register October and your initials** in the File name field.

5. Click [Save].

6. When the Backup window appears, click [OK].

7. When the Backup was completed successfully window appears, click [OK].

8. Close the Microsoft Office Accounting Data Utilities window.

9. Exit MOA or continue with Account Reconciliation.

ACCOUNT RECONCILATION

You receive a bank statement every month for your Reno Bank account (Account No. 1010, Reno Bank). The bank statement shows which checks and deposits have cleared the bank. MOA's Reconcile Account feature allows you to reconcile her bank statement. Your bank statement for her Reno Bank Account is shown here.

Statement of Account			Your Name Retailers
Reno Bank			Your address
October 1 to October 31 Account # 89123631			Reno, NV
REGULAR RENO BANK			
Previous Balance		$ 60,000.00	
1 Deposits (+)		1,500.00	
3 checks (-)		6,200.00	
Service Charges (-)	10/31	10.00	
Ending Balance	10/31	**$55,290.00**	

		DEPOSITS		
	10/4/07		1,500.00	
	CHECKS (Asterisk * indicates break in check number sequence)			
	10/2/07	Transfer	5,000.00	
	10/5/07	4002	1,000.00	
	10/30/07	4005*	200.00	

Follow these steps to reconcile your bank statement balance to Account No. 1010, Reno Bank.

1.   Go to the Banking home page. Click .

2.   In the Account field, select Account No. 1010, Reno Bank.

3.   Type **10/31/200X (use your current year)** in the Statement date field.

4.   Type **60000.00** in the Beginning balance field.

5.   Type **55290.00** in the Ending balance field.

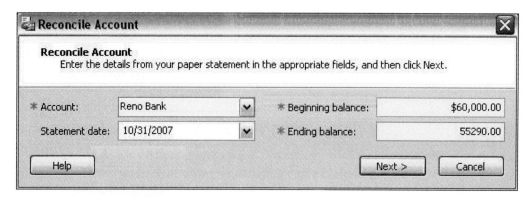

6.   Click [Next]. The Reconcile Account – Reno Bank window appears.

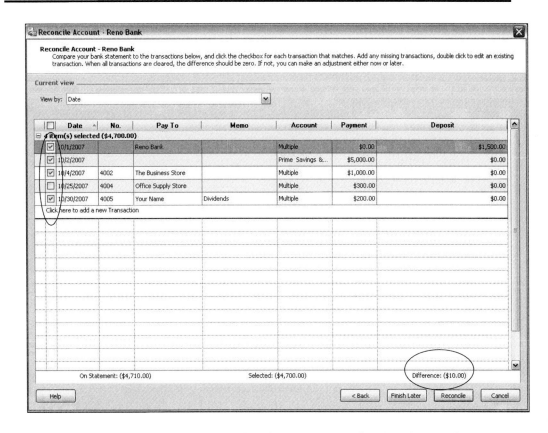

7. Click on the box next to the checks and deposits that have cleared the bank. Make sure the checks that have *not* cleared the bank remain unchecked; for example, Check No. 4003 should *not* be checked. Observe that the Difference shows ($10.00). This is the amount of the service charge.

8. Link to Click here to add a new Transaction to add the bank service charge.

9. On the Select Transaction window, select Enter bank fee.

10. Click OK.

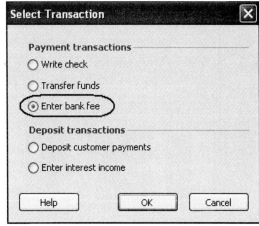

11. Type **10/31/200X (use your current year)** in the Date field.

12. Make sure Reno Bank is selected in the Bank account field.

13. In the Charge to field, select 7232, Bank/Bankcard Charges.

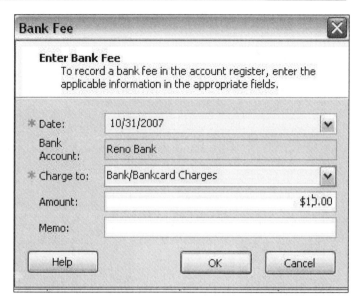

14. Type **10** in the Amount field.

15. Click .

You are returned to the Reconcile Account – Reno Bank window. Click on the box next to 10/31/200X, Bank/Bankcard Charges to place a checkmark in it. Observe that the Difference field shows $0.00. Compare your Reconcile Account – Reno Bank window to the one shown here.

16. Click Reconcile . The Reconcile completed window appears.

Reconcile completed ☒

Congratulations, your account was successfully reconciled. To print a reconciliation report for this statement, click Display Report. To close the dialog box, click Close.

Display Report   Close

18. Click Display Report . The Reconciliation Detail report appears. Compare your Reconciliation Detail report to the one shown here.

Your Name Retailers
Reconciliation Detail
Amount: Any, Bank Account: Reno Bank, Statement date: 10/31/2007
Wednesday, May 30, 2007

Type	Date	No.	Name	Amount
Reno Bank				
Opening Balance				**60,000.00**
Cleared Deposits				
Deposit	10/1/2007	1		1,500.00
Total Cleared Deposits				**1,500.00**
Cleared Withdrawals				
Fund Transfer	10/2/2007	8		(5,000.00)
Check	10/4/2007	4002	The Business Store	(1,000.00)
Check	10/30/2007	4005	Your Name	(200.00)
Bank Fee	10/31/2007	9		(10.00)
Total Cleared Withdrawals				**(6,210.00)**
Total Cleared Transactions				**(4,710.00)**
Reconciled Balance As Of Statement Date				**55,290.00**
Uncleared Withdrawals				
Check	10/25/2007	4004	Office Supply Store	(300.00)
Total Uncleared Withdrawals				**(300.00)**
Total Uncleared Transactions				**(300.00)**
Balance As Of Statement Date				**54,990.00**
Ending Balance				**54,990.00**

Compare the Ending Balance of $54,990.00 to the check register on page 87. If you deduct the bank service charge of $10 from the check register's balance, it agrees with the Account Reconciliation report: $55,000 - $10 = **$54,990.00** (ending balance on reconciliation report).

19.   Close the Reconciliation Detail window.

You have successfully completed your transactions for October. Now let's look at how these transactions were debited and credited.

PRINTING THE TRANSACTION JOURNAL

To see MOA's transaction journal, follow these steps.

1.   From the menu bar, select Reports; Company and Financial, Transaction Journal.

2.   Type **10/1/200X (use your current year)** in the From field.

3.   Type **10/31/200X (use your current year)** in the To field.

4.   The first transaction on the check register, is shown as Deposit 1, dated 10/1/200X. The other transactions dated 10/1/200X are the beginning balances that you entered from the October 1 balance sheet on page 74. Scroll down the Transaction Detail report to see all of it. The Transaction Journal is shown on the next page.

Your Name Retailers
Transaction Journal
Date Range: October 1, 2007 - October 31, 2007
Transaction type: All, No.: Any, Name: All, Account: All, Amount: Any, Void: Show
Wednesday, May 30, 2007

Type	Status	No.	Name	Date	Account	Debit	Credit	Void
Opening Balance		1		10/1/2007				
					Reno Bank	60,000.00	0.00	
					Common Stock	0.00	60,000.00	
Opening Balance		2		10/1/2007				
					Prime Savings & Loan	20,500.00	0.00	
					Common Stock	0.00	20,500.00	
Opening Balance		3		10/1/2007				
					Common Stock	0.00	2,000.00	
					Supplies	2,000.00	0.00	
Opening Balance		4		10/1/2007				
					Common Stock	0.00	7,500.00	
					Computer Equipment	7,500.00	0.00	
Opening Balance		5		10/1/2007				
					Furniture & Fixtures	5,000.00	0.00	
					Common Stock	0.00	5,000.00	
Opening Balance		6		10/1/2007				
					Prepaid Insurance	5,000.00	0.00	
					Common Stock	0.00	5,000.00	
Opening Balance		7		10/1/2007				
					Long-Term Notes Paya...	0.00	20,500.00	
					Common Stock	20,500.00	0.00	
Deposit		1		10/1/2007				
					Reno Bank	1,500.00	0.00	
					Common Stock	0.00	1,500.00	
Fund Transfer		8		10/2/2007				
					Reno Bank	0.00	5,000.00	
					Prime Savings & Loan	5,000.00	0.00	
Check	Paid	4002	The Business Store	10/4/2007				
					Accounts Payable	0.00	1,000.00	
					Accounts Payable	1,000.00	0.00	
					Reno Bank	0.00	1,000.00	
					Computer Equipment	1,000.00	0.00	
Check	Paid	4003	Office Supply Store	10/25/2007				✔
					Accounts Payable	0.00	200.00	
					Accounts Payable	200.00	0.00	
					Reno Bank	0.00	200.00	
					Supplies	200.00	0.00	
Check	Paid	4003	Office Supply Store	10/25/2007				✔
					Accounts Payable	200.00	0.00	
					Accounts Payable	0.00	200.00	
					Reno Bank	200.00	0.00	
					Supplies	0.00	200.00	
Check	Paid	4004	Office Supply Store	10/25/2007				
					Accounts Payable	0.00	300.00	
					Accounts Payable	300.00	0.00	
					Reno Bank	0.00	300.00	
					Supplies	300.00	0.00	
Check	Paid	4005	Your Name	10/30/2007				
					Accounts Payable	0.00	200.00	
					Accounts Payable	200.00	0.00	
					Reno Bank	0.00	200.00	
					Dividends	200.00	0.00	
Bank Fee		9		10/31/2007				
					Reno Bank	0.00	10.00	
					Bank/Bankcard Charges	10.00	0.00	

TRANSACTION DETAIL BY ACCOUNT

MOA's Transaction Detail by Account report is similar to a general ledger (GL). The general ledger is the Company and Financial report selection for GL Report. For purposes of seeing each account balance, follow the steps below to display the Transaction Detail by Account report.

1. From the menu bar, select Reports; Company and Financial, Transaction Detail by Account.
2. Type **10/1/200X (use your current year)** in the From field.
3. Type **10/31/200X** in the To field.

96 Chapter 3

4. The Transaction Detail by Account report is shown below. Scroll down the window to see the entire report.

Your Name Retailers
Transaction Detail by Account
Date Range: October 1, 2007 - October 31, 2007
Amount: Any, Name: All, Account: All, No.: Any, Transaction type: All, Class: All, Closing Postings: Included, Report Basis: Accrual, Void: Show
Wednesday, May 30, 2007

Type	Date	No.	Name	Memo	Amount	Balance
1010 - Reno Bank						0.00
Opening Balance	10/1/2007	1		Opening Balance	60,000.00	60,000.00
Deposit	10/1/2007	1			1,500.00	61,500.00
Fund Transfer	10/2/2007	8			(5,000.00)	56,500.00
Check	10/4/2007	4002	The Business Store		(1,000.00)	55,500.00
Check	10/25/2007	4003	Office Supply Store		(200.00)	55,300.00
Check	10/25/2007	4003	Office Supply Store		200.00	55,500.00
Check	10/25/2007	4004	Office Supply Store		(300.00)	55,200.00
Check	10/30/2007	4005	Your Name	Dividends	(200.00)	55,000.00
Bank Fee	10/31/2007	9			(10.00)	54,990.00
Total 1010 - Reno Bank					**54,990.00**	**54,990.00**
1100 - Prime Savings & Loan						0.00
Opening Balance	10/1/2007	2		Opening Balance	20,500.00	20,500.00
Fund Transfer	10/2/2007	8			5,000.00	25,500.00
Total 1100 - Prime Savings & Loan					**25,500.00**	**25,500.00**
1240 - Supplies						0.00
Opening Balance	10/1/2007	3		Opening Balance	2,000.00	2,000.00
Check	10/25/2007	4003	Office Supply Store	Store Supplies	200.00	2,200.00
Check	10/25/2007	4003	Office Supply Store	Store Supplies	(200.00)	2,000.00
Check	10/25/2007	4004	Office Supply Store	Store Supplies	300.00	2,300.00
Total 1240 - Supplies					**2,300.00**	**2,300.00**
1420 - Computer Equipment						0.00
Opening Balance	10/1/2007	4		Opening Balance	7,500.00	7,500.00
Check	10/4/2007	4002	The Business Store	Computer Storage	1,000.00	8,500.00
Total 1420 - Computer Equipment					**8,500.00**	**8,500.00**
1430 - Furniture & Fixtures						0.00
Opening Balance	10/1/2007	5		Opening Balance	5,000.00	5,000.00
Total 1430 - Furniture & Fixtures					**5,000.00**	**5,000.00**
1810 - Prepaid Insurance						0.00
Opening Balance	10/1/2007	6		Opening Balance	5,000.00	5,000.00
Total 1810 - Prepaid Insurance					**5,000.00**	**5,000.00**
2000 - Accounts Payable						0.00
Check	10/4/2007	4002	The Business Store	Computer Storage	1,000.00	1,000.00
Check	10/4/2007	4002	The Business Store		(1,000.00)	0.00
Check	10/25/2007	4003	Office Supply Store	Store Supplies	200.00	200.00
Check	10/25/2007	4003	Office Supply Store		(200.00)	0.00
Check	10/25/2007	4003	Office Supply Store	Store Supplies	(200.00)	(200.00)
Check	10/25/2007	4003	Office Supply Store		200.00	0.00
Check	10/25/2007	4004	Office Supply Store	Store Supplies	300.00	300.00
Check	10/25/2007	4004	Office Supply Store		(300.00)	0.00
Check	10/30/2007	4005	Your Name		200.00	200.00
Check	10/30/2007	4005	Your Name	Dividends	(200.00)	0.00
Total 2000 - Accounts Payable					**0.00**	**0.00**
2600 - Long-Term Notes Payable						0.00
Opening Balance	10/1/2007	7		Opening Balance	20,500.00	20,500.00
Total 2600 - Long-Term Notes Payable					**20,500.00**	**20,500.00**
3010 - Common Stock						0.00
Opening Balance	10/1/2007	1		Reno Bank	60,000.00	60,000.00
Opening Balance	10/1/2007	2		Prime Savings &...	20,500.00	80,500.00
Opening Balance	10/1/2007	3		Supplies	2,000.00	82,500.00
Opening Balance	10/1/2007	4		Computer Equip...	7,500.00	90,000.00
Opening Balance	10/1/2007	5		Furniture & Fixtu...	5,000.00	95,000.00
Opening Balance	10/1/2007	6		Prepaid Insurance	5,000.00	100,000.00
Opening Balance	10/1/2007	7		Long-Term Note...	(20,500.00)	79,500.00
Deposit	10/1/2007	1			1,500.00	81,000.00
Total 3010 - Common Stock					**81,000.00**	**81,000.00**
3110 - Dividends						0.00
Check	10/30/2007	4005	Your Name		(200.00)	(200.00)
Total 3110 - Dividends					**(200.00)**	**(200.00)**
7230 - Processing Services						0.00
7232 - Bank/Bankcard Charges						0.00
Bank Fee	10/31/2007	9			10.00	10.00
Total 7232 - Bank/Bankcard Charges					**10.00**	**10.00**
Total 7230 - Processing Services					**10.00**	**10.00**

The McGraw-Hill Companies, Inc., *Computer Accounting Essentials with Microsoft Office Accounting*

5. Close the Transaction Detail by Account report without saving.

TRIAL BALANCE

To display Your Name Retailers' trial balance follow these steps.

1. From the menu bar, select Reports; Company and Financial, Trial Balance.

2. Type **10/31/200X** in the Date field. Press <Enter>. Compare your Trial Balance with the one shown here.

Your Name Retailers
Trial Balance
As of: 10/31/2007

Wednesday, May 30, 2007

Account Name	Account No.	Debit	Credit
Reno Bank	1010	54,990.00	
Prime Savings & Loan	1100	25,500.00	
Supplies	1240	2,300.00	
Computer Equipment	1420	8,500.00	
Furniture & Fixtures	1430	5,000.00	
Prepaid Insurance	1810	5,000.00	
Long-Term Notes Payable	2600		20,500.00
Common Stock	3010		81,000.00
Dividends	3110	200.00	
Bank/Bankcard Charges	7232	10.00	
Total		**101,500.00**	**101,500.00**

3. Close the Trial Balance without saving.

FINANCIAL STATEMENTS

To display Your Name Retailers' balance sheet follow these steps.

1. From the menu bar, select Reports; Company and Financial, Profit and Loss. Type **10/1/200X to 10/31/200X (use your current year)** in the Date field. Press <Enter>. Compare your profit and loss report from and compare with the one shown on the next page.

Your Name Retailers
Profit and Loss
Date Range: October 1, 2007 - October 31, 2007
Account: All, Report Basis: Accrual, Class: All, Name: All, Closing Postings: Not Included
Wednesday, May 30, 2007

	10/1/07 - 10/31/07
Ordinary Income/Expense	
Expense	
7230 - Processing Services	
7232 - Bank/Bankcard Charges	10.00
Total 7230 - Processing Services	10.00
Total Expense	10.00
Net Ordinary Income	(10.00)
Net Income	(10.00)

2.   Close the profit and loss without saving.

3.   From the menu bar, select Reports; Company and Financial, Balance Sheet.

4.   Type **10/31/200X (use your current year)** in the Date field. Press <Enter>. Compare your Balance Sheet with the one shown here.

Your Name Retailers
Balance Sheet
As of: 10/31/2007
Report Basis: Accrual
Wednesday, May 30, 2007

	As of 10/31/07
Assets	
Current Assets	
Cash	
1010 - Reno Bank	54,990.00
1100 - Prime Savings & Loan	25,500.00
Total Cash	**80,490.00**
Other Current Assets	
1240 - Supplies	2,300.00
Total Other Current Assets	**2,300.00**
Total Current Assets	**82,790.00**
Fixed Assets	
1420 - Computer Equipment	8,500.00
1430 - Furniture & Fixtures	5,000.00
Total Fixed Assets	**13,500.00**
Other Assets	
1810 - Prepaid Insurance	5,000.00
Total Other Assets	**5,000.00**
Total Assets	**101,290.00**
Liabilities & Equity	
Liabilities	
Long Term Liabilities	
2600 - Long-Term Notes Payable	20,500.00
Total Long Term Liabilities	**20,500.00**
Total Liabilities	**20,500.00**
Equity	
3010 - Common Stock	81,000.00
3110 - Dividends	(200.00)
Net Income	(10.00)
Total Equity	**80,790.00**
Total Liabilities & Equity	**101,290.00**

5.   Close the balance sheet without saving.

6. Print the 10/1/200X to 10/31/200X cash flow statement.

Your Name Retailers
Cash Flow Statement
Date Range: October 1, 2007 - October 31, 2007
Closing Postings: Not Included
Wednesday, May 30, 2007

	10/1/07 - 10/31/07
OPERATING ACTIVITIES	
Net Income	**(10.00)**
Adjustments to reconcile net income to...	
1240 - Supplies	(2,300.00)
Net Cash provided by Operating Activities	**(2,310.00)**
INVESTING ACTIVITIES	
1420 - Computer Equipment	(8,500.00)
1430 - Furniture & Fixtures	(5,000.00)
1810 - Prepaid Insurance	(5,000.00)
Net Cash provided by Investing Activities	**(18,500.00)**
FINANCING ACTIVITIES	
2600 - Long-Term Notes Payable	20,500.00
3010 - Common Stock	81,000.00
3110 - Dividends	(200.00)
Net Cash provided by Financing Activities	**101,300.00**
Net cash change for the Period	**80,490.00**
Cash at beginning of the period	**0.00**
Cash at end of the Period	**80,490.00**

7. Close the cash flow statement without saving.

BACKING UP CHAPTER 3 DATA

Follow these steps to backup Chapter 3 data.

1. Click File; Utilities, Data Utilities.

2. In the Backup company data area, click Backup .

3. In the Backup file name field, click Browse ... . Browse to the appropriate location.

4. Type **Chapter 3 October End and your initials** in the File name field.

5. Click Save .

6. When the Backup window appears, click OK .

7. When the Backup was completed successfully window appears, click OK .

8. Close the Microsoft Office Accounting Data Utilities window.

9. Exit MOA.

SUMMARY AND REVIEW

OBJECTIVES: In Chapter 3, you used the software to:

1. Set up a new company called Your Name Retailers.
2. Edit the chart of accounts.
3. Enter beginning balances.
4. Record check register entries.
5. Void and correct an error.
6. Complete account reconciliation.
7. Print the trial balance.
8. Print the financial statements.
9. Make backup of your work.
10. Use your Internet browser to go to the book's website. (Go online to www.mhhe.com/yachtmoaessentials.

GOING TO THE NET

Access information about a chart of accounts at www.allianceonline.org. Type **chart of accounts** in the search field. Link to What should our chart of accounts include? Then, link to What are the Features of a Simple Chart of Accounts?. The URL is http://www.allianceonline.org/FAQ/financial_management/what_should_our_chart.faq/#features .

1. List the standard order that accounts are presented on the balance sheet and income statement.

2. How are account numbers organized? Why are they organized that way?

FLASHCARD REVIEW

Create the following flashcards.

1. Display the 10/31//200X transaction journal report.

2. Display the 10/1/200X to 10/31/2007 trial balance.

3. Display the 10/31/200X balance sheet.

4. Display the 10/31/200X profit and loss report.

5. Display the 10/31/200X cash flow statement.

True/Make True: Write the word True in the space provided if the statement is true. If the statement is *not* true, write the correct answer.

1. In Chapter 3, the checkbook register and October 1, 200X balance sheet are used as source documents.

    _____

    _____

2. In accounting, written evidence of a business transaction is called an account register.

    _____

    _____

3. To set up a new business, use MOA's Startup Wizard.

    _____

    _____

4. In Chapter 3, the type of business set up is Accountant/CPA.

    _____

    _____

5. The first date for recording transactions is 10/1/200X.

    _____

    _____

6. The company preference set up for undeposited funds is Account No. 1010, Reno Bank.

    _____

    _____

---

7. The total cash balance on 10/31/200X is $60,000.00.

_____

_____

Exercise 3-1: Follow the instructions to complete Exercise 3-1. You must complete Chapter 3 activities *before* you can do Exercise 3-1.

1. Print the Chart of Accounts.

2. Print the 10/1/200X to 10/31/200X transaction journal.

3. Print the 10/1/200X to 10/31/200X transaction detail by account.

Exercise 3-2: Follow the instructions below to complete Exercise 3-2.

1. Print the 10/31/200X trial balance.

2. Print the 10/31/200X balance sheet.

3. Print the 10/1/200X to 10/31/200X profit and loss report.

4. Print the 101/1/200X to 10/31/200X cash flow statement.

Analysis Question: Why are the trial balance totals different from the balance sheet totals?

Chapter 4 | Working with Inventory, Vendors, and Customers

OBJECTIVES: In Chapter 4, you use the software to:

1. Open the company, Your Name Retailers
2. Enter vendor records.
3. Enter inventory items.
4. Print the vendor list and item list.
5. Enter bills and record purchase returns.
6. Pay bills.
7. Add a vendor and non-inventory item on the fly.
8. Enter customer records and defaults.
9. Record customer sales on account, credit card sales, and sales returns.
10. Receive customer payments.
11. Make backups.[1]
12. Use your Internet browser to go to the book's website. (Go online to www.mhhe.com/moaessentials.)

GETTING STARTED

Your Name Retailers started operations on October 1, 200X (use your current year) in Reno, NV. The company is organized as a corporation. Customers purchase products from Your Name Retailers via the Internet. The three products sold by Your Name Retailers are:

➢ Podcasts (audio files).

➢ ebooks (PDF files). PDF is an abbreviation of portable document format.

➢ TV programs (video files).

---

[1] The chart in the Preface shows you the size of each backup file. Refer to this chart for backing up data. Remember, you can back up to a hard drive location or external media.

Follow these steps to open Your Name Retailers.

1. Start MOA. If Your Name Retailers does not open, from the menu bar select File; Close. The Start – Microsoft Office Accounting 200X window appears. Select Restore a backup. Restore the Chapter 3 October End and your initials sbb file. This back up was made on page 101.

2. To confirm that you are starting in the correct place, display the 10/31 trial balance. Compare your trial balance with the one printed on page 97.

3. Close the trial balance.

MERCHANDISING BUSINESSES

Merchandising businesses purchase the merchandise they sell from suppliers known as **vendors**. A vendor is a person or company from whom Your Name Retailers buys products or services. When Your Name Retailers makes purchases on account from vendors, the transactions are known as **accounts payable transactions**. Purchases made on account involve payment terms; for example, Your Name Retailers purchases inventory on account from a vendor. The vendor offers the Your Name Retailers 30 days to pay for the purchase. This is shown as Net 30 in the Payment terms field of the vendor record

MOA organizes and monitors Your Name Retailers' **accounts payable**. Accounts Payable is a group of posting accounts that show the amounts owed to vendors or creditors for goods, supplies, or services purchased on account.

When entering a purchase, you select the vendor's name and item. The vendor's address information, payment terms, and appropriate accounts are automatically debited and credited. This works similarly for accounts receivable.

Using the Vendors home page selections, the diagram on the next page illustrates entering and paying a vendor bill.

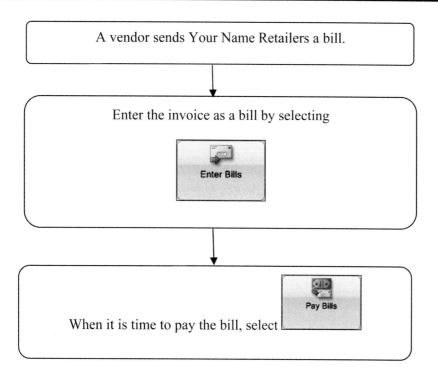

A vendor sends Your Name Retailers a bill.

Enter the invoice as a bill by selecting

Enter Bills

When it is time to pay the bill, select

Pay Bills

VENDORS

On the Vendors home page, you perform all the tasks related to vendors and payables. MOA maintains vendor records and tracks their contact information and financial details and history. The Vendors home page is the starting point for managing vendor purchases and inventory.

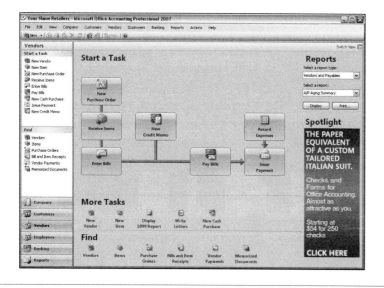

The next section shows you how to set up vendors. Follow these steps to enter vendor default information.

1. On the Navigation Pane, select  .

1. In the More Tasks area, select [New Vendor]. The Untitled – Vendor window appears. Complete the following fields:

Vendor name:	**Podcast Ltd.**
Vendor ID:	**4**
Business address:	**1341 Barrington Road**
	Los Gatos, CA 90046
Business phone number:	**(213) 555-0100**
Business fax number:	**(213) 555-0300**
E-mail 1:	**info@podcasts.net**
Web page address:	**www.podcasts.net**
Vendor since:	**1/1/200X (use your current year)**
Primary contact name:	**Howie Hansen**
Business Phone:	**(213) 555-0100, ext. 11**
E-mail:	**howie@podcasts.net**

Compare your Untitled – Vendor window to the one shown here.

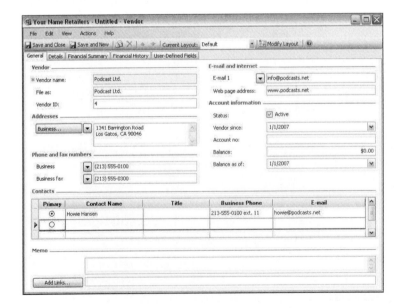

2.   Click on the Details tab. Complete the following fields:

    Credit limit: **10,000.00**
    Preferred payment method: Check
    Payment terms: Net 30

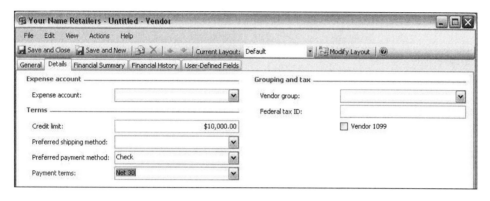

3.   Check the General and Details tab to make sure you have recorded the information correctly. Click <kbd>Save and New</kbd>.

4.   Set up the next vendor record:

        Vendor name: **eBooks Express**
        Vendor ID: 5
        Business address: **10756 NW First Street**
                                           Gig Harbor, OR 97330

        Business phone number: **(541) 555-4320**
        Business fax number: **(541) 555-8808**
        E-mail 1:   **info@ebooks.com**
        Web page address: **www.ebooks.com**
        Vendor since: **1/1/200X** (use your current year)
        Primary contact name: **Nancy Noel**
        Business Phone: **(541) 555-4320, ext. 20**
        E-mail: **nancy@ebooks.com**

     Details tab:

        Credit limit: **10,000.00**
        Preferred payment method: Check
        Payment terms: Net 30

5.   Click <kbd>Save and New</kbd>.

6.   Set up the next vendor record.

Vendor name:	TV Flix
Vendor ID:	6
Business address:	7709 Sunset Boulevard
	Burbank, CA 91501
Business phone number:	(213) 555-1690
Business fax number:	(213) 555-6320
E-mail 1:	info@tvflix.com
Web page address:	www.tvflix.com
Vendor since:	1/1/200X **(use your current year)**
Primary contact name:	Hugo Saybrook
Business Phone:	(213) 555-1690, ext. 31
E-mail:	hugo@tvflix.com

Details:

Credit limit:	10,000.00
Preferred payment method:	Check
Payment terms:	Net 30

7. Click [Save and Close] to return to the Vendors home page.

INVENTORY ITEMS

An *inventory item* is a product that is purchased for sale and is tracked in Account No. 1250, Inventory, on the balance sheet.
Because the Inventory account is increased or decreased for every purchase, sale or return, its balance in the general ledger is current. In MOA, when you purchase and receive items, they are added to inventory. When you sell items and they are added to an invoice, the items are subtracted from inventory.

On the Vendors home page, you perform all the tasks related to vendors and payables.

1. In the More Tasks area, select [New Item].

2. The Select Item Type window appears. Select Inventory.

3. Click [OK]. The Untitled – Inventory window appears. Complete these fields:

Item name: **Podcast**
Item no: 1 is completed automatically
Sales description: **audio files**
Sales price: **30.00**
Income account: Account No. 4020, Sales
Item tax: Non-taxable completed automatically
Purchase description: audio files completed automatically
Purchase price: **15.00**
Asset account: Account No. 1250, Inventory.
Preferred vendor: Podcast Ltd.
COGS account: Account No. 5015, Cost of Goods Sold
As of: 1/1/200X

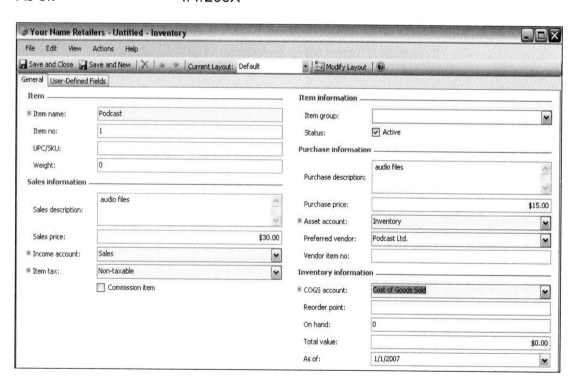

4. Click [Save and New]. When the Select Item Type window appears, make sure Inventory is selected. Click [OK].

5. The Untitled – Inventory window is ready for the next inventory item. Complete the fields shown here.

Item name:	**eBook**
Item no:	2 is completed automatically
Sales description:	**PDF files**
Sales price:	**50.00**
Income account:	Account No. 4020, Sales
Item tax:	Non-taxable completed automatically
Purchase description:	PDF files completed automatically
Purchase price:	**25.00**
Asset account:	Account No. 1250, Inventory.
Preferred vendor:	eBooks Express
COGS account:	Account No. 5015, Cost of Goods Sold
As of:	1/1/200X

6. Click [Save and New]. When the Select Item Type window appears, make sure Inventory is selected. Click [OK]. The Untitled – Inventory window is ready for the next inventory item. Complete the fields shown here.

Item name:	TV Programs
Item no:	3 completed automatically
Sales description:	video files
Sales price:	60.00
Income account:	Account No. 4020, Sales
Item tax:	Non-taxable completed automatically
Purchase description:	video files completed automatically
Purchase price:	30.00
Asset account:	Account No. 1250, Inventory.
Preferred vendor:	TV Flix
COGS account:	Account No.5015, Cost of Goods Sold
As of:	1/1/200X

7. Click [Save and Close] to return to the Vendors home page.

LISTS

You just added three vendors and three inventory items. MOA's list feature shows the details of each record.

Vendor List

The vendor list shows information about the vendors with whom you do business. When you open the list, you view the active vendors. Follow these steps to display the vendor list.

1. From the menu bar, select Vendors; Vendor Lists, Vendors. The Vendor List appears. Observe that a Tax Agency is shown. MOA includes the tax agency as a vendor. Since Your Name Retailers is located in Nevada, there is no sales tax.

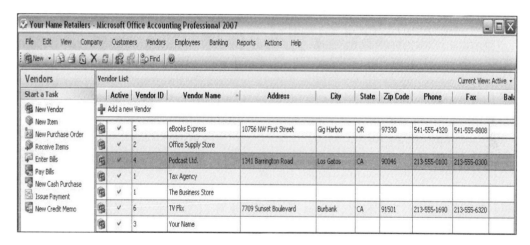

2. To see The Business Store vendor record, drill down. (Hint: Double-click on The Business Store vendor.) Since this vendor was added on the fly in the previous chapter, you need to add vendor information. The Business Store is located at 1234 Front Range Road, Reno NV 89555; telephone 775-555-1234; Vendor since 01/01/200X (use your current year); Credit limit: $5,000; Preferred payment method: Check; and Payment Terms: Net 30. Click **Save and Close** to return to the Vendors List.

3. To see Office Supply Store vendor record, drill down. Add the following vendor information: The Office Supply Store is located at

9876 Hogback Road, Reno NV 89555; telephone 775-555-9876; Vendor since 01/01/200X (use your current year); Credit limit: $5,000; Preferred payment method: Check; and Payment Terms: Net 30. Click ![Save and Close] to return to the Vendors List.

4. Now complete the Your Name (your first and last name) vendor information. Click ![Save and Close] to return to the Vendors List.

5. Click ![print icon] to print the Vendor List.

6. On the Navigation Pane, select ![Vendors] to return to the Vendors home page.

Item List

The Item List shows information about inventory items including names, numbers, descriptions, types, prices, and stock status. When you open the list, you view the active items.

Follow the steps on below to display the item list.

1. From the menu bar, select Vendors; Vendor Lists, Items. The Item List appears. If necessary, double-click on the Item No. columns to list the items in numeric order.

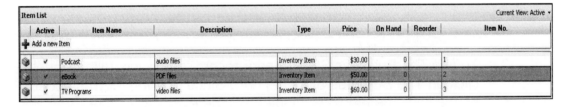

	Active	Item Name	Description	Type	Price	On Hand	Reorder	Item No.
								Current View: Active
➕ Add a new Item								
🖿	✓	Podcast	audio files	Inventory Item	$30.00	0		1
🖿	✓	eBook	PDF files	Inventory Item	$50.00	0		2
🖿	✓	TV Programs	video files	Inventory Item	$60.00	0		3

2. To see an item record, drill-down.

3. Click ![print icon] to print the Item List.

4. On the Navigation Pane, select ![Vendors] to return to the Vendors home page.

VENDOR SERVICES

MOA includes the following vendor services:

➢ Services Overview

➢ Buy Checks and Forms

➢ Bank Online

In order to complete the steps that follow, you need a live Internet connection. If needed, log on to Internet Explorer.

1. From the menu bar, select Vendors; Vendor Services, Services Overview. Websites are time and date sensitive, which means they change. As of this writing, this page appears.

2. Observe that there are links to payroll services, marketplace services, accept credit cards, payment services, buy checks and forms, accountant data transfer, credit profile services, online banking, and point of sales. These services are built into MOA.

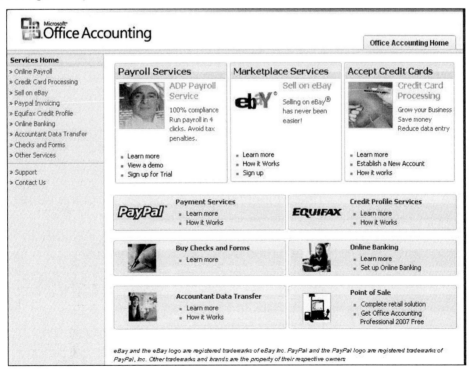

3. Link to <u>Other Services</u> to see more. (*Hint:* Remember, websites are time and date sensitive. Your website page may differ.)

4. If you select Printer-friendly version you can print the page.

    Notice that one of the links is Sell Online. MOA includes the ability to build a complete online store and automatically list products on eBay as well as the company's web site.

5. Close Internet Explorer.

6. Backup if you are working in a computer lab and transfer backup to your USB drive or continue to the next section.

VENDOR TRANSACTIONS

When entering a purchase from a vendor, you first select Enter Bills from the Vendors home page. Vendor defaults were set up earlier in this chapter. This means that vendor information is completed automatically on the Vendor Bill window.

Once you select the inventory item purchased, additional information is completed automatically. Transaction processing is dependent on which defaults are set for vendors and inventory items. In this section, you will see how MOA organizes vendor information.

On the Vendors home page, you perform all the tasks related to vendors and payables. The Vendors home page is the starting point for managing vendor purchases and inventory. In this section, you work with some of these features.

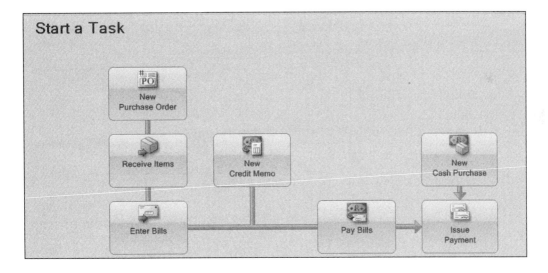

ACCOUNTS PAYABLE TASKS

In MOA, all information about a purchase is recorded in the Vendor Bill window. Then, MOA takes the necessary information from the Vendor Bill window and automatically debits and credits the transaction in the Transaction Journal.

On the Vendor Bill window, you enter bills received from vendors. Purchases from vendors are posted to both the General Ledger and to the vendors and payables reports. In accounting, vendors and payables reports are called the ***accounts payable ledger***. In MOA, vendors and payables reports track purchases. The vendors and payables reports include the following:

➤ A/P Aging Summary: An in-depth view of the amounts the company owes its vendors as of a selected date.

➤ A/P Aging Detail: Displays all the company's outstanding debt to vendors by the number of days outstanding as of a selected date.

➤ Vendor Transaction History: Shows all vendor transactions in a selected time period and calculates the vendor balance.

➤ 1099 Summary: Summarizes payments made to 1099 vendors during the last calendar year.

➤ 1099 Detail: Lists the details for all payments made to 1099 vendors.

➤ Vendor payments: Shows all vendor payments made for a selected period of time.

MOA also includes the following Purchase reports.

➤ Purchases by Vendor Summary: Summarizes items received from each vendor for a selected period of time.

➤ Purchases by Vendor Detail: Lists the items received from each vendor for a selected period of time.

➤ Purchases by Item Summary: Summarizes item purchases for a selected period of time.

➤ Purchases by Item Detail: Lists the payment status of each item received for a selected period of time.

When Your Name Retailers pays vendors, MOA's pay bills feature is used. Purchases work hand in hand with payments. Once you have entered and saved (posted) a bill, it is available when you pay bills. Then, MOA distributes the appropriate amounts.

The next section explains how to enter bills. The term bill and invoice is used interchangeably. A **bill** or **invoice** is a request for payment for products or services.

Enter Bills

The transaction you are going to record is:

Date   *Description of Transaction*

11/02   Invoice No. 5 received from Podcast Ltd. for the purchase
               of 20 audio files, $15 each, for a total of $300..

Follow these steps to record this transaction.

1.   From the Navigation Pane, select  ;
     [Enter Bills] . The Untitled – Vendor Bill window appears.
     Complete the following fields:

Date:	**11/2/200X(use your current year)**
	(Press <Tab> between fields)
No.	**5**
Vendor name:	Podcast Ltd.
Name:	Podcast
Description:	audio files is completed automatically
Qty:	**20**
Unit Price:	$15.00 is completed automatically
Line Total:	$300.00 is completed automatically

Compare your Untitled – Vendor Bill window to the one shown on the next page.

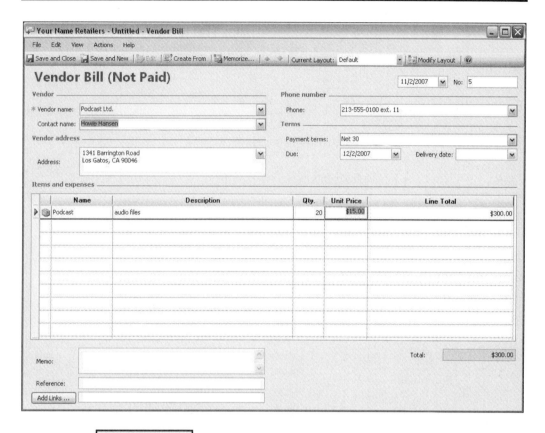

2. Click ![Save and Close]. Before completing the next transaction, let's see how MOA debited and credited this information.

3. From the menu bar, select Reports; Company and Financial, Transaction Journal. Type **11/2/200X** in the From field. The transaction was debited and credited as follows:

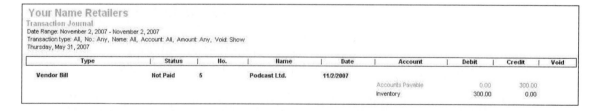

When the Inventory account is debited, it is increased. When the Accounts Payable account is debited it is also increased. Your Name Retailers owes Podcast Ltd. $300 for this purchase. Close the Transaction Journal without saving.

4.   To see how this transaction is recorded in the accounts payable
      ledger, go to the Vendors home page. In
      the Select a report type field, select
      Vendors and Payables. In the Select a
      report area, select Vendor Transaction
      History; click [Display].

5.   Type **11/2/200X** in the From field. Press
      <Tab>. The Vendor Bill for Podcast Ltd.
      appears. The Vendor Transaction History
      can be substituted for the accounts
      payable ledger.

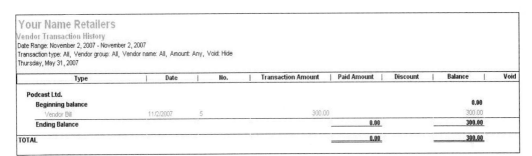

Your Name Retailers
Vendor Transaction History
Date Range: November 2, 2007 - November 2, 2007
Transaction type: All, Vendor group: All, Vendor name: All, Amount: Any, Void: Hide
Thursday, May 31, 2007

Type	Date	No.	Transaction Amount	Paid Amount	Discount	Balance	Void
Podcast Ltd.							
Beginning balance						0.00	
Vendor Bill	11/2/2007	5	300.00			300.00	
Ending Balance				0.00		300.00	
TOTAL				0.00		300.00	

6.   Close the Vendor Transaction History report without saving.

7.   Enter the following bills. Remember to save after each transaction.
      Saving posts the transaction to the appropriate accounts in the
      general ledger and accounts payable ledger.

Date   *Description of Transaction*

11/03   Invoice No. 90eB received from eBooks Express for the
                      purchase of 15 PDF files, $25 each, for a total of $375.
                      (*Hint:* In the Name field, select eBook.)

11/03   Invoice No. 210TV received from TV Flix for the purchase
                      of 25 video files, $30 each, for a total of $750. (*Hint:* In the
                      Name field, select TV Programs.)

11/05   Invoice No. 78PS received from Podcast Ltd. for the
                      purchase of 18 audio files, $15 each, for a total of $270.

Purchase Returns

Sometimes it is necessary to return merchandise that has been purchased from a vendor. When entering a purchase return, you need to record it as a new credit memo.

The following transaction is for merchandise returned to a vendor.

Date   *Description of Transaction*

11/10   Returned two video files to TV Flix Credit Memo No. CM1, for a total of $60.

Follow these steps to record a credit memo.

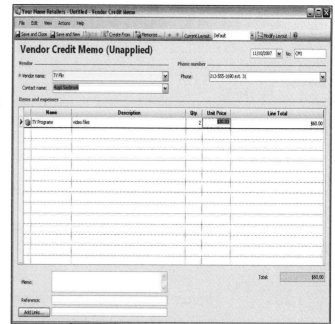

1. Click

2. Type **11/10/200X** in the date field.

3. Type **CM1** in the No. field.

4. Select TV Flix as the vendor.

5. In the Name field, select TV Programs.

6. Type **2** in the Qty. field.

7. Click [Save and Close]. Let's see how this entry is journalized. Go to Reports; Company and Financial, Transaction Journal, date is 11/10/200X. Observe that Accounts Payable/TV Flix is debited for $60. This reduces the accounts payable account balance by $60. Also, Inventory is credited for $60. This reduces the inventory account balance by the amount of the return. After viewing, close Transaction Journal without saving it.

Your Name Retailers
Transaction Journal
Date Range: November 10, 2007 - November 10, 2007
Transaction type: All, No.: Any, Name: All, Account: All, Amount: Any, Void: Show
Thursday, May 31, 2007

Type	Status	No.	Name	Date	Account	Debit	Credit	Void
Vendor Credit Memo	Unapplied	CM1	TV Flix	11/10/2007				
					Accounts Payable	60.00	0.00	
					Cost of Goods Sold	60.00	0.00	
					Cost of Goods Sold	0.00	60.00	
					Inventory	0.00	60.00	

8. To see how the accounts payable ledger records this transaction, display the Vendor Transaction History report from 11/1/200X to 11/10/200X. Observe that the balance in the TV Flix account is reduced by $60. This is indicated by the parentheses around (60.00). After viewing, close the report without saving it.

Your Name Retailers
Vendor Transaction History
Date Range: November 1, 2007 - November 10, 2007
Transaction type: All, Vendor group: All, Vendor name: All, Amount: Any, Void: Hide
Thursday, May 31, 2007

Type	Date	No.	Transaction Amount	Paid Amount	Discount	Balance	Void
eBooks Express							
Beginning balance						**0.00**	
Vendor Bill	11/3/2007	90eB	375.00			375.00	
Ending Balance				0.00		**375.00**	
Podcast Ltd.							
Beginning balance						**0.00**	
Vendor Bill	11/2/2007	5	300.00			300.00	
Vendor Bill	11/5/2007	78PS	270.00			570.00	
Ending Balance				0.00		**570.00**	
TV Flix							
Beginning balance						**0.00**	
Vendor Bill	11/3/2007	210TV	750.00			750.00	
Vendor Credit Memo	11/10/2007	CM1	(60.00)			690.00	
Ending Balance				0.00		**690.00**	
TOTAL				**0.00**		**1,635.00**	

9. Observe that the Total of the Vendor Transaction History report is $1,635. This should agree with the general ledger balance for accounts payable. (Reports; Company and Financial, GL Report, from 11/01/200X to 11/10/200X.) The general ledger balance for accounts payable is 1,635.00. This is the *same* amount that is shown on the Vendor Transaction History report.

2000 - Accounts Payable							**0.00**
Vendor Bill	11/2/2007	5	Podcast Ltd.	audio files	0.00	300.00	300.00
Vendor Bill	11/3/2007	90eB	eBooks Express	PDF files	0.00	375.00	675.00
Vendor Bill	11/3/2007	210TV	TV Flix	video files	0.00	750.00	1,425.00
Vendor Bill	11/5/2007	78PS	Podcast Ltd.	audio files	0.00	270.00	1,695.00
Vendor Credit Memo	11/10/2007	CM1	TV Flix	video files	60.00	0.00	1,635.00
Total 2000 - Accounts Payable					**60.00**	**1,695.00**	**1,635.00**

10. Close the GL Report without saving it.

Vendor Payments

Use the Pay Bills windows to pay vendor bills. The Pay Bills form displays a list of the company's unpaid vendor bills. You can choose to pay individual bills or pay all of them.

In the transaction that follows, all vendor bills are paid.

Date   *Description of Transaction*

11/20   Your Name Retailers pays all outstanding vendor bills for a total of $1,635.

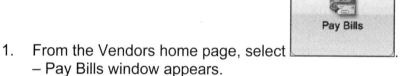

1. From the Vendors home page, select 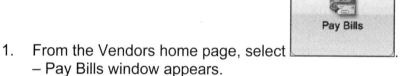. The Untitled – Pay Bills window appears.

2. Type **11/20/200X** in the date field. Press <Tab>.

3. In the Pay from field, select Account No. 1010, Reno Bank.

4. In the Payment method field, select Check.

5. Type **12/10/200X** in the Bills due on or before field.

6. In the Due Date column, click on each vendor's bill.

7. Since Your Name Retailers returned merchandise to TV Flix, link to the $0.00 in the Credits column. The Apply Credits and Payments (for TV Flix) window appears. Click on the checkbox next to the credit memo. Observe that the Total credit amount field shows $60.00.

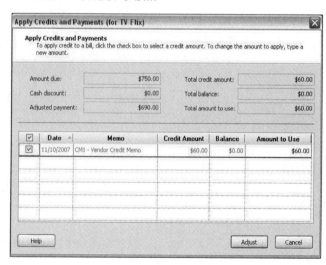

8. Click [Adjust]. You are returned to the Untitled – Pay Bill form. Observe that the Credits for TV Flix shows $60.00; the Payment column shows $690 (750 –60 = 690).

   Compare your Untitled – Pay Bills window to the one shown here. Observe that the Totals row shows $1,635. This agrees with the accounts payable balance shown on page 123.

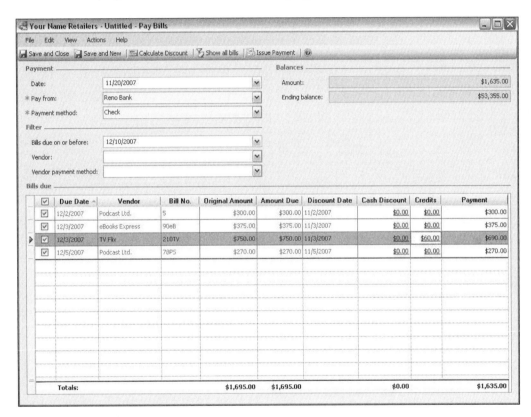

9. Click [Save and Close].

10. The Add memo and check number window appears. Read the information on this form. The Add memo and check number window is shown on the next page.

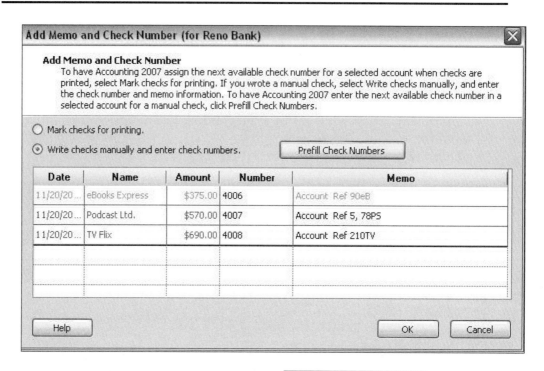

11. Select Write checks manually. Click [Prefill Check Numbers], the check numbers are added. Click [OK]. You are returned to the Vendors home page.

12. Display the GL Ledger account balance for Account No. 2000, Accounts Payable. (Reports; Company and Financial, GL Report, from 11/1/200X to 11/20/200X. If necessary, click refresh). Observe that the balance in Accounts Payable is 0.00. Check numbers are shown in the No. column because Write Checks Manually; Prefill Check Numbers was selected.

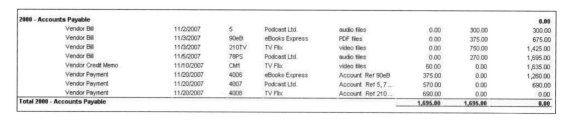

13. Display the Vendor Transaction History report from 11/1/200X to 11/20/200X. Observe that each vendor account shows a zero balance. The Vendor Transaction History report is shown on the next page.

Your Name Retailers
Vendor Transaction History
Date Range: November 1, 2007 - November 20, 2007
Transaction type: All, Vendor group: All, Vendor name: All, Amount: Any, Void: Hide
Thursday, May 31, 2007

Type	Date	No.	Transaction Amount	Paid Amount	Discount	Balance	Void
eBooks Express							
Beginning balance						0.00	
Vendor Bill	11/3/2007	90eB	375.00			375.00	
Vendor Payment	11/20/2007	4006		375.00		0.00	
Ending Balance				375.00		0.00	
Podcast Ltd.							
Beginning balance						0.00	
Vendor Bill	11/2/2007	5	300.00			300.00	
Vendor Bill	11/5/2007	78PS	270.00			570.00	
Vendor Payment	11/20/2007	4007		570.00		0.00	
Ending Balance				570.00		0.00	
TV Flix							
Beginning balance						0.00	
Vendor Bill	11/3/2007	210TV	750.00			750.00	
Vendor Credit Memo	11/10/2007	CM1	(60.00)			690.00	
Vendor Payment	11/20/2007	4008		690.00		0.00	
Ending Balance				690.00		0.00	
TOTAL				1,635.00		0.00	

Displaying the general ledger (GL report) and accounts payable ledger (Vendor Transaction History) confirms that the balance for both Account No. 2000, Accounts Payable, and each vendor is zero.

14.   To see how the vendor payments are journalized, display the 11/20/200X Transaction Journal. Observe that each vendor payment is journalized separately; for example, the November 20th vendor payment to eBooks Express shows a debit to Account No. 2000 for $375; and a credit to Account No. 1010, Reno Bank for $375. If you add the three payments together they equal, $1,635, which is the total of the three payments—375+690+570=1,635.

Your Name Retailers
Transaction Journal
Date Range: November 1, 2007 - November 20, 2007
Transaction type: All, No.: Any, Name: All, Account: All, Amount: Any, Void: Show
Thursday, May 31, 2007

Type	Status	No.	Name	Date	Account	Debit	Credit	Void
Vendor Bill	Paid	5	Podcast Ltd.	11/2/2007				
					Accounts Payable	0.00	300.00	
					Inventory	300.00	0.00	
Vendor Bill	Paid	90eB	eBooks Express	11/3/2007				
					Accounts Payable	0.00	375.00	
					Inventory	375.00	0.00	
Vendor Bill	Paid	210TV	TV Flix	11/3/2007				
					Accounts Payable	0.00	750.00	
					Inventory	750.00	0.00	
Vendor Bill	Paid	78PS	Podcast Ltd.	11/5/2007				
					Accounts Payable	0.00	270.00	
					Inventory	270.00	0.00	
Vendor Credit Memo	Applied	CM1	TV Flix	11/10/2007				
					Accounts Payable	60.00	0.00	
					Cost of Goods Sold	60.00	0.00	
					Cost of Goods Sold	0.00	60.00	
					Inventory	0.00	60.00	
Vendor Payment	Applied	4006	eBooks Express	11/20/2007				
					Accounts Payable	375.00	0.00	
					Reno Bank	0.00	375.00	
Vendor Payment	Applied	4007	Podcast Ltd.	11/20/2007				
					Accounts Payable	570.00	0.00	
					Reno Bank	0.00	570.00	
Vendor Payment	Applied	4008	TV Flix	11/20/2007				
					Accounts Payable	690.00	0.00	
					Reno Bank	0.00	690.00	

Purchasing Assets from Vendors

In the previous chapter you purchased assets for cash and used the check register as your source document. Now, along with credit purchases for inventory, assets can also be purchased on account from vendors. In the example that follows, you will see how to purchase assets on account.

Date   *Description of Transaction*

11/21   Purchased notebook computer equipment on account from The Business Store, Invoice BOS44, for a total of $1,799, terms Net 30 days.

1. Record the 11/21 using MOA's enter bills form. In the Vendor name field, select The Business Store. No. BOS 44.

2. In the Name field, select Expense 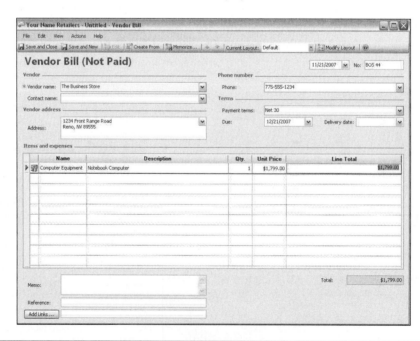. Complete the following fields:

Item name:	**Computer Equipment**
Description:	Notebook computer
Expense account:	Account No. 1420, Computer Equipment

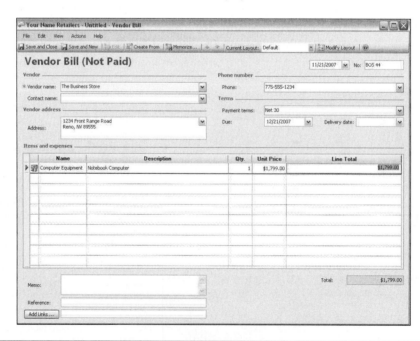

3.   Click [Save and Close].

4.   Backup your work. (*HINT:* File; Utilities, Data Utilities. [Backup])
     Name backup file **Chapter 4 Vendors and your initials**.

5.   Exit MOA or continue on to the next section.

CUSTOMERS

Now that you have purchased items from vendors, you are ready to sell that inventory. To do that, you need to learn how to use MOA's customers and receivables tasks. This section shows you how to establish customer records and defaults and explains how MOA's accounts receivable system works. ***Accounts receivable*** is a group of posting accounts that show the amounts customers owe for services or sales made on credit. Credit transactions from customers are called ***accounts receivable transactions***.

Customer receipts work similarly to paying vendor invoices. A ***customer invoice*** is defined as a request for payment to a customer for products or services sold. Once a new invoice is recorded, the receive payments form is used to record customer payments or collections.

MOA's Customers home page shows the flow of information. You will work with some of these features. From the Customers home page, MOA manages customers and receivables.

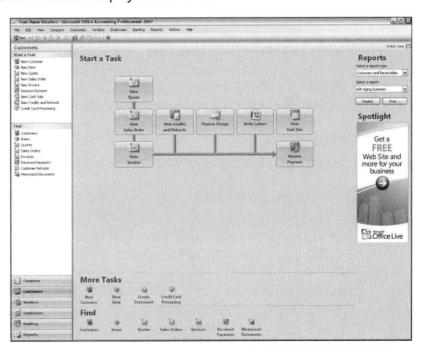

ACCOUNTS RECEIVABLE TASKS

In MOA, all information about a sale is recorded on the New Invoice form. Then, MOA takes the necessary information from the Invoice (Not Paid) window and automatically debits and credits the transaction in the Transaction Journal.

On the Invoice (Not Paid) window, you enter customer invoices. Credit sales from customers are posted to both the General Ledger and to the customers and receivables reports. In accounting, customers and receivables reports are called the *accounts receivable ledger*. MOA's customers and receivables tasks track credit sales. The customers and receivables reports include the following:

> ➢ A/R Aging Summary: Displays all the amounts owed to your company, by customer and by the number of days outstanding at a selected date.

> ➢ A/R Aging Detail: An in-depth view of the amounts your customers owe your company at a selected date.

> ➢ Customer Transaction History: Displays all customer transactions for a selected date range.

> ➢ Profitability by Customer Summary: Displays the profit made from each customer for a selected period of time.

> ➢ Profitability by Customer Detail: Calculated and details the profit margin for each customer for a selected period of time.

> ➢ Customer Refunds: Shows detailed information for all refunds that you have issued to customers in a selected date range.

MOA also includes the following Sales reports.

> ➢ Sales by Customer Summary: Displays the total sales made, by customer, for a selected period of time.

> ➢ Sales by Customer Detail: Lists all the items sold, by customer and job, for a selected period of time.

> ➤ Sales by Salesperson Summary: Displays each salesperson's total sales to customers for a selected period of time.

> ➤ Sales by Salesperson Detail: Lists net sales (before taxes) of items by each salesperson for a selected period of time.

> ➤ Sales by Item Summary: Displays total sales by item for a selected period of time.

> ➤ Sales by Item Detail: Lists all sales transactions for each item for a selected period of time.

When Your Name Retailers receives payments from customers, MOA's receive payment feature is used. Sales works hand in hand with customer payments. Once you have entered and saved (posted) a sales invoice, it is available when you receive payments. Then, MOA distributes the appropriate amounts.

CUSTOMER RECORDS

On the Customers home page, you perform all the tasks related to customers and receivables. MOA maintains your customer records and tracks their contact information and financial details. The Customers home page is the starting point for managing customer sales.

Follow these steps to set up customer records and defaults.

1. On the Navigation Pane, select 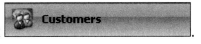 .

2. In the More Tasks area, link to [New Customer]. The Untitled – Customer window appears. Complete the fields shown here.

Customer name:	**Audio Answers**
Customer ID:	**AA1**
Business address:	**113 Aspen Drive**
	Telluride, CO 80010
Business phone:	**(303) 555-9312**
Business fax:	**(303) 555-1234**

E-mail 1:	**cathleen@audio.biz**
Web page address:	**www.audio.biz**
Customer since:	**1/1/200X**
Contact Name:	**Cathleen McClure**
Business phone:	**(303) 555-9312, ext. 1212**

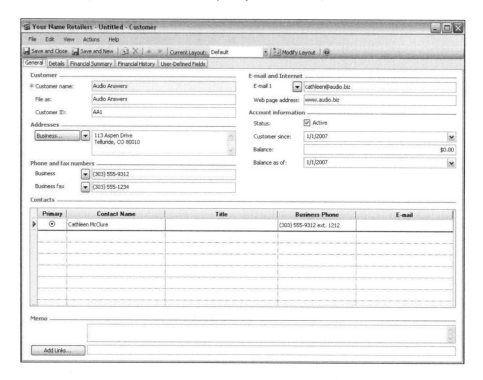

Details tab:

Credit limit:	**7,500.00**
Preferred payment method:	Check
Payment terms:	Net 30

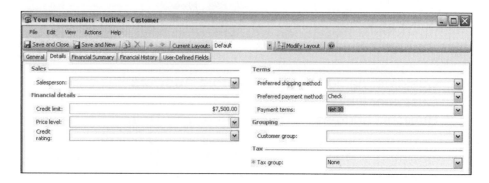

3.   Check the information recorded. Click [Save and New].

4.   Enter the following customers:

Customer name: **iPrint Design**
Customer ID: IP2
Business address: **4900 Springer Drive**
                            Palos Verdes, CA 90212
Business phone: **(310) 555-2367**
Business fax: **(310) 555-2368**
E-mail 1:   **rolo@iprint.com**
Web page address: **www.iprint.com**
Customer since: **1/1/200X**
Contact Name: **Rolo Kalm**
Business phone: **(310) 555-2364, ext. 3201**

Details tab:

Credit limit: **7,500.00**
Preferred payment method: Check
Payment terms: Net 30

Customer name: **Video Solutions**
Customer ID: **VS3**
Business address: **86113 Ginnie Blvd.**
                            Fanning Springs, FL 34688
Business phone: **(727) 555-0613**
Business fax: **(727) 555-0615**
E-mail 1:   **lh@video.com**
Web page address: **www.video.com**
Customer since: **1/1/200X**
Contact Name: **Lyman Hudson**
Business phone: **(727) 555-0613**
Details tab:

Credit limit: **7,500.00**
Preferred payment method: Check
Payment terms: Net 30

5.   Click [Save and Close] customer form to return to Customer desktop.

RECORDING CREDIT SALES

In MOA all the information about a credit sale is recorded on the Invoice (Not Paid) form. Then, MOA takes the necessary information from the window and automatically journalizes the transaction. You use MOA's New Invoice selection on the Customers home page to record credit sales to customers.

Credit sales refer to sales made to customers that will be paid for later. Your Name Retailers offers customers payment terms of Net 30 days.

Sales Invoices

The transaction you are going to record is:

Date   *Description of Transaction*

11/15/200X   Sold 5 eBooks (PDF files) on account to iPrint Design for a
              total credit sale of $250, Sales No. 1.

Follow these steps to enter the transaction.

1. If necessary on the Navigation Pane, select

. The Untitled – Invoice window appears. Complete the fields shown here.

Date: **1/15/200X**
No.:   1 is completed automatically
Customer name: iPrint Design
Name: eBook
Description: PDF files is completed automatically
Qty.:   **5**
Unit Price: $50.00 is completed automatically
Discount: 0% completed automatically
Line Total: $250.00 is completed automatically
Tax: Non-taxable is completed automatically

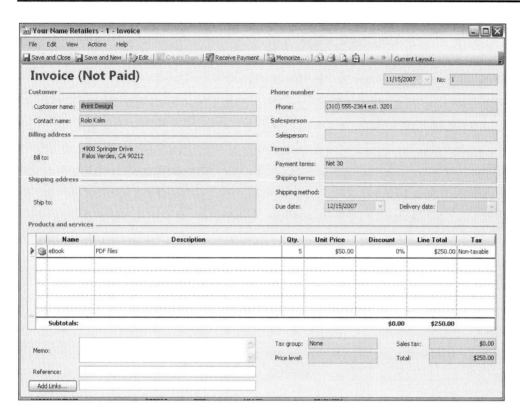

2.   Click ![Save and New] .

3.   Record the credit sales shown here.

Date	Description of Transaction
Date	*Description of Transaction*
11/15/200X	Sold 15 Podcasts (audio files) on account to Audio Answers for a total credit sale of $450, Sales No. 2.
11/15/200X	Sold 8 TV Programs (video files) on account to Video Solutions for a total credit sale of $480, Sales No. 3.

4.   Click ![Save and Close] .

5.   Look at how MOA journalizes these sales by displaying the 1/15/200X transaction journal.

Your Name Retailers
Transaction Journal
Date Range: November 15, 2007 - November 15, 2007
Transaction type: All, No.: Any, Name: All, Account: All, Amount: Any, Void: Show
Thursday, May 31, 2007

Type	Status	No.	Name	Date	Account	Debit	Credit	Void
Invoice	Not Paid	1	iPrint Design	11/15/2007				
					Accounts Receivable	250.00	0.00	
					Sales	0.00	250.00	
					Cost of Goods Sold	125.00	0.00	
					Inventory	0.00	125.00	
Invoice	Not Paid	2	Audio Answers	11/15/2007				
					Accounts Receivable	450.00	0.00	
					Sales	0.00	450.00	
					Cost of Goods Sold	225.00	0.00	
					Inventory	0.00	225.00	
Invoice	Not Paid	3	Video Solutions	11/15/2007				
					Accounts Receivable	480.00	0.00	
					Sales	0.00	480.00	
					Cost of Goods Sold	240.00	0.00	
					Inventory	0.00	240.00	

6.   Look closely at the accounts debited and credited for the sale made to In Print Design.

Type	Status	No.	Name	Date	Account	Debit	Credit	Void
Invoice	Not Paid	1	iPrint Design	11/15/2007				
					Accounts Receivable	250.00	0.00	
					Sales	0.00	250.00	
					Cost of Goods Sold	125.00	0.00	
					Inventory	0.00	125.00	

Observe that *both* the sales price, $250, and the cost of the inventory item are debited and credited. When Your Name Retailers sells PDF files the customer pays $50 each (5 PDF files were sold for a total of $250). When Your Name Retailers buys PDF files from the vendor, it pays $25 x 5 = $125. MOA tracks both the sales price *and* the purchase price when items are sold. The sales price is debited and credited to AR/customer and Sales; the cost of the item is debited and credited to Cost of Goods Sold and Inventory, respectively. This entry keeps the Inventory account up to date.

7.   Close the Transaction Journal without saving.

Inventory

Before recording more sales, let's look at the status of inventory on November 15, 200X (use your current year). Follow these steps to do that.

1. In the Reports area, select Inventory; Inventory Stock Status by Item.

2. Click [Display].

3. Type **11/15/200X** in the Date field. Press <Enter>. (*Or,* you can click refresh.) The Inventory Stock Status by Item report displays. Observe that the following quantities are on hand as of 11/15/200X:

    | eBook | PDF files | 10.00 |
    | Podcast | audio files | 23.00 |
    | TV Programs | video files | 15.00 |

4. Close the Inventory Stock Status by Item report.

Sales Returns

When a customer returns a product or requires a refund, you can create a customer credit memo with the Customer Credit Memo form.

The following transaction is for a sales return.

Date

Description of Transaction

11/17/200X

Audio Answers returned 2 Podcasts (audio files), CM01.

1. Click 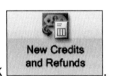.

2. Type **11/17/200X** in the date field.

3. Type **CM01** in the No. field.

4. Select Audio Answers as the customer.

5. In the Name field, select Podcast.

6. Type **2** in the Qty. field. Compare your Customer Credit Memo (Unapplied) window to the one shown here. Click [Save and Close].

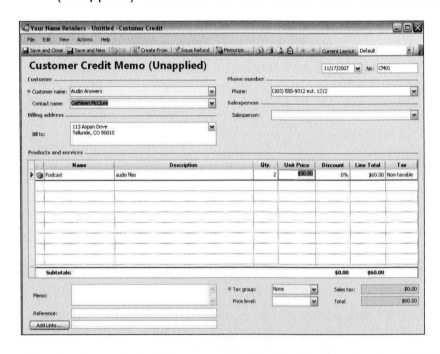

7. Let's see how this entry is journalized. Display the 11/17/200X transaction journal.

Your Name Retailers
Transaction Journal
Date Range: November 17, 2007 - November 17, 2007
Transaction type: All, No.: Any, Name: All, Account: All, Amount: Any, Void: Show
Thursday, May 31, 2007

Type	Status	No.	Name	Date	Account	Debit	Credit	Void
Customer Credit Memo	**Unapplied**	**CM01**	**Audio Answers**	**11/17/2007**				
					Accounts Receivable	0.00	60.00	
					Sales	60.00	0.00	
					Cost of Goods Sold	0.00	30.00	
					Inventory	30.00	0.00	

8. To see how the accounts receivable ledger records customer transactions, display the Customer Transaction History report from 11/1/200X to 11/17/200X. (*Hint:* Select Customers and Receivables reports; Customer Transaction History.) Observe that the balance in the Audio Answers account is reduced by the amount of the 11/17/200X return. Also, notice that the Total on the report is $1,120. This total agrees with the GL Report balance for Account No. 1200, Accounts Receivable.

Your Name Retailers
Customer Transaction History
Date Range: November 1, 2007 - November 17, 2007
Transaction type: All, Customer name: All, Customer group: All, Amount: Any, Void: Hide
Thursday, May 31, 2007

Type	Date	No.	Invoiced Amount	Paid Amount	Discount	Write-Off	Balance	Void
Audio Answers								
Beginning balance							0.00	
Invoice	11/15/2007	2	450.00		0.00	0.00	450.00	
Customer Credit Memo	11/17/2007	CM01	(60.00)		0.00	0.00	390.00	
Ending Balance				0.00			**390.00**	
iPrint Design								
Beginning balance							0.00	
Invoice	11/15/2007	1	250.00		0.00	0.00	250.00	
Ending Balance				0.00			**250.00**	
Video Solutions								
Beginning balance							0.00	
Invoice	11/15/2007	3	480.00		0.00	0.00	480.00	
Ending Balance				0.00			**480.00**	
TOTAL				0.00			**1,120.00**	

9. Close the Customer Transaction History.

10. Display the GL Report for 11/1/200X to 11/17/200X. Account No. 1200, Accounts Receivable, shows the same balance as the Customer Transaction History, $1,120.

1200 - Accounts Receivable							0.00
Invoice	11/15/2007	1	iPrint Design	PDF files	250.00	0.00	250.00
Invoice	11/15/2007	2	Audio Answers	audio files	450.00	0.00	700.00
Invoice	11/15/2007	3	Video Solutions	video files	480.00	0.00	1,180.00
Customer Credit Memo	11/17/2007	CM01	Audio Answers	audio files	0.00	60.00	1,120.00
Total 1200 - Accounts Receivable					**1,180.00**	**60.00**	**1,120.00**

11. Close the GL Report.

Credit Card Sales

Your Name Retailers accepts credit cards for customer sales. Observe that on the Customers home page in the More Tasks area, there is a Credit Card Processing link. This takes you to MOA's credit card application. With Credit Card Processing for Microsoft Office Accounting, you can accept credit card payments.

MOA can be set up to use credit cards for customer payments. In our example, you will see how MOA processes credit card transactions. In an actual business, MOA can access the online link for processing credit cards from the software. For our purposes, you will see how MOA processes credit cards but you will *not* set up the online credit card link.

The transaction you are going to record is:

Date   *Description of Transaction*

11/18   Sold 5 eBooks for $250; 8 Podcasts for $240; and 6 TV
             Programs for $360; for total credit card sales of $850.

Follow these steps to enter a new customer on the fly and credit card sales.

1.   From the Customers home page, select .

2.   Type **11/18/200X** in the date field.

3.   Accept 4 as the default invoice number.

4.   In the Customer Name field, select Add a new Customer. On the
      Customer form, complete these fields.

      Customer name: **Credit Card Sales**
      Customer ID: **CCS**
      Customer since: **1/1/2007**

      Details tab:

      Preferred payment method: Credit Card

5.   Click 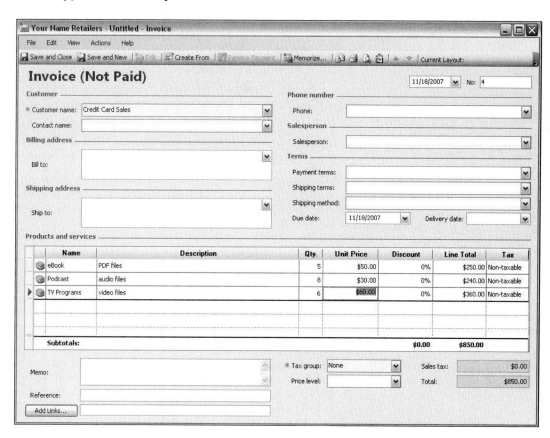 Save and Close . You are returned to the Invoice (Not Paid) form. Credit Cards Sales is shown in the Customer name field.

6.   In the Name field, select eBook.

7.   Type **5** in the Qty. field.

8.   Go to the Name field, select Podcast.

9.   Type **8** in the Qty. field.

10.   Go to the Name field, select TV Programs.

11.   Type **6** in the Qty. field.

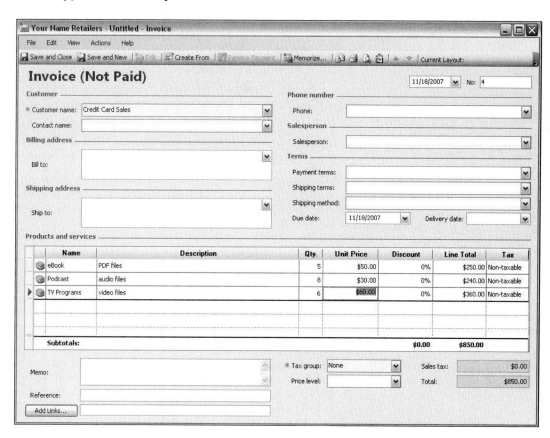

12.   Check the Invoice (Not Paid) form. Click ⊞ Save and Close . To see how this transaction is journalized, display the transaction journal for

11/18/200X. Observe that each item amount is individually debited and credited to Accounts Receivable, Sales, Costs of Goods Sold, and Inventory.

Your Name Retailers
Transaction Journal
Date Range: November 18, 2007 - November 18, 2007
Transaction type: All, No.: Any, Name: All, Account: All, Amount: Any, Void: Show
Thursday, May 31, 2007

Type	Status	No.	Name	Date	Account	Debit	Credit	Void
Invoice	Not Paid	4	Credit Card Sales	11/18/2007				
					Accounts Receivable	250.00	0.00	
					Accounts Receivable	240.00	0.00	
					Accounts Receivable	360.00	0.00	
					Sales	0.00	250.00	
					Sales	0.00	240.00	
					Sales	0.00	360.00	
					Cost of Goods Sold	125.00	0.00	
					Cost of Goods Sold	120.00	0.00	
					Cost of Goods Sold	180.00	0.00	
					Inventory	0.00	125.00	
					Inventory	0.00	120.00	
					Inventory	0.00	180.00	

RECEIVE PAYMENTS FROM CUSTOMERS

When a customer sends you a payment, you enter the customer payment on the Customer Payment form. You can then apply the payment to the invoices that are due. A payment might cover one or more invoices, or it may not completely cover an invoice. You can select which invoice to settle against a payment as well as the amount to apply to each invoice. *Or,* you can have Microsoft Office Accounting automatically apply the payment to invoices in chronological order from the oldest outstanding invoice.

In the transactions that follow, the customers pay their outstanding invoices.

Date	Description of Transaction
11/23	Received a check in full payment of Audio Answers' account, $390.
11/24	Received a check in full payment of iPrint Design's account, $250.
11/24	Received a check in full payment of Video Solutions' account, $480.

11/24   Received payments for credit card sales, $850.00. (This deposit will be verified on the November 30, 200X bank statement and account reconciliation)

Using the payment from Audio Answers as an example, follow these steps to the customer payment.

1.   From the Customers home page, select [ ]. Complete the following fields:

Date:	**11/23/200X**
No.	1 is automatically completed
Received from:	Audio Answers
Amount:	**390.00**
Payment method:	Check is automatically completed
Customer balance:	$390.00 is automatically completed
Deposit in:	Undeposited Funds is is automatically completed

2.   Audio Answers returned merchandise. Link to <u>0.00</u> in the Applied Credits column to apply the credit for the returned merchandise. On the Apply Credits and Payments (for Audio Answers) window, click on the checkmark on the credit memo row.

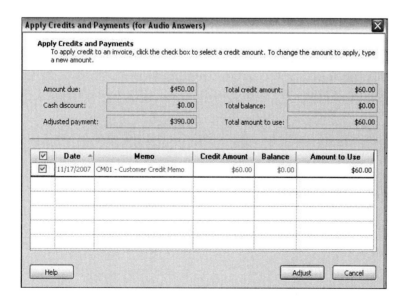

---

3. Click 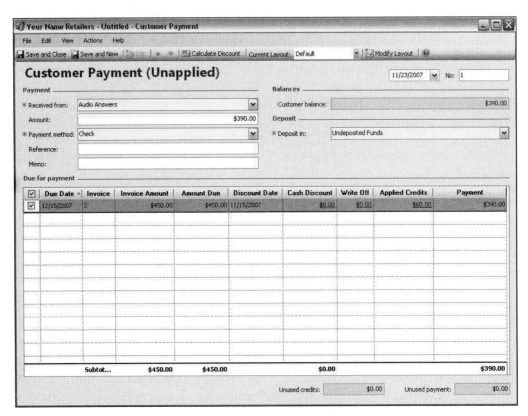 [Adjust]. You are returned to the Customer Payment form.

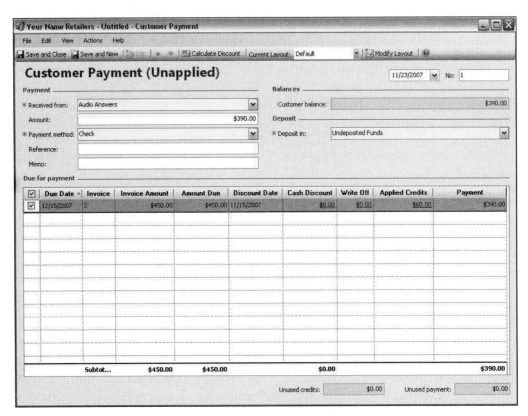

4. Click [Save and New].

5. Display the 11/23/200X to 11/24/200X Transaction Journal. When a customer payment is received, the following accounts are debited and credited. (The example shows the customer payment received from Audio Answers.)

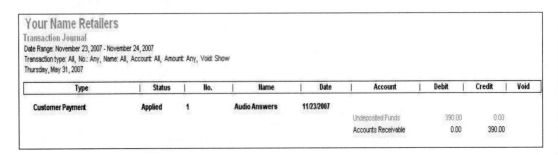

What are undeposited funds? Account No. 1005, Undeposited Funds, is a cash account for amounts received from customers but not yet deposited to the bank account. When bank deposits are made, Undeposited Funds will be credited and Reno Bank will be debited. You can think of undeposited funds as a clearing account. The undeposited funds account holds deposits until they are deposited and cleared by the bank. The November bank statement will show which customer payments cleared Account No. 1010, Reno Bank, which is Your Name Retailers' bank account.

6. Go to page 142 and record the three November 24, 200X payments received from customers. Click [Save and Close] to return to Customer desktop.

7. After you record the customer checks received on November 24 and physically deposited the 11/23 and 11/24 checks received in the Reno Bank, you make the bank deposit entry: On the Navigation Pane, click [Banking]. The Banking home page appears.

8. Click [Make Deposit].

9. Type **11/24/200X** in the date field.

10. Select Account No. 1010, Reno Bank. Place a check mark next to the 11/23 and 11/24 checks included in the deposit. (Customer checks for $390+$250+$480 were deposited.) Leave Credit Cards unchecked.

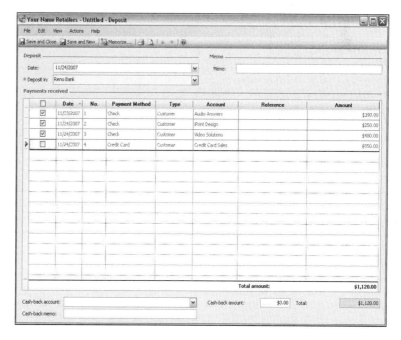

11. The Total amount of the deposit is $1,120. Compare your Untitled – Deposit window to the one shown above.

12. Click ![Save and Close]. You are returned to the Banking home page. Close the Deposit window.

13. Backup your work and Exit MOA or continue to the next section.

> **Comment:**
> Separation of duties means work is divided between different employees to insure data integrity and minimize the opportunity for wrongdoing. This is a basic internal control. For example to keep employees from stealing customer payments, the tasks: opening the mail, recording customer payments, and making deposits at the bank are assigned to three different employees.

ACCOUNT RECONCILIATION

1. To reconcile Account No. 1010 for November, use the bank statement shown below. (*HINT:* See page 90-94 for October's Account Reconciliation steps.)

Statement of Account			Your Name Retailers	
Reno Bank			Your address	
November 1 to November 30		Account # 89123631	Reno, NV	
REGULAR CHECKING				
Previous Balance	10/31	**$55,290.00**		
Deposits(+)		1,970.00		
Checks (-)		1935.00		
Service Charges (-)	11/30	10.00		
Ending Balance	11/30	55,315.00		
DEPOSITS				
	11/24	1,120.00	Customers	
	11/25	850.00	Credit Card	
CHECKS (Asterisk * indicates break in check number sequence)				
	11/3	300.00	4004	
	11/25	375.00	4006*	
	11/25	570.00	4007	
	11/25	690.00	4008	

2. After placing check marks beside the cleared deposits and checks per the bank statement, compare your screen to the following:

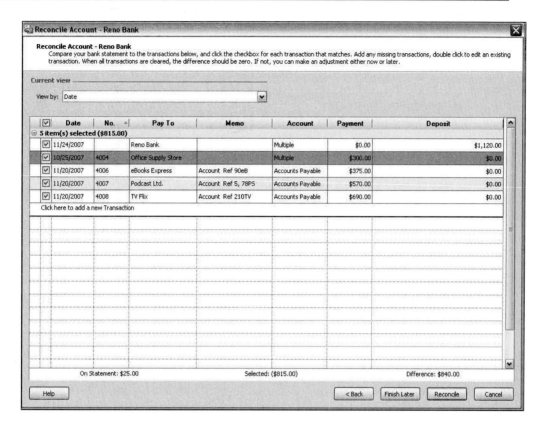

3. Notice the Difference of $840.00, Click
    Click here to add a new Transaction to record the
    $10.00 bank fee.

4. In Select Transaction window, select Enter
    bank fee. Click OK.

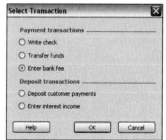

5. In Bank Fee window, Date: type
    11/30/200X (use your current
    year); Amount $10.00.
    Compare and when satisfied,
    click OK.

6. After placing a check mark beside the Bank fee of $10.00, the Reconcile Account-Reno Bank now shows a Difference of $850.00 (the amount of the credit card sales).

7. To recognize the automatic deposit by Reno Bank of the $850.00 in credit card sales, click 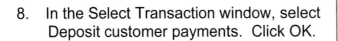.

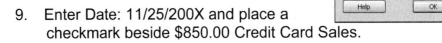

8. In the Select Transaction window, select Deposit customer payments. Click OK.

9. Enter Date: 11/25/200X and place a checkmark beside $850.00 Credit Card Sales.

10. Click .

11. After placing a check mark beside the $850.00, the Reconcile Account-Reno Bank now shows a Difference of $00.00.

12. Click Reconcile, then click Display Report.

13. Print the Reconciliation Detail report.

Your Name Retailers
Reconciliation Detail
Amount: Any, Bank Account: Reno Bank, Statement date: 11/30/2007
Thursday, May 31, 2007

Type	Date	No.	Name	Amount
Reno Bank				
Opening Balance				**55,290.00**
Cleared Deposits				
Deposit	11/24/2007	2		1,120.00
Deposit	11/25/2007	3		850.00
Total Cleared Deposits				**1,970.00**
Cleared Withdrawals				
Check	10/25/2007	4004	Office Supply Store	(300.00)
Vendor Payment	11/20/2007	4006	eBooks Express	(375.00)
Vendor Payment	11/20/2007	4007	Podcast Ltd.	(570.00)
Vendor Payment	11/20/2007	4008	TV Flix	(690.00)
Bank Fee	11/30/2007	10		(10.00)
Total Cleared Withdrawals				**(1,945.00)**
Total Cleared Transactions				**25.00**
Reconciled Balance As Of Statement Date				**55,315.00**
Ending Balance				**55,315.00**

14.   Close the Reconciliation Detail window.

REPORTS

Print the following reports. Compare your reports to the ones shown on the next pages. If you have made errors in your entries, void and edit your original entries to correct your reports.

1.   Trial Balance 11/30/200X.

Your Name Retailers
Trial Balance
As of: 11/30/2007

Thursday, May 31, 2007

Account Name	Account No.	Debit	Credit
Reno Bank	1010	55,315.00	
Prime Savings & Loan	1100	25,500.00	
Supplies	1240	2,300.00	
Inventory	1250	650.00	
Computer Equipment	1420	10,299.00	
Furniture & Fixtures	1430	5,000.00	
Prepaid Insurance	1810	5,000.00	
Accounts Payable	2000		1,799.00
Long-Term Notes Payable	2600		20,500.00
Common Stock	3010		81,000.00
Dividends	3110	200.00	
Sales	4020		1,970.00
Cost of Goods Sold	5015	985.00	
Bank/Bankcard Charges	7232	20.00	
Total		**105,269.00**	**105,269.00**

2.   Transaction Journal 11/01/200X to 11/30/200X.

Your Name Retailers
Transaction Journal
Date Range: November 1, 2007 - November 30, 2007
Transaction type: All, No.: Any, Name: All, Account: All, Amount: Any, Void: Show
Thursday, May 31, 2007

Type	Status	No.	Name	Date	Account	Debit	Credit	Void
Vendor Bill	Paid	5	Podcast Ltd.	11/2/2007	Accounts Payable	0.00	300.00	
					Inventory	300.00	0.00	
Vendor Bill	Paid	90eB	eBooks Express	11/3/2007	Accounts Payable	0.00	375.00	
					Inventory	375.00	0.00	
Vendor Bill	Paid	210TV	TV Flix	11/3/2007	Accounts Payable	0.00	750.00	
					Inventory	750.00	0.00	
Vendor Bill	Paid	78PS	Podcast Ltd.	11/5/2007	Accounts Payable	0.00	270.00	
					Inventory	270.00	0.00	
Vendor Credit Memo	Applied	CM1	TV Flix	11/10/2007	Accounts Payable	60.00	0.00	
					Cost of Goods Sold	60.00	0.00	
					Cost of Goods Sold	0.00	60.00	
					Inventory	0.00	60.00	
Invoice	Paid	1	iPrint Design	11/15/2007	Accounts Receivable	250.00	0.00	
					Sales	0.00	250.00	
					Cost of Goods Sold	125.00	0.00	
					Inventory	0.00	125.00	
Invoice	Paid	2	Audio Answers	11/15/2007	Accounts Receivable	450.00	0.00	
					Sales	0.00	450.00	
					Cost of Goods Sold	225.00	0.00	
					Inventory	0.00	225.00	
Invoice	Paid	3	Video Solutions	11/15/2007	Accounts Receivable	480.00	0.00	
					Sales	0.00	480.00	
					Cost of Goods Sold	240.00	0.00	
					Inventory	0.00	240.00	
Customer Credit Memo	Applied	CM01	Audio Answers	11/17/2007	Accounts Receivable	0.00	60.00	
					Sales	60.00	0.00	
					Cost of Goods Sold	0.00	30.00	
					Inventory	30.00	0.00	
Invoice	Paid	4	Credit Card Sales	11/18/2007	Accounts Receivable	250.00	0.00	
					Accounts Receivable	240.00	0.00	
					Accounts Receivable	360.00	0.00	
					Sales	0.00	250.00	
					Sales	0.00	240.00	
					Sales	0.00	360.00	
					Cost of Goods Sold	125.00	0.00	
					Cost of Goods Sold	120.00	0.00	
					Cost of Goods Sold	180.00	0.00	
					Inventory	0.00	125.00	
					Inventory	0.00	120.00	
					Inventory	0.00	180.00	
Vendor Payment	Applied	4006	eBooks Express	11/20/2007	Accounts Payable	375.00	0.00	
					Reno Bank	0.00	375.00	
Vendor Payment	Applied	4007	Podcast Ltd.	11/20/2007	Accounts Payable	570.00	0.00	
					Reno Bank	0.00	570.00	
Vendor Payment	Applied	4008	TV Flix	11/20/2007	Accounts Payable	690.00	0.00	
					Reno Bank	0.00	690.00	
Vendor Bill	Not Paid	BOS 44	The Business Store	11/21/2007	Accounts Payable	0.00	1,799.00	
					Computer Equipment	1,799.00	0.00	
Customer Payment	Applied	1	Audio Answers	11/23/2007	Undeposited Funds	390.00	0.00	
					Accounts Receivable	0.00	390.00	
Customer Payment	Applied	2	iPrint Design	11/24/2007	Undeposited Funds	250.00	0.00	
					Accounts Receivable	0.00	250.00	
Customer Payment	Applied	3	Video Solutions	11/24/2007	Undeposited Funds	480.00	0.00	
					Accounts Receivable	0.00	480.00	
Customer Payment	Applied	4	Credit Card Sales	11/24/2007	Undeposited Funds	850.00	0.00	
					Accounts Receivable	0.00	850.00	
Deposit		2		11/24/2007	Undeposited Funds	0.00	390.00	
					Undeposited Funds	0.00	250.00	
					Undeposited Funds	0.00	480.00	
					Reno Bank	390.00	0.00	
					Reno Bank	250.00	0.00	
					Reno Bank	480.00	0.00	
Deposit		3		11/25/2007	Undeposited Funds	0.00	850.00	
					Reno Bank	850.00	0.00	
Bank Fee		10		11/30/2007	Reno Bank	0.00	10.00	
					Bank/Bankcard Charges	10.00	0.00	

3.   Vendor List.

	Active	Vendor ID	Vendor Name	Address	City	State	Zip Code	Phone	Fax	Balance
Vendor List										Current View: Active
Add a new Vendor										
	✓	5	eBooks Express	10756 NW First Street	Gig Harbor	OR	97330	541-555-4320	541-555-8808	$0.00
	✓	2	Office Supply Store	9876 Hogback Road	Reno	NV	89555	775-555-9876		$0.00
	✓	4	Podcast Ltd.	1341 Barrington Road	Los Gatos	CA	90046	213-555-0100	213-555-0300	$0.00
	✓	1	Tax Agency							$0.00
	✓	1	The Business Store	1234 Front Range Road	Reno	NV	89555	775-555-1234		$1,799.00
	✓	6	TV Flix	7709 Sunset Boulevard	Burbank	CA	91501	213-555-1690	213-555-6320	$0.00
	✓	3	Your Name							$0.00

4.   Item List.

	Active	Item Name	Description	Type	Price	On Hand	Reorder	Item No.
Item List								Current View: Active
Add a new Item								
	✓	Podcast	audio files	Inventory Item	$30.00	17		1
	✓	eBook	PDF files	Inventory Item	$50.00	5		2
	✓	TV Programs	video files	Inventory Item	$60.00	9		3

5.   Purchase by Vendor Detail 11/01/200X to 11/30/200X.

Your Name Retailers
Purchases by Vendor Detail
Date Range: November 1, 2007 - November 30, 2007
Amount: Any, Class: All, Vendor group: All, Vendor name: All, Void: Hide
Thursday, May 31, 2007

Type	Date	No.	Item Name	Qty.	Amount	Void
eBooks Express						
Vendor Bill	11/3/2007	90eB	eBook	15.00	375.00	
Total eBooks Express					**375.00**	
Podcast Ltd.						
Vendor Bill	11/2/2007	5	Podcast	20.00	300.00	
Vendor Bill	11/5/2007	78PS	Podcast	18.00	270.00	
Total Podcast Ltd.					**570.00**	
The Business Store						
Vendor Bill	11/21/2007	BOS 44	Computer Equipment	1.00	1,799.00	
Total The Business Store					**1,799.00**	
TV Flix						
Vendor Bill	11/3/2007	210TV	TV Programs	25.00	750.00	
Vendor Credit Memo	11/10/2007	CM1	TV Programs	(2.00)	(60.00)	
Total TV Flix					**690.00**	
TOTAL					**3,434.00**	

6.   Purchase by Item Summary 11/01/200X to 11/30/200X.

Your Name Retailers
Purchases by Item Summary
Date Range: November 1, 2007 - November 30, 2007
Amount: Any, Item: All
Thursday, May 31, 2007

Item Type	11/1/07 - 11/30/07 - Qty.	11/1/07 - 11/30/07 - Am...
Inventory Items		
eBook,2	15.00	375.00
Podcast,1	38.00	570.00
TV Programs,3	23.00	690.00
Inventory Items Total	**76.00**	**1,635.00**
TOTAL	**76.00**	**1,635.00**

7. Vendor Transaction History 11/01/200X to 11/30/200X.

Your Name Retailers
Vendor Transaction History
Date Range: November 1, 2007 - November 30, 2007
Transaction type: All, Vendor group: All, Vendor name: All, Amount: Any, Void: Hide
Thursday, May 31, 2007

Type	Date	No.	Transaction Amount	Paid Amount	Discount	Balance	Void
eBooks Express							
Beginning balance						0.00	
Vendor Bill	11/3/2007	90eB	375.00			375.00	
Vendor Payment	11/20/2007	4006		375.00		0.00	
Ending Balance				375.00		0.00	
Podcast Ltd.							
Beginning balance						0.00	
Vendor Bill	11/2/2007	5	300.00			300.00	
Vendor Bill	11/5/2007	78PS	270.00			570.00	
Vendor Payment	11/20/2007	4007		570.00		0.00	
Ending Balance				570.00		0.00	
The Business Store							
Beginning balance						0.00	
Vendor Bill	11/21/2007	BOS 44	1,799.00			1,799.00	
Ending Balance				0.00		1,799.00	
TV Flix							
Beginning balance						0.00	
Vendor Bill	11/3/2007	210TV	750.00			750.00	
Vendor Credit Memo	11/10/2007	CM1	(60.00)			690.00	
Vendor Payment	11/20/2007	4008		690.00		0.00	
Ending Balance				690.00		0.00	
TOTAL				1,635.00		1,799.00	

8. Customer List.

Customer List — Current View: Active ▾

	Active	Customer ID	Customer Name	Address	City	State	Zip Code	Phone	Fax	Balance
➕ Add a new Customer										
	✔	AA1	Audio Answers	113 Aspen Drive	Telluride	CO	80010	3035559312	3035551234	$0.00
	✔	CCS	Credit Card Sales							$0.00
	✔	IP2	iPrint Design	4900 Springer Drive	Palos Verdes	CA	90212	3105552367	3105552368	$0.00
	✔	VS3	Video Solutions	86113 Ginnie Boulevard	Fanning Spri...	FL	34688	7275550613	7275550615	$0.00

9. Customer Transaction History 11/01/200X to 11/30/200X.

Your Name Retailers
Customer Transaction History
Date Range: November 1, 2007 - November 30, 2007
Transaction type: All, Customer name: All, Customer group: All, Amount: Any, Void: Hide
Thursday, May 31, 2007

Type	Date	No.	Invoiced Amount	Paid Amount	Discount	Write-Off	Balance	Void
Audio Answers								
Beginning balance							0.00	
Invoice	11/15/2007	2	450.00		0.00	0.00	450.00	
Customer Credit Memo	11/17/2007	CM01	(60.00)		0.00	0.00	390.00	
Customer Payment	11/23/2007	1		390.00	0.00	0.00	0.00	
Ending Balance				390.00			0.00	
Credit Card Sales								
Beginning balance							0.00	
Invoice	11/18/2007	4	850.00		0.00	0.00	850.00	
Customer Payment	11/24/2007	4		850.00	0.00	0.00	0.00	
Ending Balance				850.00			0.00	
iPrint Design								
Beginning balance							0.00	
Invoice	11/15/2007	1	250.00		0.00	0.00	250.00	
Customer Payment	11/24/2007	2		250.00	0.00	0.00	0.00	
Ending Balance				250.00			0.00	
Video Solutions								
Beginning balance							0.00	
Invoice	11/15/2007	3	480.00		0.00	0.00	480.00	
Customer Payment	11/24/2007	3		480.00	0.00	0.00	0.00	
Ending Balance				480.00			0.00	
TOTAL				1,970.00			0.00	

10. Profitability by Customer Summary 11/01/200X to 11/30/200X.

Your Name Retailers
Profitability by Customer Summary
Date Range: November 1, 2007 - November 30, 2007
Customer group: All, Customer name: All, Margin: Any
Thursday, May 31, 2007

Customer	Customer ID	Invoiced Amount	Cost	($) Margin	(%) Margin
Audio Answers	AA1	390.00	(195.00)	195.00	50.0%
Credit Card Sales	CCS	850.00	(425.00)	425.00	50.0%
iPrint Design	IP2	250.00	(125.00)	125.00	50.0%
Video Solutions	VS3	480.00	(240.00)	240.00	50.0%
Total Gross Profitability		**1,970.00**	**(985.00)**	**985.00**	**50.0%**

11. Sales by Customer Summary 11/01/200X to 11/30/200X. (Select Sales as the report type on the Customers home page.)

Your Name Retailers
Sales by Customer Summary
Date Range: November 1, 2007 - November 30, 2007
Customer group: All, Amount: Any, Customer name: All, Active Status: Active, Report Basis: Accrual
Thursday, May 31, 2007

Customer Name	Customer No.	Customer Group	11/1/07 - 11/30/07
Audio Answers	AA1		390.00
Credit Card Sales	CCS		850.00
iPrint Design	IP2		250.00
Video Solutions	VS3		480.00
TOTAL			**1,970.00**

12. Sales by Item Summary 11/01/200X to 11/30/200X.

Your Name Retailers
Sales by Item Summary
Date Range: November 1, 2007 - November 30, 2007
Amount: Any, Item: All, Report Basis: Accrual
Thursday, May 31, 2007

Type	Item No.	Item Group	11/1/07 - 11/30/07 - Qty.	11/1/07 - 11/30/07 - Am...
Inventory Items				
eBook	2		10.00	500.00
Podcast	1		21.00	630.00
TV Programs	3		14.00	840.00
Total Inventory Items				**1,970.00**
Total				**1,970.00**

BACK UP CHAPTER 4 DATA

1.   Backup your work. (*HINT:* File; Utilities, Data Utilities. | Backup |)
     Name your file **Chapter 4 End and your initials**.

2.   Transfer backup to your USB drive.

3.   Exit MOA or continue with the next section.

SUMMARY AND REVIEW

OBJECTIVES: In Chapter 4, you used the software to:

1.   Open the company, Your Name Retailers
2.   Enter vendor records.
3.   Enter inventory items.
4.   Print the vendor list and item list.
5.   Enter bills and record purchase returns.
6.   Pay bills.
7.   Add a vendor and non-inventory item on the fly.
8.   Enter customer records and defaults.
9.   Record customer sales on account, credit card sales, and sales
     returns.
10. Receive customer payments.
11. Make backups
12. Use your Internet browser to go to the book's website. (Go online to
     www.mhhe.com/moaessentials.)

GOING TO THE NET

Access information about MOA's vendor services by going online to
http://sba.microsoft.com/index.html. (*Hint:* From the menu bar, select
Vendors; Vendor Services, Services Overview.)

Answer the following questions.

1.   List four services offered by MOA.

2.   Link to Other Services. List 10 types of available services.

FLASHCARD REVIEW

Create the following flashcards.

1. What are the steps for adding a vendor record?

2. What are the steps for adding an inventory item?

3. What are the steps for entering a bill?

4. What are the steps for paying a bill?

5. What are the steps for entering a sales invoice?

6. What are the steps for receiving a customer payment?

7. What are the steps for applying a return of merchandise previously sold?

Multiple Choice Questions: In the space provided write the letter that best answers each questions.

_____1. A group of posting accounts that shows the amounts owed to vendors or suppliers is called:

  a. Accounts receivable.
  b. Inventory.
  c. Accounts payable.
  d. Entering bills.
  e. All of the above.

_____2. Your Name Retailers describes eBooks as:

  a. Video files.
  b. PDF files.
  c. Audio files.
  d. None of the above.
  e. All of the above.

_____3. MOA stores new company files in the following folder:

    a. Backups.
    b. Student Name.
    c. yournameretailers.sbc.
    d. Companies.
    e. None of the above.

_____4. Products that are purchased for sale are tracked in the following account:

    a. Account No. 4020, Sales.
    b. Account No. 1200, Accounts Receivable.
    c. Account No. 1250, Inventory.
    d. Account No. 4024, Merchandise.
    e. None of the above.

_____5. Which of the following shows information about inventory items?

    a. Vendor list.
    b. Trial Balance.
    c. Item list.
    d. Vendor record.
    e. None of the above.

_____6. An in-depth view of the amounts the company owes its vendors as of a selected date.

    a. Purchases by vendor detail.
    b. Invoice.
    c. Purchases by item detail.
    d. A/P aging summary.
    e. All of the above.

_____7. When merchandise is returned to the vendor, the following accounts are debited and credited:

   a. Dr. Account No. 1250, Inventory; Credit Account No. 5015, Cost of Goods Sold.
   b. Debit Account No. 5015, Cost of Goods Sold and Account No. 1250, Inventory; Credit Account No. 5015, Cost of Goods Sold and Account No. 2000, Accounts Payable/vendor.
   c. Debit Account No. 5015, Cost of Goods Sold and Account No. 2000, Accounts Payable/vendor; Credit Account No. 5015, Cost of Goods Sold and Account No. 1250, Inventory.
   d. Debit Account No. 2000/vendor; credit Account No. 5015, Cost of Goods Sold.
   e. None of the above.

_____8. When a vendor payment is made, the following accounts are debited and credited:

   a. Dr. Account No. 2000, Accounts Payable/vendor; Credit Account No. 1010, Reno Bank.
   b. Credit Account No. 1010, Reno Bank; Debit Account No. 1240, Inventory
   c. Debit Account No. 5015, Cost of Goods Sold and Credit Account No. 1010, Reno Bank.
   d. Debit Account No. 2000/vendor; credit Account No. 5015, Cost of Goods Sold.
   e. None of the above.

_____9. The term used for adding a new vendor on the record or form is called:

   a. Drill-down.
   b. A/P.
   c. Inventory item.
   d. On-the-fly.
   e. None of the above.

____10. Which report(s) shows the accounts payable balance?

    a. Purchases by vendor detail.
    b. Item list.
    c. Vendor transaction history.
    d. Trial balance.
    e. Both c. and d.

Exercise 4-1: Follow the instructions below to complete Exercise 4-1.

1. If necessary start MOA and open Your Name Retailers. Restore the Chapter 4 End and your initials.sbb file.

2. Record the following transactions during the month of December:

Date	Description of Transaction
12/21	Pay BOS44 to The Business Store for $1,799 for laptop computer purchase on 11/21. Use automatic check numbering.
12/21	Invoice No. 101eB received from eBooks Express for the purchase of 16 PDF files, $25 each, for a total of $400.
12/21	Invoice No. 352TV received from TV Flix for the purchase of 22 video files, $30 each, for a total of $660.
12/21	Invoice No. 95PS received from Podcast Ltd. for the purchase of 12 audio files, $15 each, for a total of $180.
12/23	Returned two PDF files to eBooks Express, Credit Memo No. CM2, for a total of $50.
12/24	Sold 8 eBooks (PDF files) on account to iPrint Design for a total credit sale of $400, Sales No. 5.
12/24	Sold 10 Podcasts (audio files) on account to Audio Answers for a total credit sale of $300 Sales No. 6.
12/24	Sold 12 TV Programs (video files) on account to Video Solutions for a total credit sale of $720, Sales No. 7.

12/26	Sold 4 eBooks for $200; 8 Podcasts for $240; and 6 TV Programs for $360; for total credit card sales of $800, Sale No. 8.
12/27	Video Solutions returned 2 TV Programs (video files), CM03.
12/30	Received a check in full payment of Audio Answers' account, $300.
12/30	Received a check in full payment of iPrint Design's account, $400.
12/30	Received payment for credit card sales, $800.00.
12/30	Your Name Retailers pays all outstanding vendor bills for a total of $1,190. (*Hint:* Pay from the Reno Bank account; bills due on or before 1/22/200Y (Use the year after your current year, i.e., if current year 2008, use 2009.). Remember to adjust for the 12/23/200X return to eBooks Express. Assign check numbers automatically.)
12/30	Invoice No. 152PS received from Podcast Ltd. for the purchase of 10 audio files, $15 each, for a total of $150.

3.   Continue with Exercise 4-2.

Exercise 4-2: Follow the instructions below to complete Exercise 4-2. Exercise 4-1 *must* be completed before starting Exercise 4-2.

1.   Print the following reports:

    a. Trial Balance 12/31/200X.

    b. Transaction Journal 12/1/200X to 12/31/200X.

    c. Purchase by Vendor Detail 12/1/200X to 12/31/200X.

    d. Purchase by Item Detail 12/1/200X to 12/31/200X.

    e. Vendor Transaction History 12/1/200X to 12/31/200X.

    f. Customer Transaction History 12/1/200X to 12/31/200X.

    g. Profitability by Customer Summary 12/1/200X to 12/31/200X.

    h. Sales by Customer Summary 12/1/200X to 12/31/200X. (Select Sales as the report type on the Customers home page.)

    i. Sales by Item Summary 12/1/200X to 12/31/200X.

2.   Backup. The suggested file name is **Exercise 4-2 December and your initials.sbb**.

3.   Copy backup file on to your USB drive.

ANALYSIS QUESTION: Does Your Name Retailers use the periodic or perpetual system for tracking inventory and sales?

Chapter 5

Accounting Cycle and Year End

OBJECTIVES: In Chapter 5, you use the software to:

1. Restore data from the Exercise 4-2 and your initials.sbb file. (This backup was made on page 160.)
2. Record compound journal entries.
3. Write checks for expenses.
4. Make deposits.
5. Complete account reconciliation.
6. Print a trial balance (unadjusted).
7. Record and post quarterly adjusting entries in the Journal.
8. Print adjusted trial balance and financial statements.
9. Close the fiscal year.
10. Print a Postclosing Trial Balance.
11. Make backups of Chapter 5 data[1].
12. Use your Internet browser to go to the book's website. (Go online to www.mhhe.com/moaessentials.)

GETTING STARTED:

1. Start MOA. Open Your Name Retailers.

2. If necessary, restore the Exercise 4-2 and your initials sbb file. This backup was made on page 160.

3. To make sure you are starting in the correct place, display the 12/30/200X (use your current year) trial balance. (*HINT:* Reports; Company and Financial, Trial Balance) Compare your trial balance with the one on the next page.

---

[1]The chart in the Preface shows you the size of each backup file. Refer to this chart for backing up data. Remember, you can back up to a hard drive location or external media.

Your Name Retailers
Trial Balance
As of: 12/31/2007

Thursday, May 31, 2007

Account Name	Account No.	Debit	Credit
Undeposited Funds	1005	1,500.00	
Reno Bank	1010	52,326.00	
Prime Savings & Loan	1100	25,500.00	
Accounts Receivable	1200	600.00	
Supplies	1240	2,300.00	
Inventory	1250	940.00	
Computer Equipment	1420	10,299.00	
Furniture & Fixtures	1430	5,000.00	
Prepaid Insurance	1810	5,000.00	
Accounts Payable	2000		150.00
Long-Term Notes Payable	2600		20,500.00
Common Stock	3010		81,000.00
Dividends	3110	200.00	
Sales	4020		4,070.00
Cost of Goods Sold	5015	2,035.00	
Bank/Bankcard Charges	7232	20.00	
Total		**105,720.00**	**105,720.00**

4. Close the trial balance.

COMPOUND TRANSACTIONS

A *compound transaction* is an entry that affects three or more accounts. Both the payment for payroll and the note payable payment are examples of compound transactions. Use MOA's New Journal Entry window to record compound transactions.

Date	Date of Transaction
12/31	Pay the employees in the amount of $223.00. Check No. 4013. The account distribution is:

Acct. No.	Account	Debit	Credit
7110	P/R Expenses-Employees	300.00	
2205	Payroll Liability: S/S and Medicare		63.00
2215	Payroll Liability: State, Local		14.00
1010	Reno Bank		223.00

Follow these steps to record a compound journal entry.

1. From the menu bar, select Company; New Journal Entry.

2. Record the 12/31/200X payment to employees. Refer to account distribution above for debiting and crediting the appropriate accounts. Compare your Journal Entry (New) window to the one shown here.

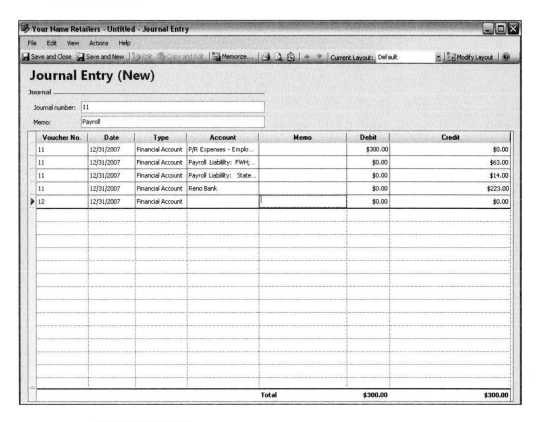

3. Click Save and New .

4. Record the note payable payment. The account distribution is shown on next page:

Date   *Date of Transaction*

12/31   Pay the note payable in the amount of $500.00. Check No. 4014. The account distribution is:

Acct. No.	Account	Debit	Credit
2600	Long-Term Notes Payable	242.00	
8150	Interest Expense	258.00	
1010	Reno Bank		500.00

5.   Save and close Journal Entry window.

WRITE CHECKS

Use MOA's Banking; Write Checks feature to issue the following checks:

12/31   Issue Check No. 4015 in the amount of $80 for cellular service. (*Hint:* Debit Account No. 7510, Telecommunications; add the vendor, Mobile One; Vendor ID, 8MO.)

12/31   Issue Check No. 4016 in the amount of $50 for Internet service. (*Hint:* Debit Account No. 7510, Telecommunications. Add the vendor, ISP; Vendor ID, 9ISP.)

12/31   Issue Check No. 4017 in the amount of $68 for telephone service. (*Hint:* Debit Account No. 7510, Telecommunications. Add the vendor, Everywhere Telephone Service; Vendor ID, 10ET.)

12/31   Issue Check No. 4018 in the amount of $111 for Electricity/Gas. (*Hint:* Debit Account No. 7815 Electricity/Gas. Add the vendor, Regional Utilities; Vendor ID, 11RU.)

12/31   Issue Check No. 4019 in the amount of $74 for Water/Garbage service. (*Hint:* Debit Account No. 7825 Water/Garbage. Add the vendor, Reno Water/Garbage; Vendor ID, 12RWG.)

12/31   Pay $200 Dividend to sole stockholder, Your Name. Check No. 4020 payable to you.

Save and close Write Checks window.

MAKE DEPOSITS

Use MOA's Banking; Make Deposits feature to make the deposits shown on the December bank statement. Remember customers mailed you checks in payment of their accounts during December and now you must physically deposit the checks into Reno Bank. (*HINT:* Account No. 1005 Undeposited Funds; Review steps 7. – 11. on page 145.)

Date   *Description of Transaction*

12/31   Make deposits in the amount of $1,500.00. This includes payments received from customers and credit card sales. The bank statement below shows each customer and credit card deposit received ($300 + $400 + $800).

Compare your Make Deposit window to the one shown here then Save and Close.

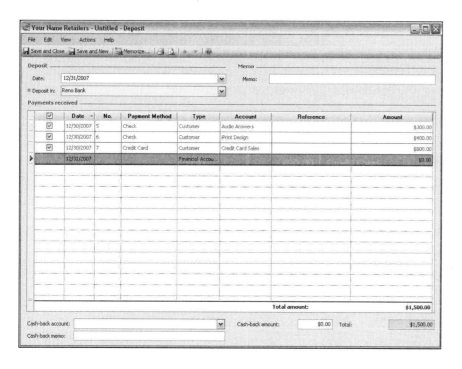

ACCOUNT REGISTER

Display the account register to see Account No. 1010, Reno Bank's activity.

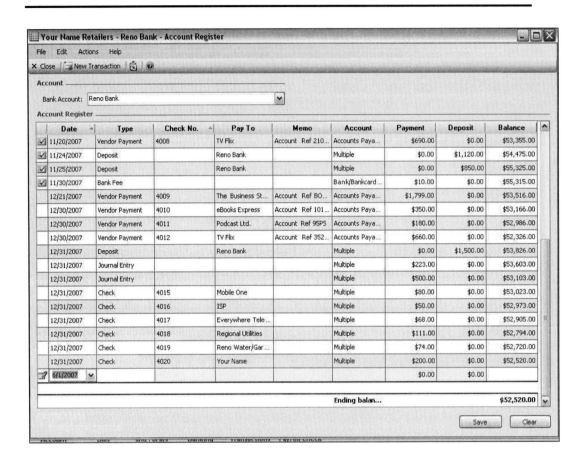

ACCOUNT RECONCILATION

You may want to review detail steps for account reconciliation, pages 146-148. Using the bank statement shown on the next page, reconcile the Reno Bank account. Remember the bank service charge of $10.00.

Follow these steps to complete account reconciliation.

1. From the Banking home page, select **Reconcile Account**. Refer to the bank statement on next page to reconcile Account No. 1010, Reno Bank on 12/31/200X.

2. Complete the Reconciliation. All checks have cleared the bank.

Statement of Account			Your Name Retailers	
Reno Bank			Your Address	
December 1 to December 31, 200X Account #0618-3201			Reno, NV	
REGULAR CHECKING				
Previous Balance	11/30	55,315.00		
Deposits		1,500.00		
Checks (-)		4,295.00		
Service Charges (-)	12/31	10.00		
Ending Balance	12/31	**$52,510**		
DEPOSITS				
	12/31	300.00	Audio Answers	
	12/31	400.00	iPrint Design	
	12/31	800.00	Credit Card	
CHECKS				
	12/23	1,799.00	4009	
	12/31	350.00	4010	
	12/31	180.00	4011	
	12/31	660.00	4012	
	12/31	223.00	4013	
	12/31	500.00	4014	
	12/31	80.00	4015	
	12/31	50.00	4016	
	12/31	68.00	4017	
	12/31	111.00	4018	
	12/31	74.00	4019	
	12/31	200.00	4020	

Observe that the Account Register ending balance shows $52,520.00. The bank statement's ending balance shows $52,510.00. The difference is the bank service charge ($10.00). Once those fees are deducted from the account register balance, the bank statement and account register agree.

Account Register Balance:	$52,520.00
Bank Service Charge:	10.00
Bank Statement Balance:	$52,510.00

3. Display the Reconciliation Detail report. Compare your Reconciliation Detail report to the one shown here.

Your Name Retailers
Reconciliation Detail
Amount: Any, Bank Account: Reno Bank, Statement date: 12/31/2007
Friday, June 01, 2007

Type	Date	No.	Name	Amount
Reno Bank				
Opening Balance				**55,315.00**
Cleared Deposits				
Deposit	12/31/2007	4		1,500.00
Total Cleared Deposits				**1,500.00**
Cleared Withdrawals				
Vendor Payment	12/21/2007	4009	The Business Store	(1,799.00)
Vendor Payment	12/30/2007	4010	eBooks Express	(350.00)
Vendor Payment	12/30/2007	4011	Podcast Ltd.	(180.00)
Vendor Payment	12/30/2007	4012	TV Flix	(660.00)
Journal Entry	12/31/2007	11		(223.00)
Journal Entry	12/31/2007	12		(500.00)
Check	12/31/2007	4015	Mobile One	(80.00)
Check	12/31/2007	4016	ISP	(50.00)
Check	12/31/2007	4017	Everywhere Telephone...	(68.00)
Check	12/31/2007	4018	Regional Utilities	(111.00)
Check	12/31/2007	4019	Reno Water/Garbage	(74.00)
Check	12/31/2007	4020	Your Name	(200.00)
Bank Fee	12/31/2007	13		(10.00)
Total Cleared Withdrawals				**(4,305.00)**
Total Cleared Transactions				**(2,805.00)**
Reconciled Balance As Of Statement Date				**52,510.00**
Ending Balance				**52,510.00**

4. Close the report.

BANK TRANSACTION REPORT

Print the following reports.

Bank Transactions from 12/1/200X to 12/31/200X. (*Hint:* From the Banking home page, select Banking as the report type, then Bank Transactions as the report.

Your Name Retailers
Bank Transactions
Date Range: December 1, 2007 - December 31, 2007
Bank Account: Reno Bank, Amount: Any, Void: Show
Friday, June 01, 2007

Type	No.	Date	Offset Account	Amount	Deposit	Withdrawal	Cleared	Balance	Name	Void
Reno Bank (USD)										
Beginning balance								**55,315.00**		
Vendor Payment	4009	12/21/2007	Accounts Payable	(1,799.00)	0.00	1,799.00	✔	53,516.00	The Business S...	
Vendor Payment	4010	12/30/2007	Accounts Payable	(350.00)	0.00	350.00	✔	53,166.00	eBooks Express	
Vendor Payment	4011	12/30/2007	Accounts Payable	(180.00)	0.00	180.00	✔	52,986.00	Podcast Ltd.	
Vendor Payment	4012	12/30/2007	Accounts Payable	(660.00)	0.00	660.00	✔	52,326.00	TV Flix	
Journal Entry	11	12/31/2007	Multiple	(223.00)	0.00	223.00	✔	52,103.00		
Journal Entry	12	12/31/2007	Multiple	(500.00)	0.00	500.00	✔	51,603.00		
Check	4015	12/31/2007	Multiple	(80.00)	0.00	80.00	✔	51,523.00	Mobile One	
Check	4016	12/31/2007	Multiple	(50.00)	0.00	50.00	✔	51,473.00	ISP	
Check	4017	12/31/2007	Multiple	(68.00)	0.00	68.00	✔	51,405.00	Everywhere Tel...	
Check	4018	12/31/2007	Multiple	(111.00)	0.00	111.00	✔	51,294.00	Regional Utilities	
Check	4019	12/31/2007	Multiple	(74.00)	0.00	74.00	✔	51,220.00	Reno Water/Ga ...	
Check	4020	12/31/2007	Multiple	(200.00)	0.00	200.00	✔	51,020.00	Your Name	
Deposit	4	12/31/2007	Undeposited Funds	1,500.00	1,500.00	0.00	✔	52,520.00		
Bank Fee	13	12/31/2007	Bank/Bankcard Charges	(10.00)	0.00	10.00	✔	52,510.00		
Ending balance								**52,510.00**		

ACCOUNTING CYCLE

Chapters 3-5 in this text work together to process the tasks in the accounting cycle for October through December. The steps of the Accounting Cycle that you do in this text are:

MOA's Accounting Cycle	
1.	Set up a company.
2.	Record transactions.
3.	Post entries.
4.	Account Reconciliation.
5.	Print the Trial Balance (unadjusted).
6.	Record and post adjusting entries.
7.	Print the Trial Balance (adjusted).
8.	Print the financial statements: balance sheet, profit and loss, cash flow statement.
9.	Close the fiscal year.
10.	Interpret accounting information.

So far in this text you have completed Steps 1. – 4. At the end of December, which is also the end of the fiscal year, you complete the remaining tasks by printing an unadjusted trial balance, recording adjusting entries, printing financial statements, and closing the fiscal year.

UNADJUSTED TRIAL BALANCE

1. Print the 12/31/200X Trial Balance (unadjusted). Compare your unadjusted trial balance to the one shown here.

Your Name Retailers
Trial Balance
As of: 12/31/2007

Friday, June 01, 2007

Account Name	Account No.	Debit	Credit
Reno Bank	1010	52,510.00	
Prime Savings & Loan	1100	25,500.00	
Accounts Receivable	1200	600.00	
Supplies	1240	2,300.00	
Inventory	1250	940.00	
Computer Equipment	1420	10,299.00	
Furniture & Fixtures	1430	5,000.00	
Prepaid Insurance	1810	5,000.00	
Accounts Payable	2000		150.00
Payroll Liability: FWH; S/S; Medicare	2205		63.00
Payroll Liability: State, Local	2215		14.00
Long-Term Notes Payable	2600		20,258.00
Common Stock	3010		81,000.00
Dividends	3110	400.00	
Sales	4020		4,070.00
Cost of Goods Sold	5015	2,035.00	
P/R Expenses - Employees	7110	300.00	
Bank/Bankcard Charges	7232	30.00	
Telecommunications	7510	198.00	
Electricity/Gas	7815	111.00	
Water/Garbage	7825	74.00	
Interest Expense	8150	258.00	
Total		**105,555.00**	**105,555.00**

2. Back up the unadjusted trial balance. Name your backup **Chapter 5 December UTB and your initials** in the File name field. (*Hint:* UTB is an abbreviation of unadjusted trial balance.)

3. Transfer a copy of your backup to your USB drive.

4. Exit MOA or continue with the next section.

END-OF-QUARTER ADJUSTING ENTRIES

It is the policy of your company to record adjusting entries at the end of the quarter to properly reflect all the quarter's business activities.

Follow these steps to record and post the adjusting entries in the journal.

1.   From the menu bar, select Company, New Journal Entry.

2.   Accept Journal No. for the journal number. (The last journal entry you made was Journal No. 13 for the December $10 Bank Fee)

3.   Type **12/31/200X (use your current year)** in the Date field.

4.   In the Account field, select the appropriate account to debit. (See transactions 1-5 on pages 171-173 below.)

5.   Type the appropriate amount in the Debit field.

6.   Select the appropriate account to credit. Make sure the Credit field shows the appropriate amount.

7.   Click [Save and New] to go to the next journal entry.

The following adjusting entries need to be recorded. Record and post these December 31, 200X adjusting entries:

1. Supplies on hand are $1,700.00. (This is Journal No. 14.)

Acct. #	Account Name	Debit	Credit
7340	Supplies (expense account)	300.00	
1240	Supplies		300.00

Computation: Supplies $2,300.00
               Office supplies on hand   - 2,000.00
               Adjustment $ 300.00

(Hint: To post your transaction, click [Save and New] after each journal entry.)

2. Adjust three months of prepaid insurance $150.00 ($50 per month x 3 months). Prepaid insurance account balance currently is $5,000.00. (This is Journal No. 15.)

Acct. #	Account Name	Debit	Credit
6150	Insurance Expense	150.00	
1810	Prepaid Insurance		150.00

3. Use straight-line depreciation for your computer equipment. Your computer equipment has a five-year service life and no salvage value. (Journal No. 16.)

   To depreciate computer equipment for the fourth quarter, use this calculation:

   $10,299 ÷ 5 years X 3/12 months = $515.00

Acct. #	Account Name	Debit	Credit
6090	Depreciation Expense	515.00	
1470	A/D-Computer Equipment		515.00

5. Use straight-line depreciation to depreciate your furniture. The furniture has a 5-year service life and no salvage value. (Journal No. 17.)

   To depreciate furniture for the fourth quarter, use this calculation:

   $5,000 ÷ 5 years X 3/12 months = $250.00

Acct. #	Account Name	Debit	Credit
6090	Depreciation Expense	250.00	
1480	A/D-Furniture & Fixtures		250.00

6. After making the end-of-quarter adjusting entries, close the Journal Entry window, then display or print the Transaction Journal for

12/31/200X. The December 31, 200X Bank Fee (Journal No. 14), along with the adjusting entries (Journal Nos. 15-21) are shown. If your Transaction Journal does *not* agree with the partial one shown below, void the appropriate journal entries.

Your Name Retailers
Transaction Journal
Date Range: December 31, 2007 - December 31, 2007
Transaction type: All, No.: Any, Name: All, Account: All, Amount: Any, Void: Show
Friday, June 01, 2007

Type	Status	No.	Name	Date	Account	Debit	Credit	Void
					Reno Bank	0.00	50.00	
					Telecommunications	50.00	0.00	
Check	Paid	4017	Everywhere Telephon...	12/31/2007				
					Accounts Payable	0.00	68.00	
					Accounts Payable	68.00	0.00	
					Reno Bank	0.00	68.00	
					Telecommunications	68.00	0.00	
Check	Paid	4018	Regional Utilities	12/31/2007				
					Accounts Payable	0.00	111.00	
					Accounts Payable	111.00	0.00	
					Reno Bank	0.00	111.00	
					Electricity/Gas	111.00	0.00	
Check	Paid	4019	Reno Water/Garbage	12/31/2007				
					Accounts Payable	0.00	74.00	
					Accounts Payable	74.00	0.00	
					Reno Bank	0.00	74.00	
					Water/Garbage	74.00	0.00	
Check	Paid	4020	Your Name	12/31/2007				
					Accounts Payable	0.00	200.00	
					Accounts Payable	200.00	0.00	
					Reno Bank	0.00	200.00	
					Dividends	200.00	0.00	
Deposit		4		12/31/2007				
					Undeposited Funds	0.00	300.00	
					Undeposited Funds	0.00	400.00	
					Undeposited Funds	0.00	800.00	
					Reno Bank	300.00	0.00	
					Reno Bank	400.00	0.00	
					Reno Bank	800.00	0.00	
Bank Fee		13		12/31/2007				
					Reno Bank	0.00	10.00	
					Bank/Bankcard Charges	10.00	0.00	
Journal Entry		14		12/31/2007				
					Supplies	300.00	0.00	
					Supplies	0.00	300.00	
Journal Entry		15		12/31/2007				
					Prepaid Insurance	0.00	150.00	
					Insurance Expense	150.00	0.00	
Journal Entry		16		12/31/2007				
					Depreciation Expense	515.00	0.00	
					A/D-Computer Equipm...	0.00	515.00	
Journal Entry		17		12/31/2007				
					Depreciation Expense	250.00	0.00	
					A/D - Furniture & Fixtur...	0.00	250.00	

7.   Close the Transaction Journal without saving.

8.   Print the 12/31/200X Trial Balance (adjusted). Compare your adjusted trial balance to the one shown on the next page.

Your Name Retailers
Trial Balance
As of: 12/31/2007

Friday, June 01, 2007

Account Name	Account No.	Debit	Credit
Reno Bank	1010	52,510.00	
Prime Savings & Loan	1100	25,500.00	
Accounts Receivable	1200	600.00	
Supplies	1240	2,000.00	
Inventory	1250	940.00	
Computer Equipment	1420	10,299.00	
Furniture & Fixtures	1430	5,000.00	
A/D-Computer Equipment	1470		515.00
A/D - Furniture & Fixtures	1480		250.00
Prepaid Insurance	1810	4,850.00	
Accounts Payable	2000		150.00
Payroll Liability: FWH; S/S; Medicare	2205		63.00
Payroll Liability: State, Local	2215		14.00
Long-Term Notes Payable	2600		20,258.00
Common Stock	3010		81,000.00
Dividends	3110	400.00	
Sales	4020		4,070.00
Cost of Goods Sold	5015	2,035.00	
Depreciation Expense	6090	765.00	
Insurance Expense	6150	150.00	
P/R Expenses - Employees	7110	300.00	
Bank/Bankcard Charges	7232	30.00	
Supplies	7340	300.00	
Telecommunications	7510	198.00	
Electricity/Gas	7815	111.00	
Water/Garbage	7825	74.00	
Interest Expense	8150	258.00	
Total		**106,320.00**	**106,320.00**

9.   Print the 10/01/200X to 12/31/200X income statement (profit and loss). Compare yours to the one shown on the next page.

Your Name Retailers

Profit and Loss

Date Range: October 1, 2007 - December 31, 2007

Account: All, Report Basis: Accrual, Class: All, Name: All, Closing Postings: Not Included

Friday, June 01, 2007

	10/1/07 - 12/31/07
Ordinary Income/Expense	
Income	
4020 - Sales	4,070.00
Total Income	**4,070.00**
Cost of Goods Sold	
5015 - Cost of Goods Sold	2,035.00
Total COGS	**2,035.00**
Gross Profit	**2,035.00**
Expense	
6090 - Depreciation Expense	765.00
6150 - Insurance Expense	150.00
7110 - P/R Expenses - Employees	300.00
7230 - Processing Services	
7232 - Bank/Bankcard Charges	30.00
Total 7230 - Processing Services	**30.00**
7340 - Supplies	300.00
7510 - Telecommunications	198.00
7810 - Utilities	
7815 - Electricity/Gas	111.00
7825 - Water/Garbage	74.00
Total 7810 - Utilities	**185.00**
Total Expense	**1,928.00**
Net Ordinary Income	**107.00**
Other Income/Expense	
Other Expense	
8150 - Interest Expense	258.00
Total Other Expense	**258.00**
Net Other Income	**(258.00)**
Net Income	**(151.00)**

10. Print the 12/31/200X balance sheet. Compare yours to the on shown on the next two pages.

Your Name Retailers
Balance Sheet
As of: 12/31/2007
Report Basis: Accrual
Friday, June 01, 2007

	As of 12/31/07
Assets	
Current Assets	
Cash	
1010 - Reno Bank	52,510.00
1100 - Prime Savings & Loan	25,500.00
Total Cash	**78,010.00**
Accounts Receivable	
1200 - Accounts Receivable	600.00
Total Accounts Receivable	**600.00**
Other Current Assets	
1240 - Supplies	2,000.00
Inventory Assets	
1250 - Inventory	940.00
Total Inventory Assets	**940.00**
Total Other Current Assets	**2,940.00**
Total Current Assets	**81,550.00**
Fixed Assets	
1420 - Computer Equipment	10,299.00
1430 - Furniture & Fixtures	5,000.00
1460 - Accumulated Depreciation	
1470 - A/D-Computer Equipment	(515.00)
1480 - A/D - Furniture & Fixtures	(250.00)
Total 1460 - Accumulated Depreciation	**(765.00)**
Total Fixed Assets	**14,534.00**
Other Assets	
1810 - Prepaid Insurance	4,850.00
Total Other Assets	**4,850.00**
Total Assets	**100,934.00**

Continued on next page....

Liabilities & Equity	
Liabilities	
Current Liabilities	
Accounts Payable	
2000 - Accounts Payable	150.00
Total Accounts Payable	**150.00**
Other Current Liabilities	
2200 - Payroll Liabilities	
2205 - Payroll Liability: FWH; S/S;...	63.00
2215 - Payroll Liability: State, Local	14.00
Total 2200 - Payroll Liabilities	**77.00**
Total Other Current Liabilities	**77.00**
Total Current Liabilities	**227.00**
Long Term Liabilities	
2600 - Long-Term Notes Payable	20,258.00
Total Long Term Liabilities	**20,258.00**
Total Liabilities	**20,485.00**
Equity	
3010 - Common Stock	81,000.00
3110 - Dividends	(400.00)
Net Income	(151.00)
Total Equity	**80,449.00**
Total Liabilities & Equity	**100,934.00**

11. Print the 10/01/200X to 12/31/200X Cash Flow Statement.

Your Name Retailers
Cash Flow Statement
Date Range: October 1, 2007 - December 31, 2007
Closing Postings: Not Included
Friday, June 01, 2007

	10/1/07 - 12/31/07
OPERATING ACTIVITIES	
Net Income	**(151.00)**
Adjustments to reconcile net income to...	
1200 - Accounts Receivable	(600.00)
1240 - Supplies	(2,000.00)
1250 - Inventory	(940.00)
1480 - A/D - Furniture & Fixtures	250.00
2000 - Accounts Payable	150.00
2205 - Payroll Liability: FWH; S/S;...	63.00
2215 - Payroll Liability: State, Local	14.00
Net Cash provided by Operating Activities	**(3,214.00)**
INVESTING ACTIVITIES	
1420 - Computer Equipment	(10,299.00)
1430 - Furniture & Fixtures	(5,000.00)
1470 - A/D-Computer Equipment	515.00
1810 - Prepaid Insurance	(4,850.00)
Net Cash provided by Investing Activities	**(19,634.00)**
FINANCING ACTIVITIES	
2600 - Long-Term Notes Payable	20,258.00
3010 - Common Stock	81,000.00
3110 - Dividends	(400.00)
Net Cash provided by Financing Activities	**100,858.00**
Net cash change for the Period	**78,010.00**
Cash at beginning of the period	**0.00**
Cash at end of the Period	**78,010.00**

Comment

If your cash flow statement or other financial statements shown on pages 175-178 *do not agree* with the textbook illustrations, drill-down to the appropriate entries. Edit the entries, then post and reprint your reports.

BACKING UP ADJUSTED DATA

1. Back up the adjusted trial balance. Name your backup **Chapter 5 ATB and your initials** in the File name field. (*Hint:* UTB is an abbreviation of unadjusted trial balance.)

2. Transfer a copy of your backup to your USB drive.

3. Exit MOA or continue with the next section.

CLOSING THE FISCAL YEAR

When you close the fiscal year, all revenue and expense accounts are moved to Account No. 3200, Retained Earnings account. Moving the expense and revenue accounts to retained earnings is called *closing the fiscal year*. Your must also close the Dividends account to Retained Earnings.

Follow these steps to close Dividends and close the fiscal year.

1. From the menu bar, select Company, New Journal Entry (Journal Entry 18). Make the following December 31, 200X closing entry, then Save and Close.

Acct. #	Account Name	Debit	Credit
3200	Retained Earnings	400.00	
3110	Dividends		400.00

2. From the menu bar, select Company; Manage Fiscal Year. The Manage Fiscal Year window appears.

3. Click 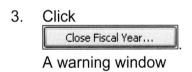 A warning window appears saying that net income will be moved to retained earnings.

> **Microsoft Small Business Accounting**
>
> ⚠ When you close this fiscal year, the net income will be moved to retained earnings. Do you want to continue?
>
> [Yes] [No]

4. Read the information on the Warning window. Since you want to close the fiscal year and move net income to retained earnings,

click 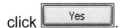.

5.   Observe that the Manage Fiscal Year window shows Closed in the Status field. Click ___Close___.

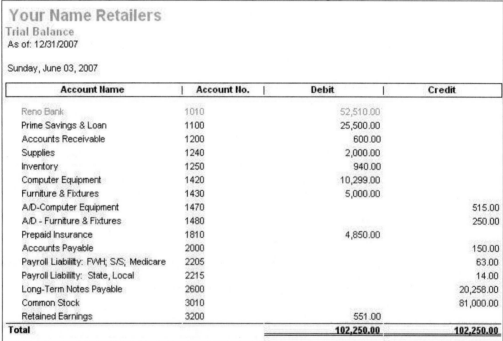

PRINTING THE POST CLOSING TRIAL BALANCE

After the fiscal year is closed, a post closing trial balance is printed. Observe that net loss in the amount of ($151.00) is moved to Retained Earnings. This net loss amount is also shown on the Balance Sheet, page 176-177. Also, observe that the post closing trial balance does *not* show dividends, revenue and expense accounts.

1.   Display or print the 12/31/200X post closing trial balance.

Your Name Retailers
Trial Balance
As of: 12/31/2007

Sunday, June 03, 2007

Account Name	Account No.	Debit	Credit
Reno Bank	1010	52,510.00	
Prime Savings & Loan	1100	25,500.00	
Accounts Receivable	1200	600.00	
Supplies	1240	2,000.00	
Inventory	1250	940.00	
Computer Equipment	1420	10,299.00	
Furniture & Fixtures	1430	5,000.00	
A/D-Computer Equipment	1470		515.00
A/D - Furniture & Fixtures	1480		250.00
Prepaid Insurance	1810	4,850.00	
Accounts Payable	2000		150.00
Payroll Liability: FWH; S/S; Medicare	2205		63.00
Payroll Liability: State, Local	2215		14.00
Long-Term Notes Payable	2600		20,258.00
Common Stock	3010		81,000.00
Retained Earnings	3200	551.00	
Total		**102,250.00**	**102,250.00**

2.   Close the post-closing trial balance without saving. Notice Retained Earnings has a debit balance since the company had a net loss and paid dividends.

BACKING UP END OF YEAR DATA

1. Back up the adjusted trial balance. Name your backup **Chapter 5 EOY and your initials** in the File name field. (*Hint:* EOY is an abbreviation of end of year.)

2. Transfer a copy of your backup to your USB drive.

3. Exit MOA or continue with the next section.

ACCOUNTANT TRANSFER

At year-end, external accountants or auditors review a company's accounting records. In this text, the accountant is your professor. It is time to send your company files via e-mail to you professor. To create the accountant transfer file, complete the following steps:

1. Open File menu; select Accountant Transfer, and click on Send Books…

2. The first Send Books window appears. Select Send books manually. Click [Next >].

3. For Select Cutoff date, type **12/31/200X** (use your current year). The Cutoff date stops you from making changes to transactions, changing company preferences, and doing many other tasks prior to the cutoff date. Click [Next >]. (Your cutoff date will differ from this screenshot.)

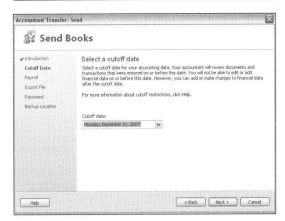

4. For Payroll, select I will run my payroll. click [Next >].

5. In Create an export file window, click [Next >]. Your date will differ.

6. In Set export file password window, click [Next >]. Do not password protect!

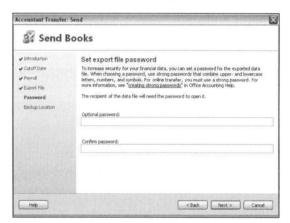

7. In Backup file window, note the back up file name and click [Export >].

8. The send books window appears and shows the progress of your export. When complete, the following window appears:

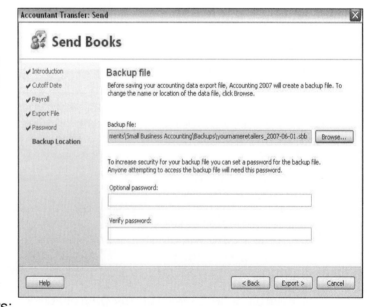

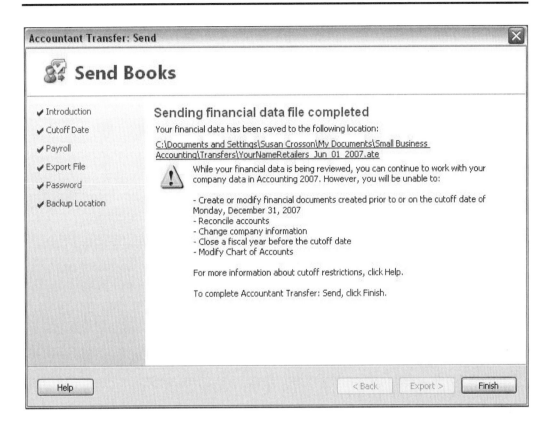

9.   Note the location of your Transfer file. Read all the tasks you are unable to do while the file is being reviewed by your professor.

10. Click [Finish].

11. IMPORTANT! Transfer a copy of your Transfers folder to your USB drive.

12. Start your e-mail program.

13. Create an e-mail message to your professor. Type **Your Name Retailers EOY** for the Subject. (Use your first and last name)

14. Attach the accountant transfer file you created this chapter (Step 8. above).

15. CC yourself on the message to be sure the message sends properly.

16. Send the message to your professor. You should receive a copy of it as well.

17. The top of Your Name Retailers screen now states:

    Your Name Retailers - Microsoft Office Accounting Professional 2007 (Books Sent To Accountant)

SUMMARY AND REVIEW

OBJECTIVES: In Chapter 5, you used the software to:

1. Restore data from the Exercise 4-2 and your initials.sbb file. (This backup was made on page 160.)
2. Record compound journal entries.
3. Write checks for expenses.
4. Make deposits.
5. Complete account reconciliation.
6. Print a trial balance (unadjusted).
7. Record and post quarterly adjusting entries in the Journal.
8. Print adjusted trial balance and financial statements.
9. Close the fiscal year.
10. Print a Postclosing Trial Balance.
11. Make backups of Chapter 5 data.
12. Use your Internet browser to go to the book's website. (Go online to www.mhhe.com/moaessentials.)

GOING TO THE NET

From MOA's menu bar, select Banking; Banking Services, Accept Credit Cards. Link to Learn More. The URL is http://sba.microsoft.com/credit.html. Complete the following.

1. What are the key benefits of MOA's credit card processing?

2. Link to Learn More in the Establish a New Merchant Account area The URL is http://sba.microsoft.com/credit_new.html.

3. Compare the price of two of the companies listed. As of this writing Chase Paymentech and PayPal are shown.

FLASHCARD REVIEW

Create the following flashcards.

1. What are the steps for entering a compound transaction?

2. What are the steps for printing the bank transaction report?

3. What are the steps for recording and posting an adjusting entry?

4. How is the fiscal year closed?

Short-answer questions: In the space provided write the answer to the question.

1. Define a compound transaction.

   _____

   _____

2. What is the account distribution for the payment made to employees?

   _____

   _____

3. What is the account distribution for the note payable payment?

   _____

   _____

4. What account is debited to pay dividends? What account is credited?

   _____

   _____

5. What account is debited to pay for cellular phone service? What account is credited?

_____

_____

_____

6. What account is debited to pay for electricity and gas? What account is credited?

_____

_____

_____

7. What account is debited to pay for water and garbage? What account is credited?

_____

_____

_____

8. What is the balance in Account No. 1005, Undeposited Funds, after the deposits are made?

_____

_____

_____

9. What is the ending balance in Account No. 1010, Reno Bank (after bank reconciliation)?

    _____

    _____

10. What is the account register and what does it show?

    _____

    _____

    _____

Exercise 5-1: Follow the instructions below to complete Exercise 5-1.

1. If necessary start MOA and open Your Name Retailers.

2. Print the Change Log report from 01/01/200X to 12/31/200X (use your current year). (*HINT:* Reports; Company and Financial, Change Log)

Exercise 5-2: Answer the questions in the space provided? Use the following abbreviations to identify reports: IS (income statement); BS (balance sheet); CFS (cash flow statement).

1. What report(s) show the net income or net loss? _____

2. What report(s) show the cash balance? _____

3. What report(s) show total fixed assets? _____

4. What report(s) show common stock? _____

5. What reports(s) show cash at the beginning of the period? _____

6. What report(s) show payroll liability accounts? _____

7. What report(s) show total expenses? _____

8. What report(s) shows the gross profit? _____

9. What report(s) show net other income/loss? _____

10. What report(s) show fixed assets? _____

11. What report(s) show net ordinary income? _____

12. What report(s) show Cost of Goods sold? _____

ANALYSIS QUESTION:

How is the December 31, 200X retained earnings balance computed? Show the computation.

OBJECTIVES: In Chapter 6, you use the software to:

1. Restore data from Chapter 5 EOY and your initials.sbb file. (This backup was made on page 181.)
2. Change the fiscal year.
3. Record one month of transactions.
4. Make bank deposit.
5. Complete account reconciliation.
6. Print a trial balance (unadjusted).
7. Make adjusting entries and print a trial balance (adjusted).
8. Print financial statements.
9. Make backups of Chapter 6 data.[1]
10. Use your Internet browser to go to the book's website. (Go online to www.mhhe.com/moaessentials.)

GETTING STARTED:

1. Start MOA. Close Company (Click File; Close Company) to view the Start-Microsoft Office Accounting window.

2. Select Restore a backup. For Backup filename browse your Backup folder to select Chapter 5 EOY and your initials backup file. Click Save.

3. In Select Company File window, click ⌐Yes⌐.

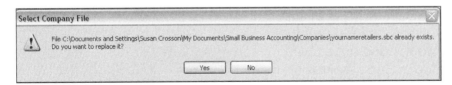

---

[1]The chart in the Preface shows you the size of each backup file. Refer to this chart for backing up data. Remember, you can back up to a hard drive location or external media.

The McGraw-Hill Companies, Inc., *Computer Accounting Essentials with Microsoft Office Accounting*

4. Confirm Database Restore shows correct Backup filename and Company, when satisfied Click [OK]. Your screen will differ.

5. The Restore, please wait screen appears.

6. When The restore process was completed successfully window appears, click [OK].

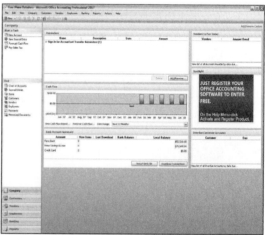

7. In the Start-Microsoft Office Accounting window, select Open an existing company.

8. Select yournameretailers, click Open to view Your Name Retailers desktop. Notice that the top of the screen does not show (Books Sent To Accountant).

9. To make sure you are starting in the correct place, display the 12/31 post closing trial balance. Compare your trial balance with the one completed in step 1, page 180.

10. Close the trial balance.

In this chapter you will apply what you have learned in this text to complete steps 2-8 in the accounting cycle for January. Remember the steps in the accounting cycle include:

Accounting Cycle
1.   Set up a company.
2.   Record transactions.
3.   Post entries.
4.   Account Reconciliation.
5.   Print the Trial Balance (unadjusted).
6.   Record and post adjusting entries.
7.   Print the Trial Balance (adjusted).
8.   Print the financial statements: balance sheet, profit and loss, cash flow statement.
9.   Close the fiscal year.
10.   Interpret accounting information.

CHANGE THE FISCAL YEAR

Before you can record transactions for January of the new fiscal year you need to change the fiscal year. Follow these steps to do that.

1.   From the menu bar, select Company; Manage Fiscal Year.

2.   Click New Fiscal Year.

3.   Enter or verify the Start and Close dates are 1/1/200Y and 12/31/200Y. 200Y is the year after your current year, i.e., if your current year is 2007, use 2008 for year 200Y.) Your year may differ from the year shown here. Click OK.

4.   The Manage Fiscal Year window appears indicating the new fiscal year is open.

5.   Close the Manage Fiscal Year window.

RECORD FIRST MONTH OF NEW FISCAL YEAR TRANSACTIONS

Record the following transactions from your Check Register for the month of January 200Y (the year you just set up as your fiscal year):

Check Number	Date	Description of Transaction	Payment	Deposit	Balance
					52,510.00
	1/2	Transfer funds (Acct. No. 1100, Prime Savings and Loan)	2,000.00		50,510.00
4021	1/3	The Business Store (Acct.1430, Furniture & Fixtures) for computer furniture	500.00		50,010.00
4022	1/4	Office Supply Store (Acct. No. 1240, Supplies)	100.00		49,910.00

Record the following vendor and customer transactions for the month of January:

Date	Description of Transaction

1/02   Invoice No. 201PS received from Podcast Ltd. for the purchase of 30 audio files, $15 each, for a total of $450.

1/03   Invoice No. 150eB received from eBooks Express for the purchase of 32 PDF files, $25 each, for a total of $800.

1/03   Invoice No. 400TV received from TV Flix for the purchase of 30 video files, $30 each, for a total of $900.

1/10   Returned two PDF files to eBooks Express Credit Memo No. CM3, $50.

1/15   Sold 10 eBooks (PDF files) on account to iPrint Design for a total credit sale of $500, Sales No. 9.

1/15   Sold 30 Podcasts (audio files) on account to Audio Answers for a total credit sale of $900, Sales No. 10.

1/15   Sold 16 TV Programs (video files) on account to Video Solutions for a total credit sale of $960, Sales No. 11.

1/17   Audio Answers returned 2 Podcasts (audio files), CM04.

1/18   Sold 10 eBooks for $500; 1 Podcasts for $30; and 12 TV Programs for $720; for total credit card sales of $1,250.

1/20   Received a $600 check from Video Solutions in payment of 12/24 credit sale less return.

1/20   Your Name Retailers pays all outstanding December and January vendor bills less any returns for a total of $2,250, Check Nos. 4023-4025. (*HINT:* eBooks Express $50 credit)

1/21   Purchased computer furniture on account from The Business Store, Invoice BOS80, for a total of $800, terms Net 30 days. (Account No. 1430 Furniture & Fixtures)

1/23	Received a check in full payment of Audio Answers' account less return, $840.
1/24	Received a check in full payment of iPrint Design's account, $500.
1/24	Received a check in full payment of Video Solution's account, $960.
1/24	Received payments for credit card sales, $1,250.
1/25	Invoice No. 175eB received from eBooks Express for the purchase of 8 PDF files, $25 each, for a total of $200.
1/25	Invoice No. 425TV received from TV Flix for the purchase of 11 video files, $30 each, for a total of $330.
1/25	Invoice No. 230PS received from Podcast Ltd. for the purchase of 6 audio files, $15 each, for a total of $90.
1/26	Returned two audio files to Podcast Ltd., CM4, $30.
1/27	Sold 16 eBooks (PDF files) on account to iPrint Design for a total credit sale of $800, Sales No. 13.
1/27	Sold 5 Podcasts (audio files) on account to Audio Answers for a total credit sale of $150 Sales No. 14.
1/27	Sold 6 TV Programs (video files) on account to Video Solutions for a total credit sale of $360, Sales No. 15.
1/27	Sold 2 eBooks for $100; 1 Podcasts for $30; and 6 TV Programs for $360; for total credit card sales of $490, Sale No. 16.
1/28	Video Solutions returned 1 TV Programs (video files), CM05.
1/29	Received a check in full payment of Audio Answers' account, $150.

1/29   Received a check in full payment of iPrint Design's account, $800.

1/29   Received payment for credit card sales, $490.00.

1/29   Your Name Retailers pays all outstanding vendor bills less any credits for a total of $1,390, Check Nos. 4026-4029.

Record the following compound entries for the month of January:

1/30   Pay the employees in the amount of $223.00. Check No. 4030. The account distribution is:

Acct. No.	Account	Debit	Credit
7110	P/R Expenses-Employees	300.00	
2205	Payroll Liability: S/S and Medicare		63.00
2215	Payroll Liability: State, Local		14.00
1010	Reno Bank		223.00

1/30   Pay the note payable in the amount of $500.00. Check No. 4031. The account distribution is:

Acct. No.	Account	Debit	Credit
2600	Long-Term Note Payable	255.00	
8150	Interest Expense	245.00	
1010	Reno Bank		500.00

Record these additional January transactions from your Check Register:

1/30   Issue Check No. 4032 to Mobile One in the amount of $80 for cellular service. (Account No. 7510 Telecommunications)

1/30   Issue Check No. 4033 to ISP in the amount of $50 for Internet service. (Account No. 7510 Telecommunications)

1/30   Issue Check No. 4034 to Everywhere Telephone Service in the amount of $68 for telephone service. (Account No. 7510 Telecommunications)

1/30   Issue Check No. 4035 to Reno Water/Garbage in the amount of $111 for Electricity/Gas. (Account No. 7815

Utilities-Electricity/Gas)

1/30   Issue Check No. 4036 to Reno Water/Garbage for $74 for
            Water/Garbage service. (Account No. 7825 Utilities-
            Water/Garbage)

1/30   Void Check No. 4035. Check should be written to Regional
            Utilities, not Reno Water/Garbage. Write check 4037 correctly to
            pay $111 electricity bill.

MAKE DEPOSIT

1/30   Make deposits in the amount of $5,390. This includes
            payments received from customers and credit card sales.

ACCOUNT REGISTER

Display the account register to see Account No. 1010, Reno Bank's
activity. Compare to one shown here. Make any corrections by voiding
the original entry and entering the correct data.

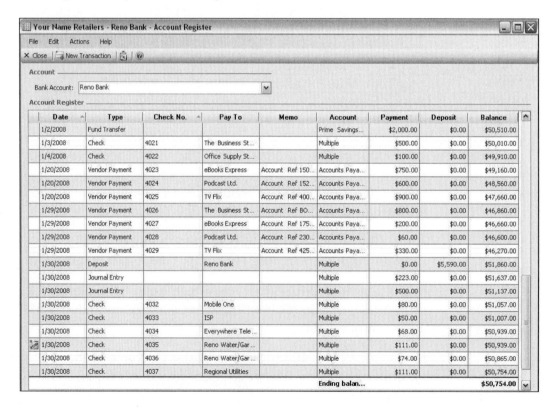

Date	Type	Check No.	Pay To	Memo	Account	Payment	Deposit	Balance
1/2/2008	Fund Transfer				Prime Savings...	$2,000.00	$0.00	$50,510.00
1/3/2008	Check	4021	The Business St...		Multiple	$500.00	$0.00	$50,010.00
1/4/2008	Check	4022	Office Supply St...		Multiple	$100.00	$0.00	$49,910.00
1/20/2008	Vendor Payment	4023	eBooks Express	Account Ref 150...	Accounts Paya...	$750.00	$0.00	$49,160.00
1/20/2008	Vendor Payment	4024	Podcast Ltd.	Account Ref 152...	Accounts Paya...	$600.00	$0.00	$48,560.00
1/20/2008	Vendor Payment	4025	TV Flix	Account Ref 400...	Accounts Paya...	$900.00	$0.00	$47,660.00
1/29/2008	Vendor Payment	4026	The Business St...	Account Ref BO...	Accounts Paya...	$800.00	$0.00	$46,860.00
1/29/2008	Vendor Payment	4027	eBooks Express	Account Ref 175...	Accounts Paya...	$200.00	$0.00	$46,660.00
1/29/2008	Vendor Payment	4028	Podcast Ltd.	Account Ref 230...	Accounts Paya...	$60.00	$0.00	$46,600.00
1/29/2008	Vendor Payment	4029	TV Flix	Account Ref 425...	Accounts Paya...	$330.00	$0.00	$46,270.00
1/30/2008	Deposit		Reno Bank		Multiple	$0.00	$5,590.00	$51,860.00
1/30/2008	Journal Entry				Multiple	$223.00	$0.00	$51,637.00
1/30/2008	Journal Entry				Multiple	$500.00	$0.00	$51,137.00
1/30/2008	Check	4032	Mobile One		Multiple	$80.00	$0.00	$51,057.00
1/30/2008	Check	4033	ISP		Multiple	$50.00	$0.00	$51,007.00
1/30/2008	Check	4034	Everywhere Tele...		Multiple	$68.00	$0.00	$50,939.00
1/30/2008	Check	4035	Reno Water/Gar...		Multiple	$111.00	$0.00	$50,939.00
1/30/2008	Check	4036	Reno Water/Gar...		Multiple	$74.00	$0.00	$50,865.00
1/30/2008	Check	4037	Regional Utilities		Multiple	$111.00	$0.00	$50,754.00
					Ending balan...			$50,754.00

ACCOUNT RECONCILATION

Use the January bank statement to reconcile the Reno Bank account.

Statement of Account Reno Bank January 1 to January 31, 200Y Account #0618-3201			Your Name Retailers Your Address Reno, NV	
REGULAR CHECKING				
Previous Balance	12/31	52,510.00		
Deposits		5,590.00		
Checks (-)		7,346.00		
Service Charges (-)	1/31	10.00		
Ending Balance	1/31	**$50,744.00**		
DEPOSITS				
	1/30	$600.00	Video Solutions	
	1/30	840.00	Audio Answers	
	1/30	500.00	iPrint Design	
	1/30	960.00	Video Solutions	
	1/30	1,250.00	Credit Card	
	1/30	150.00	Audio Answers	
	1/30	800.00	iPrint Design	
	1/30	490.00	Credit Card	
CHECKS				
	1/3	2,000.00	Transfer	
	1/4	500.00	4021	
	1/4	100.00	4022	
	1/22	750.00	4023	
	1/22	600.00	4024	
	1/22	900.00	4025	
	1/30	800.00	4026	
	1/30	200.00	4027	
	1/30	60.00	4028	
	1/30	330.00	4029	
	1/30	223.00	4030	

	1/31	500.00	4031	
	1/31	80.00	4032	
	1/31	50.00	4033	
	1/31	68.00	4034	
	1/31	74.00	4036*	
	1/31	111.00	4037	

Once the $10 Service Charge is deducted from the account register balance, the bank statement and account register agree.

Account Register Balance:	$50,754.00
Bank Service Charge:	10.00
Bank Statement Balance:	$50,744.00

Prepare the account reconciliation for January and display the report. Compare your Reconciliation Detail report to the one shown here.

Your Name Retailers
Reconciliation Detail
Amount: Any, Bank Account: Reno Bank, Statement date: 1/31/2008
Sunday, June 03, 2007

Type	Date	No.	Name	Amount
Reno Bank				
Opening Balance				**52,510.00**
Cleared Deposits				
Deposit	1/30/2008	5		5,590.00
Total Cleared Deposits				**5,590.00**
Cleared Withdrawals				
Fund Transfer	1/2/2008	21		(2,000.00)
Check	1/3/2008	4021	The Business Store	(500.00)
Check	1/4/2008	4022	Office Supply Store	(100.00)
Vendor Payment	1/20/2008	4023	eBooks Express	(750.00)
Vendor Payment	1/20/2008	4024	Podcast Ltd.	(600.00)
Vendor Payment	1/20/2008	4025	TV Flix	(900.00)
Vendor Payment	1/29/2008	4026	The Business Store	(800.00)
Vendor Payment	1/29/2008	4027	eBooks Express	(200.00)
Vendor Payment	1/29/2008	4028	Podcast Ltd.	(60.00)
Vendor Payment	1/29/2008	4029	TV Flix	(330.00)
Journal Entry	1/30/2008	22		(223.00)
Journal Entry	1/30/2008	23		(500.00)
Check	1/30/2008	4032	Mobile One	(80.00)
Check	1/30/2008	4033	ISP	(50.00)
Check	1/30/2008	4034	Everywhere Telephone...	(68.00)
Check	1/30/2008	4036	Reno Water/Garbage	(74.00)
Check	1/30/2008	4037	Regional Utilities	(111.00)
Bank Fee	1/31/2008	24		(10.00)
Total Cleared Withdrawals				**(7,356.00)**
Total Cleared Transactions				**(1,766.00)**
Reconciled Balance As Of Statement Date				**50,744.00**
Ending Balance				**50,744.00**

UNADJUSTED TRIAL BALANCE

1. Print the 1/31/200Y Trial Balance (unadjusted). Compare your unadjusted trial balance to the one shown here.

Your Name Retailers
Trial Balance
As of: 1/31/2008

Sunday, June 03, 2007

Account Name	Account No.	Debit	Credit
Reno Bank	1010	50,744.00	
Prime Savings & Loan	1100	27,500.00	
Accounts Receivable	1200	300.00	
Supplies	1240	2,100.00	
Inventory	1250	985.00	
Computer Equipment	1420	10,299.00	
Furniture & Fixtures	1430	6,300.00	
A/D-Computer Equipment	1470		515.00
A/D - Furniture & Fixtures	1480		250.00
Prepaid Insurance	1810	4,850.00	
Payroll Liability: FWH; S/S; Medicare	2205		126.00
Payroll Liability: State, Local	2215		28.00
Long-Term Notes Payable	2600		20,003.00
Common Stock	3010		81,000.00
Retained Earnings	3200	551.00	
Sales	4020		5,290.00
Cost of Goods Sold	5015	2,645.00	
P/R Expenses - Employees	7110	300.00	
Bank/Bankcard Charges	7232	10.00	
Telecommunications	7510	198.00	
Electricity/Gas	7815	111.00	
Water/Garbage	7825	74.00	
Interest Expense	8150	245.00	
Total		**107,212.00**	**107,212.00**

2. Make a Back up. Type **Chapter 6 January UTB and your initials** in the File name field for the name of your backup. (*Hint:* UTB is an abbreviation of unadjusted trial balance.)

3. Transfer a copy of your backup to your USB drive.

4. Exit MOA or continue with the next section.

END-OF-MONTH ADJUSTING ENTRIES

Your Name Retailers changed their adjusting entry policy for the new fiscal year. The new policy is to record adjusting entries at the end of each month to properly reflect all the month's business activities. Make the following adjusting entries for the month of January:

1. Supplies on hand are $1,900.00. (This is Journal and Voucher No. 25.)

Acct. #	Account Name	Debit	Credit
7340	Supplies (expense account)	200.00	
1240	Supplies		200.00

Computation: Supplies $2,100.00
               Office supplies on hand   - 1,900.00
               Adjustment $ 200.00

2. Adjust one month of prepaid insurance ($50/month). (Journal and Voucher No. 26.)

Acct. #	Account Name	Debit	Credit
6150	Insurance Expense	50.00	
1810	Prepaid Insurance		50.00

3. Use straight-line depreciation for your computer equipment. Your computer equipment has a five-year service life and no salvage value. (Journal and Voucher No. 27.)

To depreciate computer equipment for the month, use this calculation:

$10,299 ÷ 5 years X 1/12 months = $172.00

Acct. #	Account Name	Debit	Credit
6090	Depreciation Expense	172.00	
1470	A/D-Computer Equipment		172.00

4. Use straight-line depreciation to depreciate your furniture. The furniture has a 5-year service life and no salvage value. (Journal and Voucher No. 28.)

   To depreciate furniture for the month, use this calculation:

   $5,000 ÷ 5 years X 1/12 month = $83.00

Acct. #	Account Name	Debit	Credit
6090	Depreciation Expense	83.00	
1480	A/D-Furniture & Fixtures		83.00

5. You purchased new furniture during the month. Use straight-line depreciation to depreciate your furniture. The furniture has a 5-year service life and a $100 salvage value. Use the following adjusting entry. (Journal and Voucher No. 29.)

   The computation is:

   ($500 + $800 -$100)÷ 5 years X 1/12 month = $20.00

Acct. #	Account Name	Debit	Credit
6090	Depreciation Expense	20.00	
1480	A/D-Furniture & Fixtures		20.00

6. After journalizing and posting the end-of-quarter adjusting entries, close the Journal Entry window, then display or print the Transaction Journal for 1/31/200Y. If your Transaction Journal does *not* agree with the one shown on next page, void and correct.

Your Name Retailers
Transaction Journal
Date Range: January 31, 2008 - January 31, 2008
Transaction type: All, No.: Any, Name: All, Account: All, Amount: Any, Void: Show
Sunday, June 03, 2007

Type	Status	No.	Name	Date	Account	Debit	Credit	Void
Bank Fee		24		1/31/2008				
					Reno Bank	0.00	10.00	
					Bank/Bankcard Charges	10.00	0.00	
Journal Entry		25		1/31/2008				
					Supplies	200.00	0.00	
					Supplies	0.00	200.00	
Journal Entry		26		1/31/2008				
					Prepaid Insurance	0.00	50.00	
					Insurance Expense	50.00	0.00	
Journal Entry		27		1/31/2008				
					Depreciation Expense	172.00	0.00	
					A/D-Computer Equipm ...	0.00	172.00	
Journal Entry		28		1/31/2008				
					Depreciation Expense	83.00	0.00	
					A/D - Furniture & Fixtur ...	0.00	83.00	
Journal Entry		29		1/31/2008				
					Depreciation Expense	20.00	0.00	
					A/D - Furniture & Fixtur ...	0.00	20.00	

7. Close the Transaction Journal without saving.

> **Comment**
>
> If your unadjusted and adjusted trial balances *do not agree* with the textbook illustrations, drill-down to the appropriate entries. Edit the entries, then post and reprint your reports.

ADJUSTED TRIAL BALANCE

1. Print the 1/31/200Y Trial Balance (adjusted). Compare your adjusted trial balance to the one shown on next page.

Your Name Retailers
Trial Balance
As of: 1/31/2008

Sunday, June 03, 2007

Account Name	Account No.	Debit	Credit
Reno Bank	1010	50,744.00	
Prime Savings & Loan	1100	27,500.00	
Accounts Receivable	1200	300.00	
Supplies	1240	1,900.00	
Inventory	1250	985.00	
Computer Equipment	1420	10,299.00	
Furniture & Fixtures	1430	6,300.00	
A/D-Computer Equipment	1470		687.00
A/D - Furniture & Fixtures	1480		353.00
Prepaid Insurance	1810	4,800.00	
Payroll Liability: FWH; S/S; Medicare	2205		126.00
Payroll Liability: State, Local	2215		28.00
Long-Term Notes Payable	2600		20,003.00
Common Stock	3010		81,000.00
Retained Earnings	3200	551.00	
Sales	4020		5,290.00
Cost of Goods Sold	5015	2,645.00	
Depreciation Expense	6090	275.00	
Insurance Expense	6150	50.00	
P/R Expenses - Employees	7110	300.00	
Bank/Bankcard Charges	7232	10.00	
Supplies	7340	200.00	
Telecommunications	7510	198.00	
Electricity/Gas	7815	111.00	
Water/Garbage	7825	74.00	
Interest Expense	8150	245.00	
Total		**107,487.00**	**107,487.00**

2. Make a Backup. Type **Chapter 6 ATB and your initials** in the File
    name field for the name of your backup. (*Hint:* ATB is an
    abbreviation of adjusted trial balance.)

3. Transfer a copy of your backup to your USB drive.

4. Exit MOA or continue with the next section.

SUMMARY AND REVIEW

OBJECTIVES: In Chapter 6, you used the software to:

1. Restore data from Chapter 5 EOY and your initials.sbb file. (This backup was made on page 181.)
2. Change the fiscal year.
3. Record one month of transactions.
4. Make bank deposit.
5. Complete account reconciliation.
6. Print a trial balance (unadjusted).
7. Make adjusting entries and print a trial balance (adjusted).
8. Print financial statements.
9. Make backups of Chapter 6 data.
10. Use your Internet browser to go to the book's website. (Go online to www.mhhe.com/moaessentials.)

GOING TO THE NET

Access the Google search engine at www.google.com.

1. Link to News. Then click ▸Business . Link to an article of interest.
2. Write a brief essay (no more than 75 words) of what you found. Include the appropriate website address.

FLASHCARD REVIEW

Create the following flashcard.

1. What are the steps for opening a new year?

Short-answer and True/make true questions: In the space provided write the answer to the question.

1. You can complete the activities in Chapter 6 without completing Chapter 5.

_____

_____

2. Step 4 of MOA's Accounting Cycle is reconciling the bank statement.

_____

_____

3. The check register's balance does *not* show the bank service charge.

_____

_____

4. Your checkbook register and bank statement are used as source documents for recording entries.

_____

_____

5. The account reconciliation feature can reconcile the cash account(s) only.

_____

_____

6. In Chapter 6, accounting records are completed for January 1 - March 31, 200Y.

_____

_____

7. MOA includes an editing feature so that entries can be corrected.

_____

_____

6. For the period of January 1 to January 31, 200Y, Your Name Retailers net income is $_____.

7. At the end of the month, Your Name Retailers total assets are
   $_____.

8. At the end of the month, Your Name Retailers total liabilities are
   $_____.

Exercise 6-1: Follow the instructions below to complete Exercise 6-1.

If necessary start MOA and open Your Name Retailers. Restore the Chapter 6 ATB and your initials.sbb file. This backup was made on page 203.

1.   Print the 1/1/200Y to 1/31/200Y Transaction Journal.

2.   Print the Adjusted Trial Balance 1/31/200Y.

3.   Print the financial statements:

     a. Income Statement (Profit and Loss 1/1/200Y to 1/31/200Y);
     b. Balance Sheet (as of 1/31/200Y);
     c. Cash Flow Statement (from 1/01/200Y to 1/31/200Y).

4.   Print the Change Log.

Exercise 6-2:

     Transfer a copy of your Chapter 6 ATB and your initials.sbb file to your professor using the Accountant transfer feature.

ANALYSIS QUESTION:

Does Your Name Retailers have a net income or net loss for January? Explain why there is a net income or net loss. Suggest two actions to improve the running of Your Name Retailers.

Project

1

Your Name Hardware Store

In Project 1, you complete the business processes for Your Name Hardware Store, a merchandising business. Your Name Hardware Store sells shovels, wagons, and wheel barrows. It is organized as a corporation. It is the purpose of Project 1 to review what you have learned about merchandising businesses. Accounts payable, inventory, accounts receivable, and payroll transactions are included in this project as well as account reconciliation. A checklist is shown listing the printed reports that you should have at the end of this project. The step-by-step instructions also remind you to print reports at certain intervals.

SETUP

Follow these steps to complete Project 1, Your Name Hardware Store:

Step 1: Start Microsoft Office Accounting. From the menu bar, select File; Close Company.

Step 2: From the Start – Microsoft Office Accounting 2007 window, link to Set up a new company.

Step 3: Read the information on the Set up your company, Company and Preferences window. Click Next.

Step 4: Read the information on the Company Introduction window. Click Next.

Step 5: The Add company details window appears. Complete the following fields

Company name:	**Your Name Hardware Store** [Use your first and last name]
Legal name:	Your Name Hardware Store
Street:	**81 Edgewood Avenue**
City, State, Zip	**Vancouver**
State/Province:	**OR**

Zip/Postal code:	**93611**
Country/Region:	United States
Phone:	**503-555-8200**
Fax:	**503-555-8220**
E-mail:	**info@hardware.com**
Web Site:	**www.hardware.com**
Federal tax ID:	379023388

Step 6: Check the information that you just typed. Click [Next].

Step 7: The Set up accounts window appears. Accept the default for Select your business type and have Accounting 2007 suggest accounts, by clicking by clicking [Next].

Step 8: The Set up accounts (Cont.) window appears. In the Business type field, select Retail. Click [Next].

Step 9: The Select a fiscal year and start date window appears. Make these selections:

Beginning of the first fiscal year: **1/1/200X** (Use your current year)
End of first fiscal year: **2/31/200X** (Use your current year)
Start date: **1/1/200X** (Use your current year)

Step 10: Make sure the dates on the Select a fiscal year and start date window are correct. Click [Next].

Step 11: The Preferences introduction window appears. Read the information. Click [Next].

Step 12: The Select jobs preferences window appears. Accept the default for No by clicking [Next].

Step 13: The Select sales tax preferences window appears. Accept the default for No by clicking [Next]. (The State of Oregon does not have sales tax.)

Step 14: The Select form layout preferences appears. Select the default for Sells products, or both products and services. Click **Next**.

Step 15: The Select numbering preferences window appears. Click on the boxes next to Customers, Vendors, Employees, Products and Services to place a checkmark. Click **Next**.

Step 16: The Currency preferences window appears. Accept the default for No by clicking **Next**.

Step 17: The Set up payroll window appears. Your Name Hardware Store is *not* going to use the ADP payroll service. Accept the default for No by clicking **Next**.

Step 18: The Online Sales window appears. Click on the radio button next to No, do not enable online sales at this point. Click **Next**.

Step 19: The Select cash basis or accrual basis reporting window appears. Accept the default for Accrual basis reports (Recommended) by clicking **Next**.

Step 20: The Select add-ins window appears. Uncheck the four boxes in the Enabled column. Click **Next**.

Step 21: The Company details and preferences completed window appears. Click **Finish**.

Step 22: The Select company file window appears. Observe that the Companies folder is shown in the Save in field. The File name field shows yournamehardwarestore.sbc. (*Hint:* Since you used your first and last name, your File name field differs.) Click **Save**.

Step 23: When the Microsoft Office Accounting Startup Wizard progress checklist window appears, click **Close**.

COMPANY PREFERENCES

Step 24:   From the menu bar, select Company; Preferences.

Step 25:   Click Company; Tracking. Check Use change log. Then Click on System Accounts tab. In the Opening balances field, select Account No. 3010, Common Stock. Click OK.

CHART OF ACCOUNTS

Step 26: Delete the following accounts.

1220	Employee Advances
1730	Start-up Costs
3050	Owner's Equity
3115	Distrib-Life Insurance
3120	Draws

Step 27: Change the following accounts names.

1010	Checking Account	**Vancouver Bank**
1100	Savings	**First Savings & Loan**
1810	Prepaid Expense	**Prepaid Insurance**
2050	Trusts Payable	**Short-Term Notes Payable**
2205	Payroll Liability: FWH; S/S; Medicare	**Payroll Liability: S/S and Medicare**
2225	Payroll Liability: 401K	**Payroll Liability: Federal WH**
4022	Consignment Sales	**Sales-Shovels**
5015	Purchases	**Cost of Goods Sold**
7232	Bank/Bankcard Charges	**Bank Service Charges**
7234	Employment Services Fees	**Credit Card Fees Expense**

Step 28: Add these accounts.

1251	Inventory-Shovels	Inventory Asset (Inventory Subaccount)
1255	Inventory-Wheel barrows	Inventory Asset (Inventory Subaccount)
1260	Inventory-Wagons	Inventory Asset (Inventory Subaccount)
4035	Sales-Wheel barrows	Income
4040	Sales-Wagons	Income
5020	Cost of Goods Sold-Wheel barrows	Cost of Goods Sold (COGS Subaccount)
5025	Cost of Goods Sold-Shovels	Cost of Goods Sold (COGS Subaccount)
5030	Cost of Goods Sold-Wagons	Cost of Goods Sold (COGS Subaccount)

Step 29:   You purchased Your Name Hardware Store in December of last year. Use the Balance Sheet below to record the beginning balances.

Your Name Hardware Store Balance Sheet January 1, 200X (Your current year)		
ASSETS		
Current Assets		
1010 - Vancouver Bank	$ 80,000.00	
1100 - First Savings & Loan	15,000.00	
Total Current Assets		$95,000.00
Fixed Assets		
1430 – Furniture and Fixtures	6,000.00	
Total Fixed Assets		6,000.00
Other Assets:		
1810 – Prepaid Insurance	2,900.00	
Total Other Assets		2,900.00
Total Assets		$103,900.00

LIABILITIES AND STOCKHOLDERS' EQUITY		
2050 - Short-Term Notes Payable	4,000.00	
2600 - Long-Term Notes Payable	5,500.00	
Total Liabilities		$9,500.00
3010 - Common Stock		94,400.00
Total Liabilities and Equity		$103,900.00

VENDORS

Step 30:   Enter the following vendors.

Vendor name:	**AAA Shovels**
Vendor ID:	**AAA111**
Business address:	**3000 First Avenue**
	Santa Cruz, CA 90036
Business phone number:	**(310) 555-2243**
Business fax number:	**(310) 555-2245**
E-mail 1:	**info@aaa.biz**
Web page address:	**www.aaa.biz**
Vendor since:	**1/1/2007**
Primary contact name:	**Tim Newton**
Business Phone:	**(310) 555-2243, ext. 10**
E-mail:	**tim@aaa.biz**

Details tab:
Credit limit:	**15,000.00**
Preferred payment method:	Select Check
Payment terms:	Select Net 30

Vendor name:	**BBB Wheel barrows**
Vendor ID:	**BBB112**
Business address:	**46011 Mesquite Street**
	El Paso, TX 76315
Business phone number:	**(915) 555-3000**
Business fax number:	**(915) 555-3100**
E-mail 1:	**info@BBB.com**
Web page address:	**www.BBB.com**
Vendor since:	**1/1/2007**
Primary contact name:	**Baker Bayou**
Business Phone:	**(915) 555-3000**
E-mail:	**BB@BBB.com**

Details tab:
Credit limit:	**15,000.00**
Preferred payment method:	Select Check
Payment terms:	Select Net 30

Vendor name: **CCC Wagons**
  Vendor ID: **CCC113**
  Business address: **2301 Dirt Road**
                           Dugout, AZ 86003
  Business phone number: **(928) 555-2288**
  Business fax number: **(928) 555-2299**
  E-mail 1:   **info@CCC.net**
  Web page address: **www.CCC.net**
  Vendor since: **1/1/2007**
  Primary contact name: **Caitlin Conner**
  Business Phone: **(928) 555-2288**
  E-mail: **caitlin@CCC.net**

  Details tab:
  Credit limit: **15,000.00**
  Preferred payment method: Select Check
  Payment terms: Select Net 30

INVENTORY ITEMS

Step 31:   Enter the following inventory items.

Item name: **Shovels**
Item no.   1
Sales description: **Shovels**
Sales price: **30.00**
Income account: Account No. 4022, Sales-Shovels
Purchase price: **15.00**
Asset account: Account No. 1251, Inventory-
                          Shovels

Preferred vendor: AAA Shovels
COGS account: Select Account No. 5025, Cost of
                          Goods Sold-Shovels

Item name: **Wheel barrows**
Item No.   2
Sales description: **Wheel barrows**
Sales price: **100.00**
Income account: Account No. 4035, Sales-Wheel
                          barrows
Purchase price: **75.00**

Asset account:	Account No. 1255, Inventory-Wheel barrows
Preferred vendor:	BBB Wheel barrows
COGS account:	Select Account No. 5020, Cost of Goods Sold-Wheel barrows

Item name:	**Wagons**
Item No.	3
Sales description:	Wagons
Sales price:	**50.00**
Income account:	Account No. 4040, Sales-Wagons
Purchase price:	**20.00**
Asset account:	Account No. 1260, Inventory-Wagons
Preferred vendor:	CCC Wagons
COGS account:	Select Account No. 5030, Cost of Goods Sold-Wagons

CUSTOMERS

Step 32: Enter the following customers.

Customer name:	**Dawn Bright**
Customer ID:	**DB001**
Business address:	**1800 W. Peoria Avenue Vancouver, OR 92731**
Business phone:	**(503) 555-8630**
Business fax:	**(503) 555-8632**
E-mail 1:	**db@myemail.com**
Web page address:	**www.myemail.com/bright**
Customer since:	**1/1/2007**
Contact Name:	**Dawn Bright**
Business phone:	**(503) 555-8630**

Details tab:	
Credit limit:	**10,000.00**
Preferred payment method:	Check
Payment terms:	Net 30

Customer name: **Roy Lars**
Customer ID: **RL002**
Business address: **603 Nature Drive**
                            Eugene, OR 97401
Business phone: **(541) 555-7845**
Business fax: **(541) 555-9001**
E-mail 1:   **roy@mail.biz**
Web page address: **www.mail.biz/larsR**
Customer since: **1/1/2007**
Contact Name: **Roy Lars**
Business phone: **(541) 555-7845**

Details tab:
Credit limit: **10,000.00**
Preferred payment method: Check
Payment terms: Net 30

Customer name: **Shar Watsonville**
Customer ID: **SW003**
Business address: **3455 West 20th Avenue**
                            Eugene, OR 97402
Business phone: **(541) 555-9233**
Business fax: **(541) 555-9235**
E-mail 1:   **sharon@email.com**
Web page address: **www.email.com/watsonville**
Customer since: **1/1/2007**
Contact Name: **Shar Watsonville**
Business phone: **(541) 555-9233**

Details tab:
Credit limit: **10,000.00**
Preferred payment method: Check
Payment terms: Net 30

Customer name: **Credit Card Sales**
Customer ID: **CCS**
Customer since: **1/1/2007**

Details tab:
Preferred payment method: Credit Card

BACKUP

Step 33:   Make a backup. Use **Your Name Hardware Store Begin.sbb** as the filename.

TRANSACTIONS

Step 34:   Record the following transactions. Assume all vendor payments and checks issued for expenses are paid with Vancouver Bank's online banking service. All transactions occur during January of your current year.

Date	Description of Transaction
1/06	Invoice No. 74A was received from AAA Shovels for 25 shovels at $15 each, $375.
1/06	Invoice No. 801 was received from CCC Wagons for 30 wagons at $20 each, $600.
1/06	Invoice No. ER555 was received from BBB Wheel barrows for 32 wheel barrows at $75 each, $2,400.
1/10	Made credit card sales of $1,020: 4 shovels, $120; 5 wheel barrows, $500; 8 wagons, $400. Credit card sales are deposited in Vancouver Bank; No. 1.
1/12	Made credit card sales of $740: 5 wagons, $250; 4 wheel barrows, $400; and 3 shovels, $90; No. 2.
1/12	Sold one shovel to Dawn Bright on account, Sales No. 3
1/17	Made credit card sales, $910: 3 wagons, $150; 2 shovels, $60; 7 wheel barrows, $700; No. 4.
1/20	Your Name Hardware Store pays all outstanding vendor bills for a total of $3,375.00. (*Hint:* The required payment method is Check from Vancouver Bank; bills due on or before 2/18; assign check numbers automatically.)
1/21	Made credit card sales of $1,430: 6 shovels, $180; 8 wheel barrows, $800; 9 wagons, $450; No. 5.

1/21   Issued Check No. 4 to Stevens Rentals for $1,350 in payment of rent. (*Hint:* Use Banking; Write Checks from the Vancouver Bank Account; add vendor as needed; uncheck To be printed. Account No. 7310 Rent.)

1/22   Sold one wagon to Shar Watsonville on account, No. 6.

1/24   Invoice No. 88A was received from AAA Shovels for 15 shovels at $15 each, $225.

1/24   Invoice No. 962 was received from CCC Wagons for 18 wagons at $20 each, $360.

1/24   Invoice No. ER702 was received from BBB Wheel barrows for 20 wheel barrows at $75 each, $1,500.

1/26   Made credit card sales of $1,080: 6 shovels, $180; 6 wheel barrows, $600; 6 wagons, $300; No. 7.

1/27   Issued Check No. 5 to Diane Bellweather for $245 in payment of Short-Term Notes Payable. (*Hint:* Add vendor.)

1/27   Issued Check to Vancouver Bank for $175.80 in payment of Long-Term Notes Payable; Journal No. 7. Use the following account distribution:

Acct. No.	Account	Debit	Credit
2600	Long-Term Notes Payable	140.00	
8150	Interest Expense	35.80	
1010	Vancouver Bank		175.80

(*Hint:* Use the New Journal Entry form; Journal No. 7.)

1/27   Pay the employees in the amount of $3,967.63; Journal No. 8. The account distribution is:

Acct. No.	Account	Debit	Credit
7110	P/R Expenses-Employee	5,000.00	
2205	Payroll Liabilities: S/S and Medicare		382.50
2215	Payroll Liabilities: State, Local		95.87
2225	Payroll Liabilities: Federal WH		554.00
1010	Vancouver Bank		3,967.63

1/27	Issued Check No. 8 to Rainer Utilities for $225.65 in payment of electricity and gas. (*Hint:* Add new vendor, Account No. 7815 Utilities-Electricity/Gas.)
1/29	Made credit card sales of $1,020: 4 shovels, $120; 5 wheel barrows, $500; 8 wagons, $400; No. 8.
1/30	Receive payments for credit card sales, $6,200.00.
1/30	Received a check in full payment of Dawn Bright's account, $30.
1/30	Received a check in full payment of Shar Watsonville's account, $50.
1/30	Make deposits to Vancouver Bank in the amount of $6,280 ($6,200 from credit card sales; $30 and $50 from customer sales.) The bank statement on next page shows each customer and credit card deposit received.

BACKUP

Step 35:   Back up. The suggested filename is **Your Name Hardware Store January**.

BANK RECONCILATION

Step 36: Complete account reconciliation for Account No. 1010, Vancouver Bank.

Statement of Account Vancouver Bank January 1 to January 31 Account No. 937522			Your Name Hardware Store 81 Edgewood Ave. Vancouver, OR 92711	
REGULAR CHECKING				
Previous Balance	12/31	$80,000.00		
Deposits		6,280.00		
Checks (-)		9,339.08		
Service Charges (-)	1/31	25.00		
Credit Card Fee[1] (-)	1/31	124.00		
Ending Balance	1/31	**$76,791.92**		
DEPOSITS				
	1/30	30.00	Dawn Bright	
	1/30	50.00	Shar Watsonville	
	1/30	6,200.00	Credit Card	
CHECKS				
	1/20	600.00	1	
	1/20	375.00	2	
	1/20	2,400.00	3	
	1/21	1,350.00	4	
	1/27	245.00	5	
	1/27	175.80	6	
	1/27	3,967.63	7	
	1/28	225.65	8	

[1]Vancouver Bank charges 2 percent for credit card sales. The total credit card sales for the month are $6,200 x .02 = $124.00.

The McGraw-Hill Companies, Inc., *Computer Accounting Essentials with Microsoft Office Accounting*

REPORTS

Step 37: Print the reconciliation detail report.

Step 38: Print the bank transactions.

Step 39: Print the trial balance.

Step 40: Print the vendor list; customer list; and item list.

Step 41: Print the transaction journal.

Step 42: Print the transaction detail by account report.

Step 43: Print the vendor transaction history.

Step 44: Print the customer transaction history.

Step 45: Print the financial statements: Profit and Loss, Balance Sheet, and Cash Flow Statement.

BACKUP

Step 46: Make a backup of Project 1, Your Name Hardware Store. Use **Your Name Hardware Store Financial Statements.sbb** as the file name.

	CHECKLIST OF PRINTOUTS, Your Name Hardware Store
	Ask your professor how these should be turned in…
	Reconciliation Detail
	Bank Transactions
	Trial Balance
	Vendor List
	Customer List
	Item List
	Transaction Journal
	Transaction Detail by Account
	Vendor Transaction History
	Customer Transaction History
	Inventory Stock Status by Item Report
	Profit and Loss
	Balance Sheet
	Cash Flow Statement

Student Name_____**Date**_____

CHECK YOUR PROGRESS: PROJECT 1, Your Name Hardware Store

1. What are the total debit and credit balances on the Trial Balance? _____

2. What are the total assets on January 31? _____

3. What is the balance in the Vancouver Bank account on January 31? _____

4. How much is total income on January 31? _____

5. How much net income (net loss) is reported on January 31? _____

6. What is the balance in the Inventory-Shovels account on January 31? _____

7. What is the balance in the Inventory-Wheel barrows account on January 31? _____

8. What is the balance in the Inventory-Wagons account on January 31? _____

9. What is the balance in the Short-Term Notes Payable account on January 31? _____

10. What is the balance in the Common Stock account on January 31? _____

11. What are the total expenses reported on January 31? _____

12. Were any Accounts Payable incurred during the month of January? (Circle your answer.)   YES   NO

Project 2

Student-Designed Merchandising Business

You have learned how to complete the accounting cycle for merchandising businesses. Project 2 gives you a chance to create a merchandising business of your own.

You select retail as the business type, edit your business's Chart of Accounts, create beginning balances and transactions, and complete MOA's computer accounting cycle. Project 2 also gives you an opportunity to review the software features learned so far.

Before you begin, you should design your business. You will need the following:

1. Company information that includes business name, address, and telephone number.

2. Select retail as the business type.

3. A Chart of Accounts: 80 accounts minimum, 110 accounts maximum.

4. A Balance Sheet for your business.

5. One month's transactions for your business. These transactions must include accounts receivable, accounts payable, inventory, sales, and dividends. You should have a minimum of 25 transactions; a maximum of 35 transactions. These transactions should result in a net income.

6. Complete another month of transactions that result in a net loss.

A suggested checklist of printouts is shown on the next page.

PROJECT 2
CHECKLIST OF PRINTOUTS
Ask your professor how these should be turned in…
Reconciliation Detail
Bank Transactions
Trial Balance
Vendor List
Customer List
Item List
Transaction Journal
Transaction Detail by Account
Vendor Transaction History
Customer Transaction History
Inventory Stock Status by Item Report
Profit and Loss
Balance Sheet
Cash Flow Statement
Change Log

<table>
<tr><td>Chapter
7</td><td>Microsoft Office
Accounting Tools and
Fixed Assets</td></tr>
</table>

OBJECTIVES: In Chapter 7, you use the accounting tools that come with the MOA software to:

1. Start Microsoft Office Accounting (MOA).
2. Open the product-based sample company, Northwind Traders.
3. Use Microsoft Office Accounting Analysis Tools—Excel Pivot Tables.
4. Use Microsoft Office Accounting Analysis Tools—Access Reports.
5. Use Fixed Assets Manager.
6. Use Accountant View.
7. Use your Internet browser to go to the book's website. (Go online to www.mhhe.com/moaessentials.)

In Chapter 7, you become familiar with some of the MOA features and tools that make many of the necessary tasks and analyses in running a business easier to do. These MOA innovations allow you to use advanced features like Pivot Tables and Access Reports that are found in other Office suite products or do fixed asset accounting with ease. In this chapter, Word, Excel, and Access are used and should be install on your computer to complete this chapter.

GETTING STARTED

1. Start Microsoft Office Accounting.

2. From the File pull down menu, select Open Company. (*Hint:* These instructions assume a company opened when you started MOA.)

3. Select the sampleproductcompany file in the Select Company File window, then click Open.

4. When the title bar shows Northwind Traders – Microsoft Office Accounting Professional 2007, the product based sample company is open.

Northwind Traders - Microsoft Office Accounting Professional 2007

USING MICROSOFT OFFICE ACCOUNTING ANALYSIS TOOLS

You can quickly use analysis tools like Excel pivot tables and Access reports to view MOA data in meaningful ways because MOA is preloaded with some Excel and Access templates. You do not need to know much about Excel or Access to use these templates but you do need to have the Excel and Access programs on your computer. The MOA Analysis Tools window shows the different types of pre-built Excel Pivot Tables and Access Reports that are available for you to use to analyze company data.

The following steps assume the [Display] button is active (*not* grayed out). If you *cannot* click Display, in the Company Name field, click Open, then select the sampleproductcompany to open it. Northwind Traders should appear in the Company Name field. (*Hint:* See Getting Started on the previous page.)

EXCEL PIVOT TABLES

Excel PivotTables allows data to be organized so it can be moved around to see how the various data pieces relate to each other. The Analysis Toolbox provides two Excel PivotTable reports. The Sales Analysis PivotTable allows you to view sales data by customer, items sold, and time period. The Purchases Analysis PivotTable allows you to view your purchase data by vendor, items purchases, and time period. PivotTables make pattern, relationship, and trend analyses easier to do. To begin working with MOA PivotTables, complete the following steps.

1. If Northwind Traders, the product based sample company in Microsoft Office Accounting is not open, open it. (*Hint:* See Getting Started on the previous page.)

2. Open the separate Data Analysis Tools program. Click **start**; All Programs, Microsoft Office, Microsoft Office Accounting 2007 Tools, Analysis Tools.

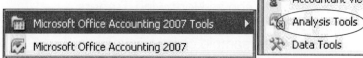

3. The MOA Analysis Tools window appears for Northwind Traders.

4. Select the Sales Analysis Excel Pivot Table by highlighting and click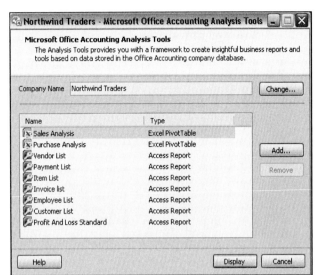

Display .

5. The Please wait window appears. Be patient as the workbook is created, the database is connected, and the data is fetched.

6. The Microsoft Excel - SalesReports1 Sales Cube window appears. (Your dates may differ from the window shown here.)

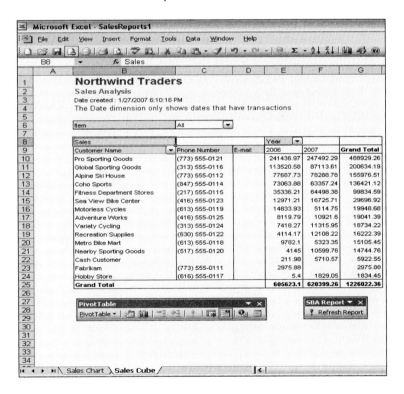

Observe that there are two tabs at the bottom of the chart. Sales Cube is selected above; Sales Chart is selected in step 7.

7.   To view the sales data graphically, select the Sales Chart tab and the graph appears.

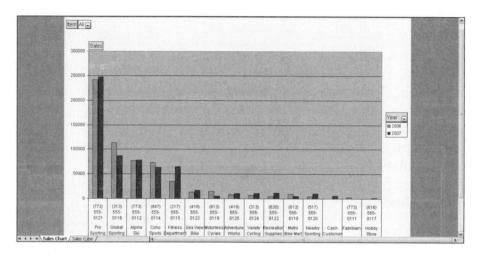

8.   To change the sales data shown in the cube or graph, use the Item, Sales, Year, or Customer pull down menus to make selections. For example, for Item pick Service Item and click OK.

9.   The data appears in sales cube or sales graph. Data displayed in this way could easily answer the question, Northwind Traders sells services to which customers and how much have they bought in the past two year? Further selections could drilldown by customer or by service item for more specific information.

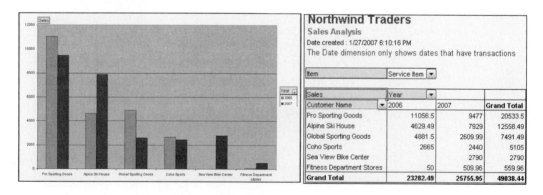

10.   From Excel's menu bar, click File, Save As.

11. Create a Your Name Chapter 7 folder on your Desktop if you have not yet done so and select it for the Save As field.

12. Type **Services Sales Report and your first and last name** in the File name field. The Save as type field displays Microsoft Office Excel Workbook.

13. Click Save.

14. Print both the Services Sales Report Your First and Last Name's Sales Chart and Sales Cube. If a Security Warning pops up, check the box and click Enable Macros.

15. Close Excel. (If at a later time, you open this Excel file and a window prompts that the SQL server does not exist, click ⬛ OK ⬛.)

ACCESS REPORTS

Access is a database program that you can use to create reports. The Analysis Tools provides pre-built Access reports for your use. You can also edit existing reports or create your own new reports. To begin working with Access reports, complete the following steps.

1. If Northwind Traders, the product based sample company in Microsoft Office Accounting is not open, open it. (*Hint:* See Getting Started.)

2. If the separate Data Analysis Tools program is not open, open it. (*Hint:* Click ⬛ **start** ⬛; All Programs, Microsoft Office, Microsoft Office Accounting 2007 Tools, Analysis Tools.)

3. In the MOA Analysis Tools window for Northwind Traders select the Payment List Access Report and click Display.

4. The Please wait window appears. Be patient as the report is created. Click OK to any Security Alert windows.

5. When the report appears, click on the Multiple pages icon [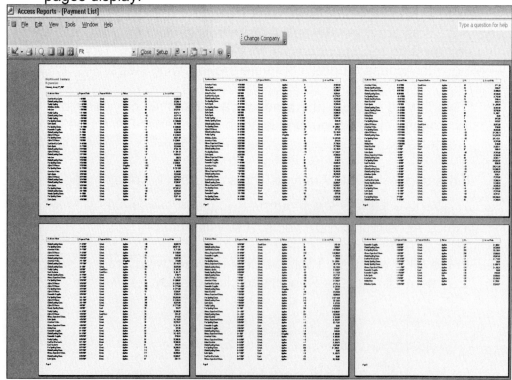] so 6 pages display.

6. Click on the Office links icon and publish the payment list in Microsoft Office Word (the pull down menu choices also include Excel). In a few moments, the payment list appears as a Word document.

7. From Word's menu bar, click File, Save As.

8. In the Save in field, select your desktop folder, Your Name Chapter 7.

9. Type **Payments List and your First and Last name** in the File name field. In the Save as type field select Word Document.

10. Click Save.

11. Print your Word document.

12. Return to MOA by exiting Word, Access and MOA Analysis Tools.

USING FIXED ASSETS TOOLS

In accounting, when a business acquires a fixed asset such as a building or equipment, it uses that asset to produce income. Since fixed assets generally provide the business benefits that last for more than a year, the business spreads the fixed asset's cost over its useful life. **Depreciation** is the process of allocating this cost expiration over a fixed asset's useful life. MOA Fixed Asset Manager allows you to add new fixed assets, dispose assets, calculate, and post depreciation into Microsoft Office Accounting. You add a new fixed asset and depreciate it using Fixed Asset tools. To begin working with Fixed Assets, complete the following steps.

1. If Northwind Traders, the product based sample company in Microsoft Office Accounting is not open, open it. (*Hint:* See Getting Started.)

2. From the menu bar, select Fixed Assets; Fixed Asset Manager. (If Fixed Assets has not been previously used, it will install. If a window prompts to restart MOA, do that; then open the product based sample company, Northwind Traders.)

3. When the Fixed Asset Manager window appears, notice its Toolbar displays buttons for New Fixed Asset, Dispose Fixed Asset, Post Depreciation, and Help. The Fixed Asset Navigation Pane allows you to Start a Task or work with Reports.

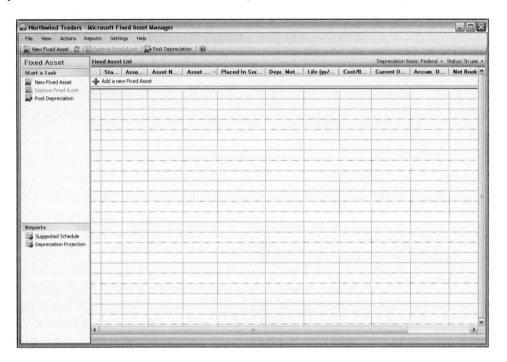

4. To add a fixed asset, complete the following steps:

   a. On the Toolbar, click New Fixed Asset.
   b. When the Untitled-Fixed Asset window appears, complete the fields as follows: Asset name: type **Auto;** Asset class: select **Auto 1;** Notice Asset ID, Date of purchase, and Placed in service is automatically completed; Asset account: select **Property and Equipment**; Depr./Amortization expense account: select **Depreciation Expenses/Equipment**; Accum. Depr./Amortization account: select **Accum. Depr. Property and Equipment;** and Cost/Other Basis: type **20,000.00.** Compare your window to the one below (Your Date of Purchase and Placed in service dates will differ.)

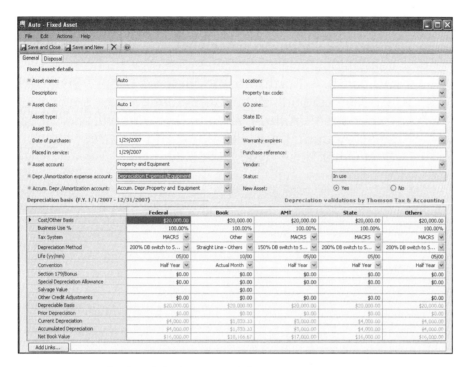

c. When satisfied, click Save and Close. You are returned to Fixed Asset Manager; notice your new auto is listed.

5. To view the projected depreciation expense under all the various methods used for financial and tax purposes for the year, from the menu bar, click Fixed Assets; Fixed Asset Projection. The following report appears.

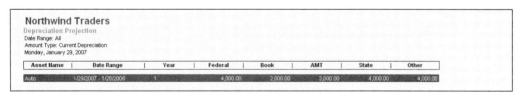

6. Select File; Close to exit report. Do not save.

7. Add another fixed asset.
   a. From the menu bar, click Fixed Assets; Fixed Asset Manager, New Fixed Asset.

   b. In the Untitled-Fixed Asset window complete the fields as follows: Asset name: type **Old Furniture;** Asset class: select **Furniture and Fixtures-nonrentals;** Date of purchase: type **today's date but a year ago** (i.e. type **1/29/2006** if today's date is 1/29/2007), Placed in service date automatically completes; Asset account: select **Office/Store Furniture and Fixtures**; Depr./Amortization expense account: select **Depreciation Expenses/Furniture**; Accum. Depr./Amortization account: select **Accum. Depr. Furniture and Fixtures;** and Cost/Other Basis: type **10,000.00**.

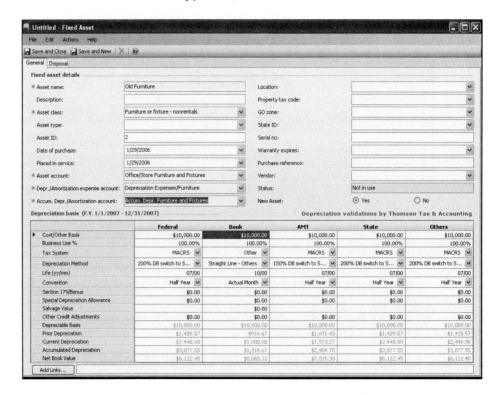

c. When satisfied, click Save and Close.

d. Read the window prompt, then click [Yes] when the following window appears.

e. When you return to Fixed Asset Manager, notice old furniture is listed under auto.

8. To depreciate a fixed asset, like the old furniture, complete the following steps:

   a. In the Start Task list, click Post Depreciation. The Fixed Asset Depreciation Wizard appears. For the Depreciation through date type **12/31/200X** (200X should be 2007 if that is your current year.) Click Next > .

   b. Review Depreciation Run window to verify the depreciation amounts. Observe that the Depr. Amt. column shows $4,000.00 for Auto and $2,448.98 for Old Furniture. Click Next > .

   c. Type **2448.98** in the debit column for Depreciation Expenses/Furniture. Type **2448.98** in the credit column for Accum. Depr. Furniture and Fixtures.

   d. Type **4000.00** in the debit column for Depreciation Expenses/Equipment. Type **4000.00** in the credit column for Accum. Depr. Property and Equipment. Confirm that debits equal credits. You *cannot* post if debits do *not* equal credits. The Depreciation Run window shown below lists entries for both Auto and Old Furniture.

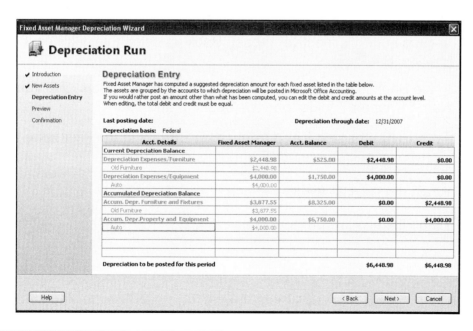

e. Preview entry carefully. Remember once an entry is posted it cannot be changed. When satisfied, click [Next >].
f. The Preview window shows the entries for depreciation; click [Post]. Wait while entry is posted and records are updated.
g. When Confirmation window appears, click [Finish]. You are returned to the Fixed Asset Manager window.

9. In the Navigation Pane, link to Suggested Schedule. In a moment, it displays.

10. Print the Suggested Schedule.

11. Return to MOA desktop by closing Suggested Depreciation Schedule and Fixed Asset Manager.

BACK UP CHAPTER 7 DATA

Follow these steps to back up.

1. Click [start]; All Programs, Microsoft Office, Microsoft Office Accounting 2007 Tools, Data Tools.

2. In the Backup company data area, click [Backup]. (*HINT:* If your backup button is inactive, Close. Back up using File; Utilities, Data Utilities, Backup.)

3. In the Backup file name field, click [Browse ...]. Browse to the Your Name Chapter 7 folder on your Desktop and open it.

4. Type **END Chapter 7 and your three initials** in the File name field. Click [Save].

5. When the Backup window appears, click [OK].

6. When the window prompts, Backup was completed successfully, click [OK].

7. Close the MOA Data Utilities window.

8. Make a backup copy on your USB drive in a folder called Your Name Chapter 7 folder.

   a. Start Windows Explorer (*Hint:* Right-click Start; left-click Explore).

   b. Display your external media (i.e., USB drive in the left pane of Windows Explorer and the Your Name Chapter 7 folder in the right pane. Highlight the Your Name Chapter 7 folder and drag it on to the external media to copy it.

   c. Double click on your external media to display its contents to confirm that you successfully copied the Your Name Chapter 7 folder and its contents. Close Windows Explorer.

9. Exit MOA or continue with the next section.

EXPLORING THE ACCOUNTANT VIEW

Accountant View is also located in the separate program, Microsoft Office Accounting 2007 Tools that installed with MOA. It allows accountants access to tasks they perform for or on behalf of their clients. Accountants can import, export, and view their clients' books as well as manage their clients' payroll. Follow these steps to explore the Accountant View desktop.

1. Click ![start]; All Programs, Microsoft Office, Microsoft Office Accounting 2007 Tools, Accountant View.

2. The Accountant View desktop appears. From it, accountants can work with the accounts and records of multiple clients. The desktop contains several different panes.

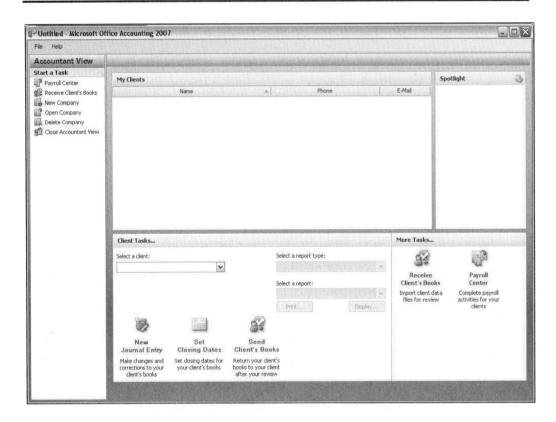

a. The Start a Task navigation pane on the left gives the accountant easy access to common tasks such as the payroll processing, receiving client's books, creating a new company, opening a company's records, deleting a company's records, and closing the accountant view.

b. The My Clients pane lists client contact information. A client's books can be opened by clicking on their name in this pane. Clients can be added to the Accountant View by importing their books or creating a new company.

c. The Client Task pane provides icons that can be selected to create or edit journal entries, set closing dates, or return books to clients. Client reports can also be displayed or printed. A more tasks side pane allows for accountant customization.

3. On the Accountant View desktop under Other Tasks, click Receive Client's Books to start the Accountant Transfer Wizard. The wizard allows clients to continue

using MOA while their accountant makes adjustments to their books. When the accountant sends the client's books back, the accountant changes will seamlessly update the client's books.

4.   In the Welcome to Accountant Transfer: Receive window, select Receive books manually. Click Next.

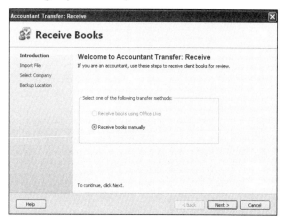

5.   In select import file, click Browse. Go to your Transfers folder on your USB drive.

6.   Select the Your Name Retailers transfer file you made at yearend and emailed to your professor and yourself. (*HINT:* Chapter 5) Your file name will differ (since you used your first and last name) from what is shown here. Click Open.

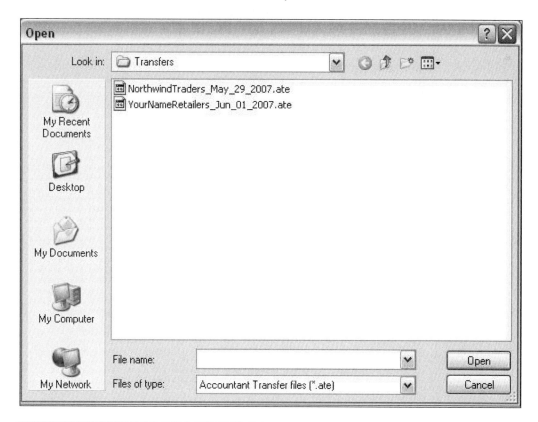

7. Verify the import file. Click Next.

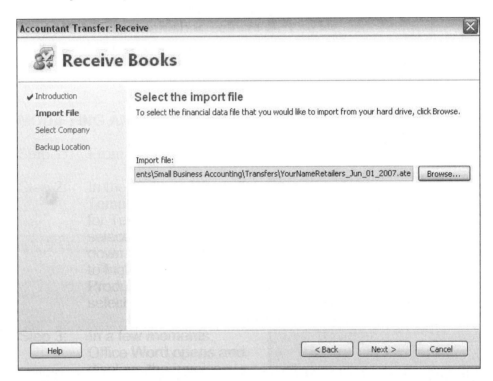

8. In Provide Password screen since there is no password, click Next.

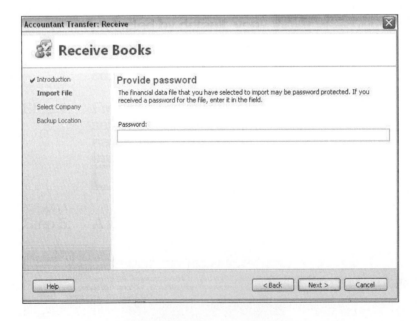

9. In Select a Company window, click Browse.

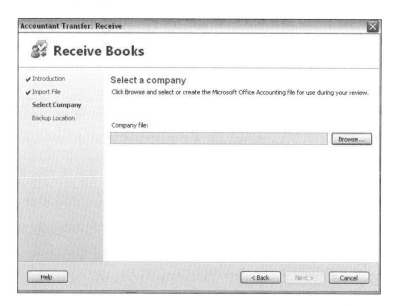

10. Type **EOY Review Your Name Retailers** (use your first and last name) for File Name. Click Save.

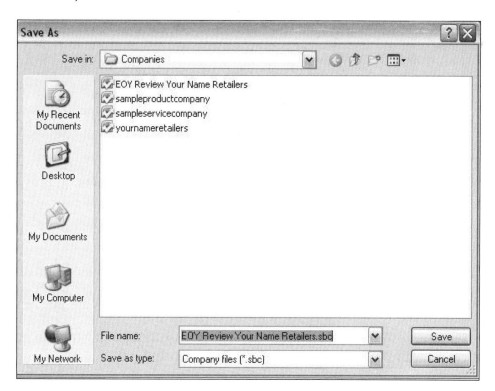

11. A screen will ask if you want to create a new company. Click Yes.

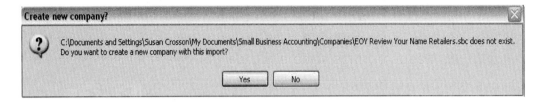

12. If asked to create a backup, browse to select your Backup folder.

13. Click Import to receive Your Name Retailers transfer file into the created EOY Review Your Name Retailers company.

14. When receiving financial data file complete, the following window appears:

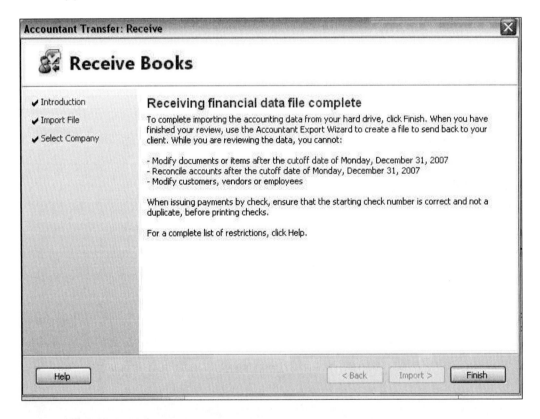

15. Click Finish to return to the Accountant View desktop. You can now work with the company data that was imported.

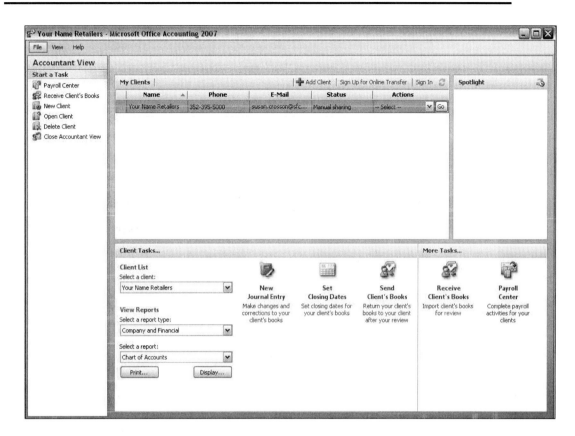

16.   Notice the top of the Accountant view window indicates you are the accountant:

17.   To print the Post Closing Trial Balance, in Client Tasks; Client List:

a.   Select Your Name Retailers for client.
b.   Select Company and Financial for report type.
c.   Select Trial Balance for report.
d.   Click Display.
e.   Compare your 12/31/200X Post Closing Trial balance to the one shown on the next page.

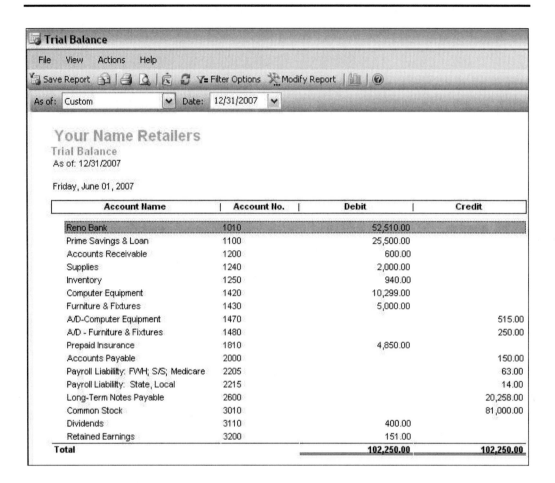

17. Close the Trial Balance and the Accountant View.

SUMMARY AND REVIEW

OBJECTIVES: In Chapter 7, you used the accounting tools to:

1. Start Microsoft Office Accounting (MOA).
2. Open product-based sample company, Northwind Traders.
3. Use Microsoft Office Accounting Analysis Tools—Excel Pivot Tables.
4. Use Microsoft Office Accounting Analysis Tools—Access Reports
5. Use Fixed Assets Manager.
6. Use Accountant View.
7. Used your Internet browser to go to the book's website. (Went online to www.mhhe.com/moaessentials.)

GOING TO THE NET

From MOA's menu bar, select Help; Microsoft Office Accounting Help, and search for Excel Pivot Tables to answer these questions.

1. Why is MOA's system of permissions for accessing data a security feature?
2. To use MOA, is a Microsoft Windows user name and password required?
3. List the preset user roles in MOA.
4. Which preset role has the most privileges? Which preset role has the least privileges?

FLASHCARD REVIEW

Create the following flashcards.

1. What are the steps to use MOA Analysis Tools?

2. What are the steps to add a new fixed asset?

Short-answer questions: In the space provided write the answer to the question.

1. What are the three tools found in Microsoft Office Accounting 2007 Tools?

   _____

   _____

2. What basic maintenance tasks can be done using Data Tools?

   _____

   _____

3. List two advantages to using the Analysis Tools templates?

    _____

    _____

4. Why use Excel Pivot Tables?

    _____

    _____

5. List the types of Access Reports?

    _____

    _____

6. Why are fixed assets depreciated?

    _____

    _____

7. What tasks does the Fixed Asset Manager allow you to do?

    _____

    _____

8. What tasks does Accountant View allow you to do?

    _____

    _____

9. Explain how to import a client file into Accountant View?

_____

_____

10. Explain how to display a client report in Accountant View?

_____

_____

Exercise 7-1: Follow the instructions below to complete Exercise 7-1. If necessary start MOA and open Northwind Traders.

1. Print the Services Sales Report Your First and Last Name—both the Sales Chart and Sales Cube. (Step 14 of the Excel Pivot Tables section)

2. Print Payments List Your First and Last Name as a Word document. (Step 11 of the Access Reports section.)

3. Print Suggested Schedule of Depreciation. (Step 10 of the Using Fixed Assets Tools section.)

Exercise 7-2: After opening Fabrikam, Inc. (the sample service company) in MOA and the MOA Analysis Tools, answer the following questions in the space provided.

1. Is Patricia Doyle a customer, vendor, or employee? _____

2. Is Randall Boseman a customer, vendor, or employee? _____

3. Is Ray Chow a customer, vendor, or employee? _____

4. What is the outstanding balance owed to the Washington State Department o Revenue? _____

5. How much does the School of Fine Art owe? _____

6. What is Stefan Delmarco's job title? _____

7. What is the price of Roofing Materials; what Type is it? _____

8. What was the amount of Invoice 1011; who was the customer? _____

9. Invoice 1079 to customer Katie Jordan is for what job? Has it been paid? _____

10. What company is the preferred vendor overall that the company purchases from the most? _____

ANALYSIS QUESTION: Explain why there are so many different ways MOA must keep track of fixed assets and its associated depreciation.

Chapter 8

Integration with Microsoft Office—Excel and Word

OBJECTIVES: In Chapter 8, you use the software to:

1. Start Microsoft Office Accounting (MOA).
2. Open product-based sample company, Northwind Traders.
3. Backup sample company database.
4. Copy report data to an Excel spreadsheet.
5. Modify report data and create a graph before copying data to Excel.
6. Use the Write Letter wizard to create a letter.
7. Protect Word documents.
8. Use your Internet browser to go to the book's website. (Go online to www.mhhe.com/moaessentials.)

Since Microsoft Office Accounting is a Microsoft Office program, it works well with Excel and Word to create graphs, spreadsheets and business documents. For example, if you have Microsoft Office (specifically XP or Vista) installed on your computer, you can copy a MOA report or financial statement to an Excel spreadsheet. Or, with MOA's letter writing wizard you can also easily customize common business letters to your vendors, customers, or employees.

This chapter describes several procedures for adding Microsoft Office Accounting data to Microsoft Office applications. You must have Word and Excel on your computer to do this chapter. You will notice that some of the features of Excel (graphing) or Word (mail merge) have been integrated into Microsoft Office Accounting. The three steps of the Write Letter wizard will also be explained. You will also create and modify reports in Excel, Word, and Microsoft Office Accounting 2007 and learn how to secure these documents.

GETTING STARTED:

1. Start Microsoft Office Accounting.

2. From the File menu, select Open Company. (*Hint:* These instructions assume a company opened when you started MOA.)

3. Select the sampleproductcompany file in the Select Company File window, then click ☐ Open .

4. When the title bar shows Northwind Traders – Microsoft Office Accounting Professional 2007, the product based sample company is open.

Northwind Traders - Microsoft Office Accounting Professional 2007

BACKUP NORTHWIND TRADERS

Before you make any changes to Northwind Traders, backup the sample company data. If you need to start over for any reason, opening this back up company allows you a fresh start.

1. Click File; Utilities, Data Utilities.

2. In the Backup company data area, click Backup .

3. In the Backup file name field, click Browse ... to locate your desktop and create a folder called **Your Name Chapter 8**.

4. Type **Northwind Traders, your three initials, and the date** in the File name field.

   | File name: | Northwind Traders SVC_2007-01-23 | ▼ | Save |
   | Save as type: | Backup Files (*.sbb) | ▼ | Cancel |

5. Click Save .

6. When the Backup window appears, click [OK]. *Do not password protect!* (Businesses use passwords to protect backups from unauthorized use.)

7. After several minutes, when the window prompts, Backup was completed successfully, click [OK].

8. Close the Microsoft Office Accounting Data Utilities window.

COPYING MICROSOFT OFFICE ACCOUNTING REPORT DATA TO MICROSOFT EXCEL

Follow these steps to learn how to copy Northwind's balance sheet and income statement data to Microsoft's spreadsheet program, Excel.
To begin, Northwind Traders desktop should be displayed.

Balance Sheet

1. On the Navigation pane, click 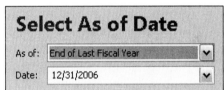.

2. For the Select a Report, click Balance Sheet.

3. Under the Select As of Date, pick As of: End of Last Fiscal Year. The date will fill-in automatically. Click [Display].

Select As of Date	
As of:	End of Last Fiscal Year
Date:	12/31/2006

4. When Balance Sheet displays, verify Report Basis: Accrual, As of: End of Last Fiscal Year, and Date: 12/31/XXXX.

5. From Toolbar, select Modify Report.

6. When the Modify Report pane displays on the right side, click Headers and Footers and place a check mark next to Footer, replace (Footer 1) in the box with your **First and Last Name**.

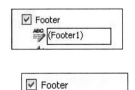

7. On the menu bar, select File; Print Preview to verify that your first and last name displays next to the page number at the bottom of the page. Close the Print Preview.

8. On the menu bar, select Actions; Export to Excel.

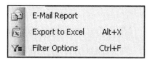

E-Mail Report		
Export to Excel	Alt+X	
Filter Options	Ctrl+F	

9. The Excel program will start and copy the Northwind Trader's balance sheet into a blank worksheet. Compare yours to the one shown below.

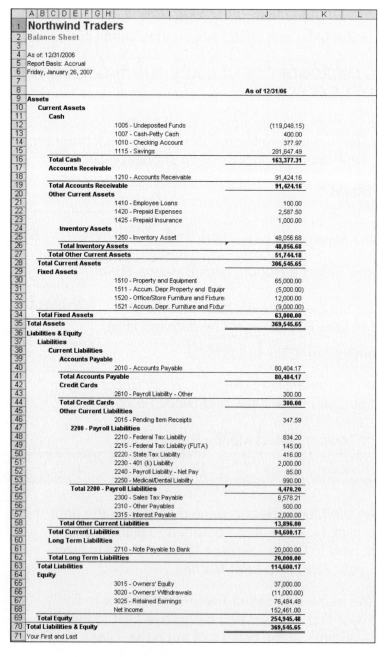

	A B C D E F G H	I	J	K L
1	**Northwind Traders**			
2	Balance Sheet			
3				
4	As of: 12/31/2006			
5	Report Basis: Accrual			
6	Friday, January 26, 2007			
7				
8			**As of 12/31/06**	
9	**Assets**			
10	**Current Assets**			
11	**Cash**			
12		1005 - Undeposited Funds	(119,048.15)	
13		1007 - Cash-Petty Cash	400.00	
14		1010 - Checking Account	377.97	
15		1115 - Savings	281,647.49	
16	**Total Cash**		**163,377.31**	
17	**Accounts Receivable**			
18		1210 - Accounts Receivable	91,424.16	
19	**Total Accounts Receivable**		**91,424.16**	
20	**Other Current Assets**			
21		1410 - Employee Loans	100.00	
22		1420 - Prepaid Expenses	2,587.50	
23		1425 - Prepaid Insurance	1,000.00	
24	**Inventory Assets**			
25		1250 - Inventory Asset	48,056.68	
26	**Total Inventory Assets**		**48,056.68**	
27	**Total Other Current Assets**		**51,744.18**	
28	**Total Current Assets**		**306,545.65**	
29	**Fixed Assets**			
30		1510 - Property and Equipment	65,000.00	
31		1511 - Accum. Depr.Property and Equipr	(5,000.00)	
32		1520 - Office/Store Furniture and Fixture	12,000.00	
33		1521 - Accum. Depr. Furniture and Fixtur	(9,000.00)	
34	**Total Fixed Assets**		**63,000.00**	
35	**Total Assets**		**369,545.65**	
36	**Liabilities & Equity**			
37	**Liabilities**			
38	**Current Liabilities**			
39	**Accounts Payable**			
40		2010 - Accounts Payable	80,404.17	
41	**Total Accounts Payable**		**80,404.17**	
42	**Credit Cards**			
43		2610 - Payroll Liability - Other	300.00	
44	**Total Credit Cards**		**300.00**	
45	**Other Current Liabilities**			
46		2015 - Pending Item Receipts	347.59	
47	**2200 - Payroll Liabilities**			
48		2210 - Federal Tax Liability	834.20	
49		2215 - Federal Tax Liability (FUTA)	145.00	
50		2220 - State Tax Liability	416.00	
51		2230 - 401 (k) Liability	2,000.00	
52		2240 - Payroll Liability - Net Pay	85.00	
53		2250 - Medical/Dental Liability	990.00	
54	**Total 2200 - Payroll Liabilities**		**4,470.20**	
55		2300 - Sales Tax Payable	6,578.21	
56		2310 - Other Payables	500.00	
57		2315 - Interest Payable	2,000.00	
58	**Total Other Current Liabilities**		**13,896.00**	
59	**Total Current Liabilities**		**94,600.17**	
60	**Long Term Liabilities**			
61		2710 - Note Payable to Bank	20,000.00	
62	**Total Long Term Liabilities**		**20,000.00**	
63	**Total Liabilities**		**114,600.17**	
64	**Equity**			
65		3015 - Owners' Equity	37,000.00	
66		3020 - Owners' Withdrawals	(11,000.00)	
67		3025 - Retained Earnings	76,484.48	
68		Net Income	152,461.00	
69	**Total Equity**		**254,945.48**	
70	**Total Liabilities & Equity**		**369,545.65**	
71	Your First and Last			

10. Now that Northwind's balance sheet is in Excel format, you can use Excel's features.

11. From Excel's menu bar, click File, Save As.

12. In the Save in field, select your desktop folder named Your Name Chapter 8.

13. The File name field displays Book1.xls. The Save as type field displays Microsoft Excel Worksheet. Highlight the file name. Type **balance sheet and your first and last name** in the File name field.

14. Click [Save]. Excel automatically adds the extension .xls to the file name.

15. Minimize the Excel window. You are returned to Northwind Traders—Microsoft Office Accounting. If the balance sheet report is still open, close it without saving. Northwind Trader's Select a Report window appears. (*Hint:* You can also click on Reports in the Navigation pane to display the Select a Report window.)

Income Statement

1. From the Select a Report window, click Profit and Loss (another term for the Income Statement).

2. Under the Select Date Range, select Range: Last Fiscal Year and the dates will fill-in automatically. Compare your screen, when satisfied, click [Display].

3. When Profit and Loss displays, verify Report Basis: Accrual, Date Range: Last Fiscal Year.

4. On the Toolbar, click Modify Report.

5. When the Modify Report pane displays on the right side, click Header and Footer and place a check mark next to Footer, replace (Footer 1) in the box with your **First and Last Name**.

6. On the menu bar, select File; Print Preview to verify that your first

and last name displays next to the page number at the bottom of the pages.

7. Close the Print Preview.

E-Mail Report		
Export to Excel	Alt+X	
Filter Options	Ctrl+F	

8. On the menu bar, select Actions; Export to Excel.

9. The Excel program will start and copy the Northwind Trader's profit and loss into a blank worksheet. Compare yours to the one shown below.

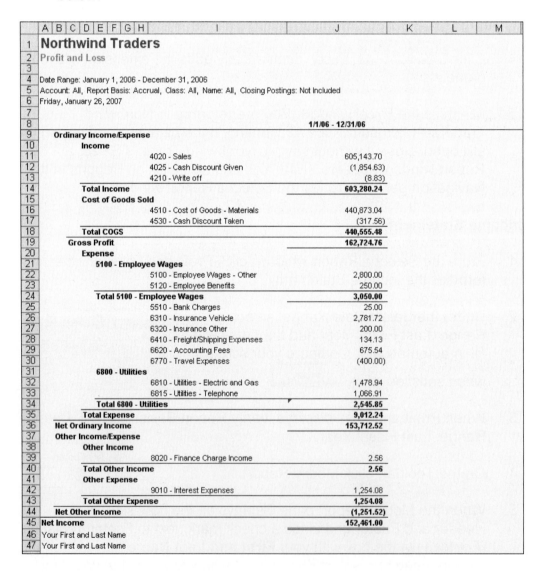

	A B C D E F G H	I	J	K	L	M
1	**Northwind Traders**					
2	Profit and Loss					
3						
4	Date Range: January 1, 2006 - December 31, 2006					
5	Account: All, Report Basis: Accrual, Class: All, Name: All, Closing Postings: Not Included					
6	Friday, January 26, 2007					
7						
8			1/1/06 - 12/31/06			
9	Ordinary Income/Expense					
10	Income					
11		4020 - Sales	605,143.70			
12		4025 - Cash Discount Given	(1,854.63)			
13		4210 - Write off	(8.83)			
14	**Total Income**		**603,280.24**			
15	**Cost of Goods Sold**					
16		4510 - Cost of Goods - Materials	440,873.04			
17		4530 - Cash Discount Taken	(317.56)			
18	**Total COGS**		**440,555.48**			
19	**Gross Profit**		**162,724.76**			
20	Expense					
21	**5100 - Employee Wages**					
22		5100 - Employee Wages - Other	2,800.00			
23		5120 - Employee Benefits	250.00			
24	**Total 5100 - Employee Wages**		**3,050.00**			
25		5510 - Bank Charges	25.00			
26		6310 - Insurance Vehicle	2,781.72			
27		6320 - Insurance Other	200.00			
28		6410 - Freight/Shipping Expenses	134.13			
29		6620 - Accounting Fees	675.54			
30		6770 - Travel Expenses	(400.00)			
31	**6800 - Utilities**					
32		6810 - Utilities - Electric and Gas	1,478.94			
33		6815 - Utilities - Telephone	1,066.91			
34	**Total 6800 - Utilities**		**2,545.85**			
35	**Total Expense**		**9,012.24**			
36	**Net Ordinary Income**		**153,712.52**			
37	Other Income/Expense					
38	Other Income					
39		8020 - Finance Charge Income	2.56			
40	**Total Other Income**		**2.56**			
41	Other Expense					
42		9010 - Interest Expenses	1,254.08			
43	**Total Other Expense**		**1,254.08**			
44	**Net Other Income**		**(1,251.52)**			
45	**Net Income**		**152,461.00**			
46	Your First and Last Name					
47	Your First and Last Name					

10. Now that Northwind's income statement is in Excel format, you can use Excel's features to create a graph or to make changes.

11. On the Excel toolbar, click on the Graph icon ⬚.

12. The Chart Wizard—Step 1 of 4—Chart Type window appears. Highlight Chart Type: Pie and Chart sub-type: Pie (it's the first chart sub-type). Click | Next > |.

13. In Chart Wizard—Step 2 of 4, click in the Date Range box then left click as you move your mouse over your numbers in column J of your Excel worksheet to highlight all the numbers. Select for Series in: Columns. Below is a partial example of this step. If pie chart does not appear, click | Next > |.

14. Compare your pie chart to the one below. Click | Next > |.

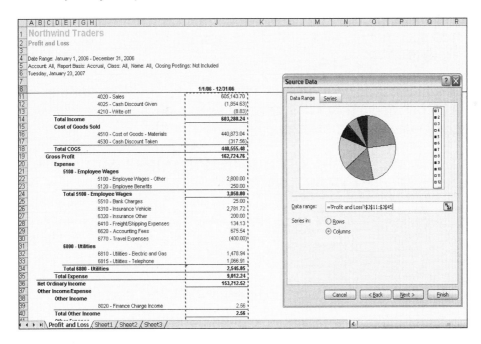

15. In Chart Wizard—Step3 of 4—Chart Options, type **Your Name Last Fiscal Income Statement** in the Title box. Click | Next > |.

16. In Chart Wizard—Step 4 of 4—Chart Location, select As Object in: Profit and Loss. Click | Finish |.

17. Position graph below the Profit and Loss Statement by dragging it.

18. From Excel's menu bar, click File, Save As.

19. In the Save in field, select your desktop folder named Your First and Last Name Chapter 8.

20. The File name displays Book1.xls. The Save as type field displays Microsoft Excel Worksheet. Highlight the file name. Type **Last Fiscal Income Statement and your first and last name** in the File name field.

21. Click [Save]. Excel automatically adds the extension .xls to the file name.

22. Close Excel. You are returned to Northwind Traders—Microsoft Office Accounting 2007. If the profit and loss report is still open, close it without saving. Do not save the changes you made to the profit and loss statement in Microsoft Office Accounting 2007--Northwind Traders.

23. Exit MOA; drag your desktop folder, Your Name Chapter 8 to your external media (i.e., USB drive) to keep a backup of your work, or continue with the next section.

MODIFYING MICROSOFT ACCOUNTING REPORTS AND ADDING GRAPHS BEFORE EXPORTING TO MICROSOFT EXCEL

1. If necessary, drag the Your Name Chapter 8 folder from your external media (i.e., USB drive) to your Desktop and start Microsoft Office Accounting.

2. Open the sample product company, Northwind Traders.

3. From Northwind's menu bar, select Reports; Company and Financials, and Profit and Loss Statement. (Or, from the Navigation pane, click Reports, then in Select a Report click on Profit and Loss Statement.)

4. For the Select Date Range, pick Range: All, and leave the From and To boxes blank. Click [Display].

5.   When Profit and Loss displays, verify Report Basis: Accrual, Date Range: All. Notice the displayed report covers more than one year.

6.   On the toolbar select Modify Report.

7.   When the Modify Report pane displays on the right side, click on Header and Footer and place a check mark next to Footer, delete (Footer 1) from box and type your **First and Last Name** in the box.

8.   In the Modify Report pane, click Columns. For Display Columns By, select Year by highlighting the radio button. For Compare To, place a check mark next to the % of Income box. Compare your Modify Report pane with the one shown here.

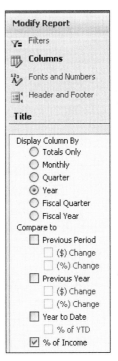

9.   If screen does not automatically refresh, click on the Refresh icon ⟳ which is located on the toolbar.

10. The comparative profit and loss statement by year displays along with the (%) of income.

11. On the toolbar, click on graph icon ⊞ which is located next to Modify Report.

12. Comparative graphs as well as the profit and loss statements display. Compare your graph to the one in the partial report below.

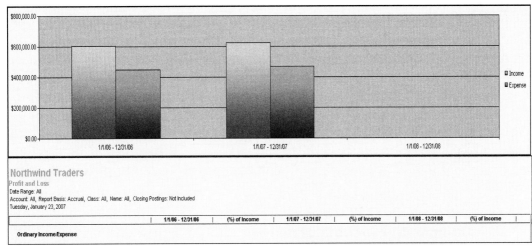

13. To save your
    comparative profit
    and loss statement
    in Northwind
    Traders, from the
    Toolbar, click File;
    Save Report As. In

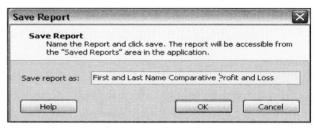

the Save Report Window type your **First and Last name**

comparative profit and loss. Compare and click OK .

14. On the toolbar, click on the Export to Excel icon to export to
    Excel (or from the Menu bar, select Actions; Export to Excel).

15. The Excel program will start and copy the Northwind Trader's profit
    and loss into a blank worksheet. Scroll down the Excel spreadsheet
    to see the partial one shown below.

18	Total COGS	440,555.48		447,461.79		0.00
19	Gross Profit	162,724.76		170,435.62		0.00
20	Expense					
21	5100 - Employee Wages					
22	5100 - Employee Wages - Other	2,800.00	0.46%	0.00	0.0%	0.00	0.0%
23	5110 - Wages	0.00	0.0%	6,020.00	0.97%	0.00	0.0%
24	5120 - Employee Benefits	250.00	0.04%	0.00	0.0%	0.00	0.0%
25	Total 5100 - Employee Wages	3,050.00		6,020.00		0.00	
26	5510 - Bank Charges	25.00	0.0%	0.00	0.0%	0.00	0.0%
27	5710 - Repairs and Maintenance Expense	0.00	0.0%	47.63	0.0%	0.00	0.0%
28	6100 - Depreciation					
29	6120 - Depreciation Expenses/Equipment	0.00	0.0%	1,750.00	0.26%	0.00	0.0%
30	6125 - Depreciation Expenses/Furniture	0.00	0.0%	525.00	0.08%	0.00	0.0%
31	Total 6100 - Depreciation	0.00		2,275.00		0.00	
32	6210 - Office Supplies	0.00	0.0%	103.47	0.01%	0.00	0.0%
33	6310 - Insurance Vehicle	2,781.72	0.46%	695.43	0.11%	0.00	0.0%
34	6320 - Insurance Other	200.00	0.03%	0.00	0.0%	0.00	0.0%
35	6410 - Freight/Shipping Expenses	134.13	0.02%	158.54	0.02%	0.00	0.0%
36	6620 - Accounting Fees	675.54	0.11%	5,940.00	0.96%	0.00	0.0%
37	6760 - Other Expenses	0.00	0.0%	240.00	0.03%	0.00	0.0%
38	6770 - Travel Expenses	(400.00)	(0.06%)	0.00	0.0%	0.00	0.0%
39	6800 - Utilities					
40	6810 - Utilities - Electric and Gas	1,478.94	0.24%	130.62	0.02%	0.00	0.0%
41	6815 - Utilities - Telephone	1,066.91	0.17%	80.50	0.01%	0.00	0.0%
42	Total 6800 - Utilities	2,545.85		211.12		0.00	
43	6910 - Rental Expenses					
44	6915 - Leased Facilities	0.00	0.0%	7,500.00	1.21%	0.00	0.0%
45	Total 6910 - Rental Expenses	0.00		7,500.00		0.00	
46	Total Expense	9,012.24		23,191.19		0.00	
47	Net Ordinary Income	153,712.52		147,244.43		0.00	
48	Other Income/Expense					
49	Other Income					
50	8010 - Gain or Loss on Sale of Assets	0.00	0.0%	200.00	0.03%	0.00	0.0%
51	8020 - Finance Charge Income	2.56	0.0%	5.79	0.0%	0.00	0.0%
52	8030 - Interest Income	0.00	0.0%	7,403.13	1.19%	0.00	0.0%
53	Total Other Income	2.56		7,608.92		0.00	
54	Other Expense					
55	9010 - Interest Expenses	1,254.08	0.2%	15.00	0.0%	0.00	0.0%
56	Total Other Expense	1,254.08		15.00		0.00	
57	Net Other Income	(1,251.52)		7,593.92		0.00	
58	Net Income	152,461.00		154,838.35		0.00	
59	Your First and Last Name					
60	Your First and Last Name					

16. From Excel's menu bar, click File, Save As.

17. In the Save in field, select your desktop folder named Your Name
    Chapter 8.

18. The File name displays Book1.xls. The Save as type field displays
    Microsoft Excel Worksheet. Highlight the file name. Type
    Comparative Income Statement and your first and last name in

the File name field.

19. Click [_S_ave]. Excel automatically adds the extension .xls to the file name.

20. Close Excel. You are returned to Northwind Traders—Microsoft Office Accounting 2007. Close any open reports.

21. Exit MOA. Drag your desktop folder, Your Name Chapter 8, to external media (i.e., USB drive) to have a backup of your work, or continue with the next section.

MICROSOFT OFFICE ACCOUNTING AND MICROSOFT WORD

Microsoft Office Accounting 2007 contains Microsoft Word templates that can be used to correspond with customers, vendors, or employees. How many templates you have will depend on your version of Microsoft Office software. If you have the most current version of Office, you will have the most templates and options for modifying the templates. Older versions of Office software will have fewer choices.

Here are some examples of available Word templates: Credit memo, Customer statement, Finance charge, Invoice product, Invoice service, Online sales receipt, Packaging slip, Sales receipt, Purchase order, Quote, Online order, and Sales order.

In this section you will prepare a letter to an employee congratulating them on being selected as the employee of the month.

1. If necessary, drag Your Name Chapter 8 folder from your external media to your desktop and start Microsoft Office Accounting.

2. Open the sample product company, Northwind Traders.

3. From Northwind Trader's menu bar, select Employees; Write Letters.

4. The Write Letters Wizard begins. Read the information about the wizard's three steps. Click [_N_ext >].

5. In the Select letter template window, highlight employee appreciation letter.doc to select it, then click Next > .

6. In the Select Employees window, place a check mark next to Brenda Diaz, then click Next > .

7. In the Add a Signature window, type **Congratulations on being selected employee of the month!** And add your **First and Last name** for the signature. Compare your window to the one below.

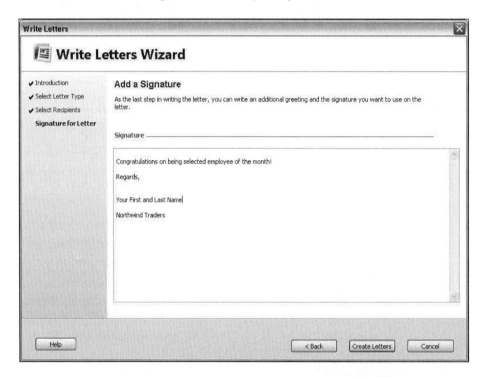

8. Review the letter. When satisfied, click Create Letters . Word will then open and display the letter complete with letterhead, date, the employee's name and address, and your additions. Compare your letter to the one created in Word on the next page. (Your date will differ.)

Northwind Traders
1234 Main St.
Fargo, ND 32801
Ph: (701) 555-0141   Fax: (701) 555-0142

1/26/2007

Brenda Diaz
5678 5th St
Chicago, IL 44444

Dear Brenda Diaz:

Please accept our thanks and gratitude for being such a valuable employee. Your hard work and dedication make our business strong and contribute significantly to customer satisfaction.

Congratulations on being selected employee of the month!

Regards,

Your First and Last Name

Northwind Traders

---

9. Click File; Save As. In the Save in field, select Your Name Chapter 8 folder on the Desktop. For the file name, type **Brenda Diaz letter and your First and Last Name**. Then click [_S_ave]. Word saves your letter in your folder.

10. Exit Word.

11. Exit Microsoft Office Accounting.

12. Drag your desktop folder, Your Name Chapter 8, to external media (i.e., USB drive); or continue with the next section.

PROTECTING MICROSOFT WORD DOCUMENTS

Protecting your business documents from unauthorized changes and providing internal controls to deter wrong-doing are essential in any business today. In this section, you will make a Word document read-only and require a password to open or modify it. You can also password protect excel documents in these ways.

Read-only Documents

1.   If necessary, start Word. Open the file for the Brenda Diaz letter. (*Hint:* Browse to Your Name Chapter 8 folder on the Desktop and select the file named, Brenda Diaz letter and your First and Last Name.)

2.   On the Tools menu, click Options.

3.   Click Security or Save tab. (Depends on the version of Word on your computer.)

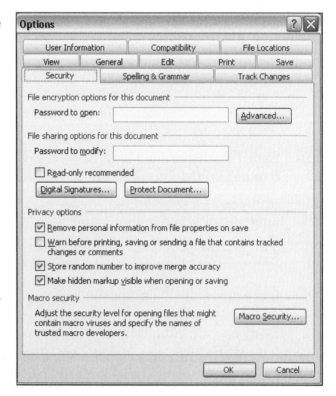

4.   Check the Read-only recommended check box, and then click OK.

5.   Click Save.

6.   Now if a user opens this read-only document, they can only change it or save it by giving the file a different name using the Save As command.

Password Protected Documents

1. If necessary, start Word. Open the file for the Brenda Diaz letter. (*Hint:* Browse to Your Name Chapter 8 folder on the Desktop and select the file named, Brenda Diaz letter and your First and Last Name.)

2. Since the file is a Read-only document, you must first save it under a different file name before using it. Click File; Save As. In the Save field, select the Your Name Chapter 8 folder on the Desktop and name the file **Password protected your First and Last Name**.

3. On the Tools menu, click Protect Document.

4. The Protect Document task pane is where you set formatting or editing restrictions and password protect them. How this task pane looks may vary with your version of Word. To restrict tracked changes edits to only those persons that know the password, check the Editing Restrictions box and select Tracked changes from the pull-down menu, then click Yes, Start Enforcing Protection .

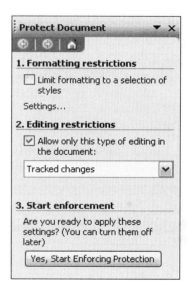

5. When the Start Enforcing Protection window appears, enter and re-enter a password. Read the Caution before clicking OK. (Write down your password _____)

6. Save the document.

7. Now if anyone tries to open or modify this document, they must enter the correct password to do so.

8. Exit Word and MOA.

9. Drag the Your Name Chapter 8 folder from your Desktop on to your external media (i.e., USB drive) or continue with the next section.

> **Read me: Security Passwords**
> Use strong passwords not weak ones. A strong password mixes uppercase and lower case letters, numbers, and symbols and is 8 or more characters in length. It is critical for you to remember your passwords since neither Microsoft nor your professor can retrieve them. Store passwords that you write down in a secure place away from the information they are helping to protect.

SUMMARY AND REVIEW

OBJECTIVES: In Chapter 8, you used the software to:

1.   Start Microsoft Office Accounting (MOA).
2.   Open product-based sample company, Northwind Traders.
3.   Backup sample company database.
4.   Copy report data to an Excel spreadsheet.
5.   Modify report data and create a graph before copying data to Excel.
6.   Use the Write Letter wizard to create a letter.
7.   Protect Word documents.
8.   Used your Internet browser to go to the book's student edition website. (Go online to www.mhhe.com/moaessentials.)

GOING TO THE NET

From MOA's menu bar, select Help; Microsoft Office Accounting Help, search for Security and Privacy in Microsoft Office Accounting related topics and answer the following questions.

1.   What is authentication?
2.   Explain two security best practices.
3.   Go to one of the Additional resources links and summarize what you learned.
4.   In your own words, what does the Privacy Statement say?

FLASHCARD REVIEW

Create the following flashcards.

1. What are the steps to export a MOA report to excel?

2. What are the steps for using the Write Letters Wizard?

3. What are the steps to make a Word document read-only?

4. What are the steps to password protect a Word or Excel document?

Short-answer questions: In the space provided write the answer to the question.

1. List two advantages of having Microsoft Office Accounting 2007 integrated with Microsoft Office suite.

    _____

    _____

2. Why is it good to backup the sample company before starting?

    _____

    _____

3. Why should a business password protect their backups?

    _____

    _____

4. How do you graph report data in Microsoft Office Accounting?

    _____

    _____

5. List the two ways to export MOA reports to Excel.

    _____

    _____

6. List at least three ways to modify a report.

    _____

    _____

7. What types of letters can you write to employees if you use the Letter Wizard?

    _____

    _____

8. What types of letters can you write to customers if you use the Letter Wizard?

    _____

    _____

9. What types of letters can you write to vendors if you use the Letter Wizard?

    _____

    _____

10. What can you do to protect Word documents?

    _____

    _____

Exercise 8-1: Follow the instructions below to complete Exercise 8-1.

If necessary, drag the Your Name Chapter 8 folder from your external media on to your Desktop, start MOA, and open Northwind Traders.

1.   Open Excel and print the following:

   a.   The balance sheet you saved in Step 14 in the Copying Microsoft Office Accounting Data to Microsoft Excel section. (*Hint:* The file name is balance sheet your first and last name.)

   b.   The income statement and graph you saved in Step 21 in the Copying Microsoft Office Accounting Data to Microsoft Excel section. (*Hint:* The file name is income statement your first and last name.)

   c.   The comparative income statement you saved in Step 19 in the Modifying Microsoft Office Reports and Adding Graphs Before Exporting to Microsoft Excel section. (*Hint:* The file name is comparative income statement your first and last name.)

2.   Open Word and print the following:

   The password protected letter to Brenda Diaz you saved in Step 6 in the Protecting Microsoft Word Documents section. (*Hint:* The file name is password protected your first and last name.)

Exercise 8-2: Follow the instructions below to complete Exercise 8-2.

1.   If necessary, drag the Your Name Chapter 8 folder from your external media on to your Desktop and start Microsoft Office Accounting.

2.   From the File menu, select Open Company.

3.   Select the sampleservicecompany file in the Select Company File window, then click Open.

268   Chapter 8

4. When the title bar shows Fabrikam, Inc. – Microsoft Office Accounting 2007, the service based sample company is open.

5. From Fabrikam's menu bar, select Reports; Company and Financials, and Balance Sheet. (Or, from the Navigation pane, click Reports, then in Select a Report click on Balance Sheet.)

6. For the Select Date Range, pick Range: End of Last Year, notice the Date automatically fills with 12/31/XXXX. Click Display.

7. Balance Sheet displays. Verify Report Basis: Accrual. Change the Report basis to the Cash basis, use the Report Basis pulldown menu to select Cash.

8. Click Modify Report. When the Modify Report pane displays, click Headers and Footers and place a check mark next to Footer, replace (Footer 1) in the box with your **First and Last Name**.

9. Then in the Modify Report pane, click Columns. For Display Columns By, select Quarter by highlighting the radio button.

10. The cash basis balance sheets by quarter for last year displays.

11. Click on the Export to Excel icon to export to Excel (or from the Menu bar, select Actions; Export to Excel).

12. The Excel program will start and copy Fabrikam, Inc.'s cash basis quarterly balance sheets into a blank worksheet.

13. Print the Excel worksheet. Be sure to set up the report to print landscape and scaling to fit one page tall by one page wide. (*Hint:* File; Page Setup.)

14. Save. (*Hint:* File; Save As.) In the Save in field, select your desktop folder named Your Name Chapter 8. Type **Exercise 8-2 Cash Balance Sheet and your first and last name** in the File name field. Click Save.

15. Close Excel. You are returned to Fabrikam, Inc.—Microsoft Office Accounting 2007.

16. If you are not returned to the cash basis quarterly balance sheets, re-display it.

17. On the toolbar, click on graph icon .

18. Print the cash basis quarterly balance sheets and graph by clicking on Print icon. It is several pages long.

19. Change Report Basis to Accrual.

20. Click on the Print icon to print the accrual basis quarterly balance sheets and graph. It is several pages long.

21. Close the Balance Sheet. Do not save any changes.

22. In the Navigation Pane, Select Company.

23. From Fabrikam, Inc's menu bar, select Customers; Write Letters.

24. The Write Letters Wizard begins. Click Next.

25. In the Select a letter template window, highlight collection letter—final notice.doc to select it, then click Next.

26. When the Select Customer window appears; select for Filter options: Active; and select for Date range: 90+ days. Place a check mark next to Katie Jordan, then click Next.

27. In the Add a Signature window, type **Legal proceedings begin next week!** And add your **First and Last name** for the signature. When satisfied, click Create Letters.

28. Word will then open and display the collection letter to Katie Jordan.

29. On the Tools menu, click Options.

30. Click Security or Save tab.

31. Check the Read-only recommended check box, and then click OK.

32. Click Save.

33. Print letter.

34. Save the letter. Click File; Save As. In the Save in field, select Your Name Chapter 15 folder on the Desktop. For the file name, type: **Exercise 8-2 Letter and your First and Last Name**. Then click Save.

35. Exit Microsoft Office Accounting.

36. Drag the Desktop folder, Your Name Chapter 8, on to your external media (i.e., USB drive) so that you have a portable backup of your work.

EXERCISE 8-2
CHECKLIST OF PRINTOUTS

	Fabrikam, Inc.'s cash basis quarterly balance sheets in Excel (Step 13)
	Fabrikam, Inc.'s cash basis quarterly balance sheets and graph in MOA (Step 18)
	Fabrikam, Inc.'s accrual basis quarterly balance sheets and graph in MOA (Step 20)
	Customer Letter (Step 33)

ANALYSIS QUESTION: Which is correct, a cash or accrual income statement? What is the difference?

Project 3
Student-Designed Forms

Project 3 gives you a chance to create customized customer and vendor forms for a business of your own. You select one of several template themes to make your forms more appealing. Then, you customize Word templates by adding your company logo, letterhead, and slogan. Most of the tasks you do are performed using Microsoft Word which must be installed on your computer. If you need help, consult the Word help menu.

You are able to do this customization by editing the Word template's XML tags. Office Word templates in Microsoft Office Word 2003 or later use a technology called *Extensible Markup Language (XML)* to identify fields into which data about specific transactions or persons can be inserted. The tags which surround the data add meaning and allow the data to be processed as information. XML resembles HTML, the technology used to publish pages on the World Wide Web. You do not need to know much about XML technology since Office Accounting 2007 provides a customized set of XML tags that you see in the Word Document Actions pane when you open one of the templates.

Office Accounting 2007 comes with two sets of templates which can be found under the path C:\Documents and Settings\All Users\Templates\ Office Accounting 2007\.[1] A basic set for use with Office XP (or earlier) is located in the Basic Templates folder and another set in the Templates folder is for use with Office 2003 (or later). Before you begin, you should review these folders. Notice the different types of customer and vendor templates that are available and how the different themes change the look of the form. Some of the templates that you will find include: Credit Memo, Customer Statement, Finance Charge, Invoice Product, Invoice Service, Online Sales Receipt, Packaging Slip, etc.

At the end of Project 3, a checklist is shown listing the printed forms you should have. The project's step-by-step instructions remind you to print the forms. Your professor may require these be turned in for a grade.

---

[1] In the Microsoft Vista operating system, the templates are located under C:\ProgramData\Microsoft\Windows\Templates\Office Accounting 2007\Templates\.

GETTING STARTED

Start MOA. From menu bar, select File; Open Company. In the Select Company File window, double click on the sampleproductcompany file in the Companies folder to select it. The Northwind Traders desktop will appear.

MODIFYING AN INVOICE TEMPLATE

Step 1:   From the Company menu, select Manage Word Templates.

Step 2:   In the Manage Word Templates dialog box, for Template types select Invoice.   Scroll down Templates Name to highlight Invoice Product - B&W.doc to select it. Click Modify.

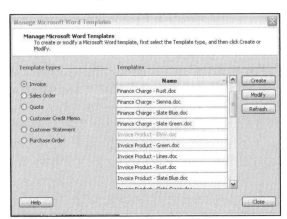

Step 3:   In a few moments, Office Word opens and displays the Invoice Product – B&W (Read-only) document. Since templates are write-protected by default, you must first rename the template before you can edit or customize it.

Step 4:   From the File menu, select Save As. For file name, type **Your Name Invoice B&W**. Click Save.

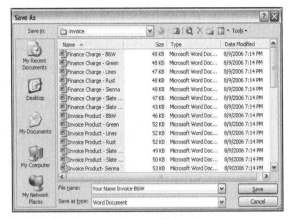

Step 5:   A warning box may appear. Read and click OK.

Step 6: Notice the Word Document Actions pane on the right side of your screen. These are the XML tags that can be customized. Hide the XML tags in the document by removing the check mark from the Show XML tags in the document check box.

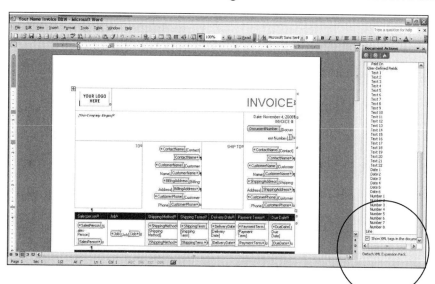

Step 7: Compare your document to the one below and then recheck the Show XML tags in the document check box:

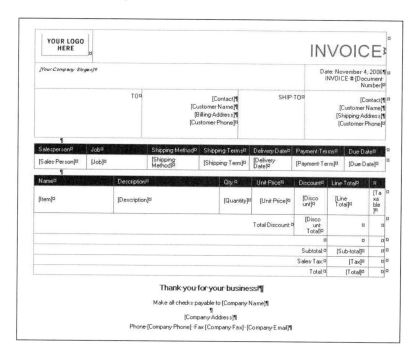

Step 8:   Add a graphic or clipart to your invoice by placing your mouse in the Your Logo Here placeholder. On your toolbar, select Insert; Picture, and either From File or Clip Art. Navigate to the location of a clipart or graphics file you like and select it. Your selection will now appear as your Company's logo. You can repeat this step to insert different graphic images.

Step 9:   Add a company slogan to your template by placing your mouse anywhere in the Your Company Slogan text box. The Your Company Slogan box is located just below your Logo. Type the following phase: **Accounting is the language of business!** Then format as you want.

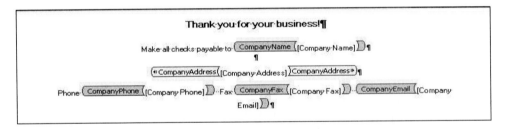

Step 10:   Scroll to the lower part of the template to modify it.

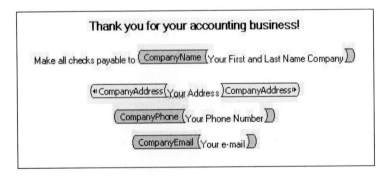

Step 11:   Add your **first and last name Company, address, phone number, and e-mail** information, as well as your thanks for the **accounting** business.   Compare your modifications to the following screenshot. Remember to remove the brackets as you enter your information. Delete the Fax field and tags.

Step 12: Uncheck the Show XML tags in document check box and view
the layout and how information will be displayed in your
finished invoice template. When you are satisfied, click Save.

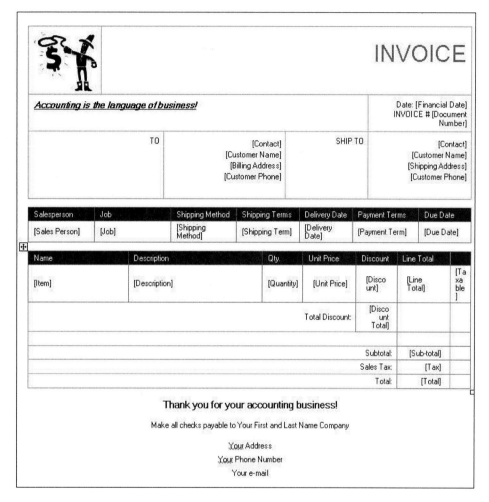

Step 13: Print your customized Invoice.

Step 14: Return to the MOA Manage Microsoft
Word Template dialog box and Click
Refresh. (Click OK to any Privacy
Warnings.) Your customized Invoice will
appear in the list of available templates.

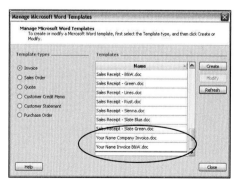

Step 15: Click Close to return to the MOA
desktop.

MODIFYING A PURCHASE ORDER TEMPLATE

Step 1:   From the Company menu, select Manage Word Templates.

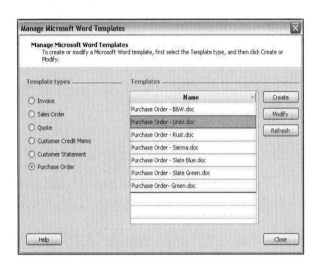

Step 2:   In the Manage Word Templates dialog box, for Template types select Purchase Order. Scroll down Templates Name to highlight Purchase Order - Lines.doc to select it. Click Modify.

Step 3:   In a few moments, Office Word opens and displays the Purchase Order – Lines (Read-only) document. Since templates are write-protected by default, you must first rename the template before you can edit or customize it.

Step 4:   From the File menu, select Save As. For file name, type **Your Name Purchase Order - Lines**. Click Save.

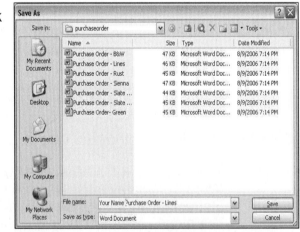

Step 5:   A warning box may appear. Read and click OK.

Step 6:   Add a graphic or clipart to your purchase order by placing your mouse in the Your Logo Here placeholder. On your toolbar, select Insert; Picture, and either From File or Clip Art. Navigate to the location of a clipart or graphics file you like and select it. Your selection will now appear as your Company's logo.

Step 7:   Add a company slogan to your template, place your mouse anywhere in the Your Company Slogan text box. The Your Company Slogan box is located just below your Logo. Type the following phase: **Accounting is the language of business!** Then format as you want.

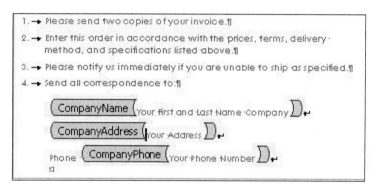

Step 8:   Modify the Ship To fields to show **your first and last name Company, your address, and your phone number** information. Remember to remove the brackets as you enter your first and last name Company, your address, and your phone number.

Step 9:   Modify your purchase order instructions located at the bottom of the form to show **your first and last name Company, your address, and your phone number**. Delete the Fax field. Compare yours to the one shown here. Remember to remove the brackets as you enter your information.

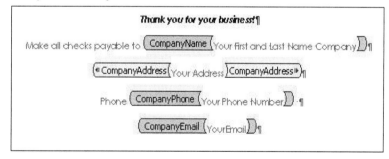

Step 10:   Modify the bottom of your purchase order form to show **your first and last name Company, your address, your phone number, and your email**. Delete the Fax field.

Step 11: Compare your Purchase Order to the one shown below. When you are satisfied, click Save.

Step 12: Print your customized Purchase Order.

Step 13: Return to the MOA Manage Microsoft Word Template dialog box and Click Refresh. (Click OK to any Privacy Warnings.) Your customized Purchase Order will appear in the list of available templates.

Step 14: Click Close. You return to the MOA desktop.

PROJECT 3
CHECKLIST OF PRINTOUTS
Ask your professor if these should be turned in…

	Invoice
	Purchase Order

Appendix A | Troubleshooting

Appendix A includes troubleshooting tips for Microsoft Office Accounting 2007 (MOA). These troubleshooting tips are included on the textbook website at www.mhhe.com/moaessentials.

The Troubleshooting tips in Appendix A include the following:

- Backup/Restore
- Change the Fiscal Year
- Identify the Company Database
- Attach Database
- Delete a Company Database
- Delete Microsoft Office Accounting

BACKUP/RESTORE

A. What if your computer does *not* have the appropriate .sbc file in the Companies folder? (When a company is created in MOA, the extension .sbc is added to the company name.)

If you need to transport data to another computer, *or,* the computer you are using in the lab does *not* have the company set up, use the steps shown below to restore data and set up the company at the same time. (*Hint:* Detailed steps for backing up, locating the backup file, and restoring are in Chapter 1.)

    1.   Start MOA. If necessary, select File; Close Company.
    2.   From the Start – Microsoft Office Accounting 2007 window, link to Restore a backup.
    3.   In the Backup filename field, browse to the location of the backup file.
    4.   In the Restore backup file to field, click Browse ... .
    5.   In the File name field, type the name of the company. Click Save .

6. When the window appears that says the company does not exist? Do you want to create it?, click [Yes]. This sets up the .sbc file in the Companies folder. When an MOA company is set up and saved, .sbc is automatically added as the extension.)

B. What should I do if I receive an error message when I try to restore a .sbb backup file?

1. Exit MOA.
2. Start MOA. When restoring backup files, remember to link to Restore a Backup from the startup menu. To go to the startup menu, from MOA's menu bar select File; Close Company. This takes you to the Start – Microsoft Office Accounting 2007 window. Link to Restore a backup.
3. In the Backup filename field, browse to the location of the backup file.
4. In the Restore backup file to field, click [Browse ...].
5. Select the appropriate company name. (Or, type the company name if it does *not* exist on the computer you are using.)
6. Complete the steps to restore the file. (Detailed steps for restoring files are in Chapter 1.)

C. Where are my backup files?

MOA's default location for backup files is: My Documents\Small Business Accounting\Backups. Backup files end in the extension, .sbb. If a Backups folder does *not* exist, the authors suggest you create one. You may also backup to the desktop; other hard drive or network location; or external media.

The location of the My Documents folder is:

C:\Documents and Settings\Computer Name[this could be identified as Administrator or your first and last name]\My Documents\Small Business Accounting.

D. Where are my company files?

MOA's default location for company files is: My Documents\Small Business Accounting\Companies. Company files end in the extension, sbc.

E.   Can I restore an Small Business Accounting 2006 zipped Backup File to Microsoft Office Accounting 2007?

Yes. Follow the steps shown.

1.   Start Microsoft Office Accounting. If a company opens, select File; Close Company.
2.   From MOA's startup window, select Restore a backup.
3.   In the Backup filename field, click Browse ... .
4.   In the Files of type field, select Version 1.0 Backup Files (*.zip).
5.   In the Look in field, go to the location of your Small Business Accounting 2006 backup files. (Small Business Accounting 2006 backup files end in the extension .zip).
6.   Select the file you want to restore.
7.   When the window prompts you to convert the file to Microsoft Office 2007 follow the screen prompts to do that.
8.   If necessary type the appropriate company name in the Restore backup file to field.
9.   Open the appropriate company.

CHANGE THE FISCAL YEAR

In Chapter 3, you set up a merchandising business. Then in Chapters 4 and 5, you record transactions for the fourth quarter of 200X (the current year). In Chapter 6, you record transactions for January 200Y (the year after your current year). In order to record transactions for January 200Y, you need to change the fiscal year from 200X to 200Y.

1.   From the menu bar, select Company; Manage Fiscal Year.

2.   Click New Fiscal Year.

3.   Enter or verify the Start and Close dates are 1/1/200Y and 12/31/200Y. 200Y is the year after your current year, i.e., if your current year is 2007, use 2008 for year 200Y.) Your year may differ from the year shown here. Click OK .

4.   The Manage Fiscal Year window appears indicating the new fiscal year is open.

5.   Close the Manage Fiscal Year window.

IDENTIFY THE COMPANY DATABASE

What is the company database path for Microsoft Office Accounting?

1. From the Windows desktop, double-click My Computer. Go to C:\Program Files\Microsoft SQL Server\MSSQL.1\MSSQL\Data.
2. The database files for MOA companies are identified with two extensions:

   .sbd – Small Business Database
   .sbl – Small Business Log

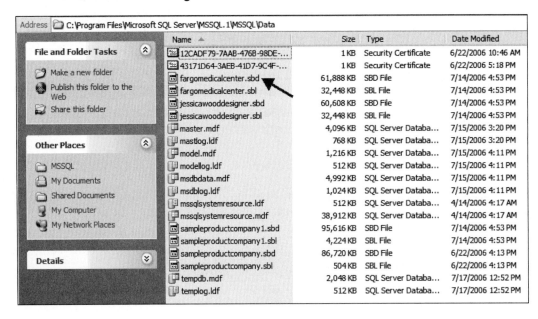

ATTACH DATABASE

Go to the help window, in the Search field type **attach**, then List Topics. Read the information on this window to learn how to attach the database file.

Attach Database dialog box: options and information

In the Attach Database dialog box, you can attach a database by selecting a data file, providing a name for it, and then attaching it to Microsoft Office Accounting.

To open the Attach Database dialog box, point to Utilities on the File menu, and then click Data Utilities. On the Accounting 2007 Data Tools dialog box, click the Advanced tab, and then click Attach.

- Data file to attach: To select a small business data (.sbd) file to attach to MOA, click [Browse ...]. (Go to C:\Program Files\Microsoft SQL Server\\MSSQL.1\MSSQL\data.

- Corresponding log file: After you select a data file to attach to MOA, the data file's corresponding small business log (.sbl) file appears in this field. The log file is located in the same folder as the data file.

- Database name: After you select a data file to attach to MOA, a default name appears in this field. You can edit this name.

- Create new company file (.sbc) that links to this database: To create a new small business company (.sbc) file that links to the database, select this check box.

- Attach: Click to attach the database to MOA.

DELETE A COMPANY DATABASE

There are two ways to delete a company database.

1. From File; Utilities, Data Utilities.
2. From the Microsoft Office Accounting 2007 startup window.

If you want to remove a company from Microsoft Office Accounting, delete the data file and then delete the associated company file, which is stored by default in the My Documents\Small Business Accounting\Companies folder of the administrator who set up your company in Microsoft Office Accounting.

Note: You cannot delete a company database when it is in use. If you want to delete an open company file, you must close it first.

You must have administrator access to delete a company.

To delete the data file:

1.   On the File menu, select Utilities; Data Utilities.

2.   In the Data Tools dialog box, under Delete a company, click 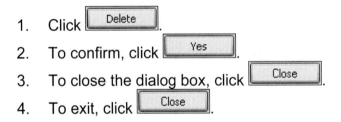 Delete .

      Note: If the Delete command appears dimmed, it is unavailable. You do not have sufficient access to use it.

3.   In the Delete a Database dialog box, select the file name.

      Note: You cannot delete the database that is currently open. Select File; Close company to close the open company.

1.   Click Delete .

2.   To confirm, click Yes .

3.   To close the dialog box, click Close .

4.   To exit, click Close .

To delete the associated company file:

1.   Log in to Windows as the Administrator who installs and sets up the software.
2.   On the Start menu, point to Documents, and then click My Documents.
3.   Click the Small Business Accounting folder to open it.
4.   Click the Companies folder to open it.
5.   Select the company file name.
6.   On the File menu, click Delete .
7.   To confirm, click Yes .

How do I delete a company from the Microsoft Office Accounting 2007 Startup window?

1. Start MOA. If a company starts, click File; Close.
2. From the Microsoft Office Accounting 2007 start up window, link to

    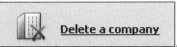.
3. The Look in Field shows the Companies folder. (If *not*, go to the location of your company files. Company files end in the extension, sbc.)
4. Double-click on the file you want to delete. When the window prompts, Are you sure you want to delete the selected company and the associated database?, click 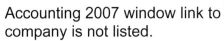.
5. To check that the company is deleted, from the Start – Microsoft Office

    Accounting 2007 window link to 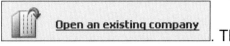. The company is not listed.

DELETE MICROSOFT OFFICE ACCOUNTING 2007

To delete Microsoft Office Accounting, do the following:

Step   1:   Make a backup of any data files that you have created.

Step   2:   Exit Microsoft Office Accounting.

Step   3:   From the Start menu, select Control Panel, then Add or Remove Programs.

Step   4:   Remove the add-ins—Microsoft Office Accounting ADP Payroll Addin, Equifax Addin, Fixed Asset Manager, PayPay Addin.

Step   5:   Remove Microsoft Office Accounting 2007.

Step   6:   Select Change/Remove to confirm that you want to remove the Microsoft Office Accounting program files. (If necessary, click Yes to All to delete shared files.)

Step   7:   Select the Microsoft Small Business Connectivity Components. Click Remove.

Step   8:   Remove the Microsoft SQL Server Native Client; Microsoft SQL Server Setup Support Files (English); and Microsoft SQL Server VSS writer.

Step   9:   Delete the Small Business Accounting folder. (The default location is My Documents.)

Step 10:   Empty the Recycle bin.

Appendix B — Review of Accounting Principles

Appendix B is a review of basic accounting principles and procedures. Standard accounting procedures are based on the double-entry system. This means that each business transaction is expressed with one or more debits and one or more credits in a journal entry and then posted to the ledger. The debits in each transaction must equal the credits.

The double-entry accounting system is based on the following premise: each account has two sides—a debit (left) side and credit (right) side. This is stated in the *accounting equation* as:

Assets = Liabilities + Equities

Assets are the organization's resources that have a future or potential value. Asset accounts include: Cash, Accounts Receivable, Office Supplies, Prepaids, Inventory, Investments, Equipment, Land, Buildings, etc.

Liabilities are the organization's responsibilities to others. Liability accounts include: Accounts Payable, Notes Payable, Unearned Rent, etc.

Equities are the difference between the organization's assets and liabilities. Equity accounts for organizations that are sole proprietorships or partnerships include: Capital and Withdrawals. Equity accounts for organizations that are corporations include contributed capital accounts like Common Stock which represent external ownership and Retained Earnings which represent internal ownership interests. Temporary equity-related accounts known as revenue and expense accounts recognize an organization's income producing activities and the related costs consumed or expired during the period.

Since assets are on the left side of the accounting equation, the left side of the account increases. This is the usual balance, too; assets increase on the left side and have a debit balance. Liabilities and Equities accounts are on the right side of the equation. Therefore, they increase on the right side and normally carry credit balances.

The McGraw-Hill Companies, Inc., *Computer Accounting Essentials with Microsoft Office Accounting*

Another way to show the accounting equation and double-entry is illustrated below.

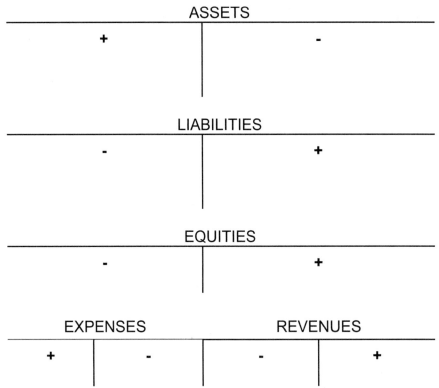

Each element of the accounting equation, Assets, Liabilities, and Equities, behaves similarly to their placement in the equation. Assets have debit balances; Liabilities have credit balances; Equities have credit balances; Expenses have debit balances because they decrease equity; and Revenues have credit balances because they increase equity.

In computerized accounting it is important to number each account according to a system. This is called the Chart of Accounts. The Chart of Accounts is a listing of all the general ledger accounts. The MOA chart of accounts shows the account number, Name, Type (this classifies the accounts for financial statements) and Balance. To see the chart of accounts, from the menu bar select Company; Company Lists, Chart of Accounts. If necessary, widen the columns to see the Name, Type, or Balance Total columns. A partial chart of account is shown on the next page for merchandising business.

Active	No.	Name	Type	Balance
	1005	Undeposited Funds	Cash Account	$0.00
✓	1010	Portland Bank	Bank	$87,635.72
✓	1100	First Savings & Loan	Bank	$15,000.00
✓	1200	Accounts Receivable	Accounts Receivable	$0.00
✓	1230	Deposits	Other Current Asset	$0.00
✓	1240	Federal Income Tax Receivable	Other Current Asset	$0.00
✓	1250	Inventory-Mountain Bikes	Inventory Asset	$2,100.00
✓	1255	Inventory-Road Bikes	Inventory Asset	$1,275.00
✓	1260	Inventory-Children's Bikes	Inventory Asset	$360.00
✓	1420	Interior	Fixed Asset	$0.00
✓	1430	Furniture & Fixtures	Fixed Asset	$6,000.00
✓	1450	Vehicle	Fixed Asset	$0.00
✓	1460	Accumulated Depreciation	Fixed Asset	$0.00
✓	1475	A/D-Interior	Fixed Asset	$0.00
✓	1480	A/D - Furniture & Fixtures	Fixed Asset	$0.00
✓	1490	A/D - Vehicle	Fixed Asset	$0.00
✓	1730	Organization Costs	Other Asset	$500.00
✓	1740	Accum. Amortization	Other Asset	$0.00
✓	1810	Prepaid Insurance	Other Asset	$2,400.00
✓	2000	Accounts Payable	Accounts Payable	$4,560.00
✓	2010	Pending Item Receipts	Current Liability	$0.00
✓	2050	Short-Term Notes Payable	Current Liability	$3,755.00
✓	2200	Payroll Liabilities	Current Liability	$1,032.37
✓	2205	Payroll Liability: S/S and Medicare	Current Liability	$382.50
✓	2210	Payroll Liability: FUTA	Current Liability	$0.00
✓	2215	Payroll Liability: State, Local	Current Liability	$95.87
✓	2220	Payroll Liability: SUTA	Current Liability	$0.00
✓	2225	Payroll Liability: Federal WH	Current Liability	$554.00
✓	2230	Payroll Liability: Profit Sharing	Current Liability	$0.00
✓	2235	Payroll Liability: Medical & Dental	Current Liability	$0.00
✓	2240	Payroll Liability: Section 125	Current Liability	$0.00
✓	2245	Payroll Liability: Union Dues	Current Liability	$0.00
✓	2250	Payroll Liability: Other	Current Liability	$0.00

Report information in the form of financial statements is important to accounting. The Balance Sheet reports the financial position of the business on a specific date. It shows that assets are equal to liabilities plus equities—the accounting equation. The Profit & Loss shows the difference between revenue and expenses for a specified period of time (month, quarter, year). The Income Statement is another name for Profit & Loss. Microsoft Office Accounting tracks revenue and expense data for an entire year. At the end of the year when all revenue and expense accounts are closed, the resulting net income or loss is moved into the equity account, Retained Earnings. For corporations, the Statement of Retained Earnings shows this in the account's activity during the year. The Statement of Cash Flows reports the operating, financial, and investing activities for the period. It shows the sources of cash coming into the business and the destination of the cash going out.

The most important task you have is accurately recording transactions into the appropriate accounts. Microsoft Office Accounting helps you by organizing the software into Customer, Vendor, and Banking Home pages. By selecting the appropriate Home page and icon (for example, Banking—Write Checks, Make Deposit, Reconcile Account), you can record transactions into the right place using easy-to-complete forms. Once transactions are entered, Microsoft Office Accounting keeps this information in a database. Then the data is organized into journal entries or transaction listings, account or ledger activities, report preparation, and analysis.

One of the most important tasks is deciding how to enter transactions. Recording and categorizing business transactions will determine how Microsoft Office Accounting uses that information. For instance, observe that the chart of accounts shows Account 1010 – Portland Bank, classified as a Bank Type; Account No. 1200 Accounts Receivable is Accounts Receivable. The Type column classifies the account for the financial statements—Asset, Liability, and Equity accounts go on the balance sheet; Income, Cost of Goods Sold, and Expense accounts go on the Profit & Loss Statement.

As you work with Microsoft Office Accounting, you see how the accounts, recording of transactions, and reports work together to provide your business with the information necessary for making informed decisions.

Another important aspect of accounting is determining whether the basis for recording transactions is cash or accrual. In the cash basis method, revenues and expenses are recognized when cash changes hands. In other words, when the customer pays for their purchase, the transaction is recorded. When the resource or expense is paid for by the business, the transaction is recorded.

In the accrual method of accounting, revenues and expenses are recognized when they occur. In other words, if the company purchases inventory on April 1, the transaction is recorded on April 1. If inventory is sold on account on April 15, the transaction is done on April 15 *not* when cash is received from customers. Accrual basis accounting is seen as more accurate because assets, liabilities, revenues, and expenses are recorded when they actually happen.

The chart on the next page summarizes Appendix B, Review of Accounting Principles.

ACCOUNTING EQUATION:	Assets =	Liabilities +	Owners Equities +	Revenues –	Expenses
Definition:	Something that has future or potential value "resources"	Responsibilities to others "Payables" "Unearned"	Internal and External ownership	Recognition of value creation	Expired, used, or consumed costs or resources
Debit Rules: DR	Increase	Decrease	Decrease	Decrease	Increase
Credit Rules:CR	Decrease	Increase	Increase	Increase	Decrease
Account Types and Examples	**Current Assets:** Cash, Marketable Securities, Accounts Receivable, Inventory, Prepaids **Plant Assets:** Land, Buildings, Equipment, Accumulated Depreciation **Noncurrent Assets:** Investments, Intangibles	**Current Liabilities:** Accounts Payable, Unearned Revenue, Advances from Customer **Noncurrent or Long-term Liabilities:** Bonds Payable, Notes Payables, Mortgage Payable	**Sole Proprietor:** (both internal and external) Name, Capital; Name, Withdrawals **Partnership:** (both internal and external) Partner A, Capital; Partner A, Withdrawals, etc. **Corporation:** External: Common Stock, Preferred Stock, Paid-in Capital Internal: Retained Earnings, Dividends	**Operating Revenue:** Sales: Fees Earned, Rent Income, Contract Revenue **Other Revenue:** Interest Income	**Product/Services Expenses:** Cost of Goods Sold, Cost of Sales **Operating Expenses:** Selling Expenses, Administrative Expense, General Expense, Salary Expense, Rent Expense, Depreciation Expense, Insurance Expense **Other Expenses:** Interest Expense

	Assets		Liabilities		Owners Equities		Revenues		Expenses	
T-Account Rules	Acquire resources	Consume resources	Pay bills Recognize earnings	Buy on credit Receive cash or other assets before earning it	Internal: Net Loss External: Owners reduce ownership thru withdrawals or dividends	Internal: Net Income External: Investment made by owners in company	Sales returns Sales discount given	Sales Earned Income	Resources consumed expired used	
	increase	*decrease*	*decrease*	*increase*	*decrease*	*increase*	*decrease*	*increase*	*Increase*	*decrease*

Basic Financial Statements:

Income Statement
Revenue−Expense=Net Income (NI) or Loss (NL)
(Prepare first)

Statement of Equity
Beginning* + NI (or −NL) − (Dividends or Withdrawals) = Ending*
*for Sole Proprietors and Partnerships use "Capital" and Withdrawals
for Corporations use "Retained Earnings" and Dividends
(Prepare second)

Balance Sheet
Assets=Liabilities + Equities
(Prepare third)

Statement of Cash Flows
Operating+/-Investing+/-Financing+Beginning Cash=Ending Cash
(Prepare last)

Appendix C — Glossary

Appendix C lists a glossary of terms used in *Computer Accounting Essentials with Microsoft Office Accounting*. The number in parentheses refers to the textbook page. Appendix C is also included on the textbook website at www.mhhe.com/moaessentials, link to Student Edition, then Glossary.

accounting equation	The accounting equation is stated as assets = liabilities + owner's equity. (Appendix B, p. 287)
accounts payable	The money a company owes to a supplier or vendor. (p. 106)
accounts payable ledger	Shows the account activity for each vendor. (p. 118)
accounts payable transactions	Purchases of merchandise for resale, assets, or expenses incurred on credit from vendors. (p. 106)
accounts receivable	Money that is owed by customers to the business. (p. 129)
accounts receivable ledger	Shows the account activity for each customer. (p.130)
accounts receivable transactions	Credit transactions from customers. (p. 129)
assets	The economic resources and other properties that a business owns. (p. Appendix B, p. 287)
backing up	Saving your data to a hard drive location or external media. (p. 12)

balance sheet	Lists the types and amounts of assets, liabilities, and equity as of a specific date. (p. 73)
bill	A request for payment for products or services. (See invoice.) (p. 119)
change log	The Change Log tracks who changed company data and what changes are made. This ability to monitor changes occurring in the accounting system and who is doing them is an essential internal control. (See internal control.) (p. 41)
chart of accounts	A list of a company's general ledger accounts. (p. 21)
closing the fiscal year	Moving the expense and revenue accounts to retailed earnings. (p. 179)
compound transaction	An entry that affects three or more accounts. (p. 162)
content pane	Displays information on your company. (p. 21)
credit sales	Refers to sales made to customers that will be paid for later. (p. 134)
customer invoice	A request for payment to a customer for products or services sold. (p. 129)
default	A predefined setting. You can accept the default option settings, or you can change them to suit your own preferences. (p. 13)
depreciation	The process of allocating the cost of a fixed assets over their expected useful lives. (p. 231)
dialog box	A window that appears when the system requires further information. You type information into dialog boxes to communicate with the program. Some dialog boxes display warnings and messages. (p. 23)

ellipsis (...)	A punctuation mark consisting of three successive periods (...). Choosing a menu item with an ellipsis opens a dialog box. See glossary item, dialog box. (p. 23)
equity	The difference between the assets and liabilities or what the business has left after the debts are paid. (Appendix B, p. 287)
Extensible Markup Language (XML)	A technology to identify fields into which data can be inserted. The tags which surround the data add meaning and allow it to be processed as information. (p. 271)
external media	Examples of external media include floppy disks; CD-R; DVD-R; USB drive; Zip disks. External media of this type can be used for backing up Microsoft Office Accounting data. (p. 13)
find	The find list contains links to records and accounts for the company. (p. 21)
graphical user interface (GUI)	The general look of a program is called its graphical user interface. The key is the Windows environment: the mouse, icons, toolbars, menus, and a navigation pane. One of the benefits of Windows is that it standardizes terms and operations used in software programs. (p. 19).
internal control	An integrated system of people, processes, and procedures that minimize or eliminate business risks, protect assets, ensure reliable accounting, and promote efficient operations. (p. 41.)
inventory item	A product that is purchases for sale and is tracked in a merchandise inventory account. (p. 110)
invoice	A request for payment to a customer for products and/or services sold.. (See bill.) (p. 119)

liabilities	The business's debts. (Appendix B, p. 287)
menu bar	A horizontal bar below the title bar on a window that contains the names of menus. (p. 20)
navigation pane	The pane on the left side of the MOA window that includes the Start a Tasks list, the Find List, and the navigation buttons. (p. 21)
navigation buttons	Links in the Navigation Panel for the home pages: Company, Customers, Vendors, Employees, Banking, and Reports. (p. 22)
restore	Previously backed up data can be restored or retrieved. (p. 13)
start a task	The start a task list contains links to help manage company. (p. 21)
statement of financial position	Another name for balance sheet. (See balance sheet). (p. 73)
system date	Today's date or the current date. (p. 85)
taskbar	In Windows XP, the Start button and taskbar are located at the bottom of your screen. (p. 20)
title bar	The top line of every window is a bar which contains the name of the application or menu in that window. (p. 20)
toolbar	A horizontal bar at the top of a software program window that contains buttons and options you can use to carry out commands. If a button appears dimmed, it is unavailable. (p. 20)
vendors	A person or company from whom your company buys products or services. (p. 106)

Index